NOTIONS OF GENRE

NOTIONS OF GENRE

Writings on Popular Film before Genre Theory

EDITED BY BARRY KEITH GRANT AND MALISA KURTZ

UNIVERSITY OF TEXAS PRESS *Austin*

Requests for permission to reproduce material from this work should be sent to:
Permissions
University of Texas Press
P.O. Box 7819
Austin, TX 78713–7819
http://utpress.utexas.edu/index.php/rp-form

♾ The paper used in this book meets the minimum requirements of
ANSI/NISO Z39.48-1992 (R1997) (Permanence of Paper).

Library of Congress Cataloging-in-Publication Data

Names: Grant, Barry Keith, 1947- editor. | Kurtz, Malisa, editor.
Title: Notions of genre : writings on popular film before genre theory /
edited by Barry Keith Grant and Malisa Kurtz.
Description: First edition. | Austin : University of Texas Press, 2016.
Includes index.
Identifiers: LCCN 2016003757
  ISBN 978-1-4773-0375-7 (cloth : alk. paper)
  ISBN 978-1-4773-1108-0 (pbk. : alk. paper)
  ISBN 978-1-4773-1109-7 (library e-book)
  ISBN 978-1-4773-1110-3 (non-library e-book)
Subjects: LCSH: Film genres. | Motion picture plays—History and criticism.
Motion picture authorship.
Classification: LCC PN1995 .N68 2016 | DDC 791.43/6—dc23
LC record available at http://lccn.loc.gov/2016003757

doi:10.7560/303757

CONTENTS

ACKNOWLEDGMENTS

The editors wish to thank the following: the Office of the Dean of Social Sciences at Brock University and the Council for Research in Social Sciences for research grants to complete the manuscript. University librarian Justine Cotton provided invaluable research assistance and, once more, Dan Barnowski provided technical help. At the University of Texas Press, senior acquisitions editor Jim Burr offered support from the outset and helpful advice throughout the process of manuscript preparation and publication, editorial assistant Sarah B. McGavick helped us navigate the labyrinth of copyright clearances, and managing editor Robert Kimzey ably served as our project manager. Freelance editor Annette Wenda gave the manuscript the careful copyediting it needed.

INTRODUCTION

BARRY KEITH GRANT AND MALISA KURTZ

IN THE CONVOLUTED NARRATIVE of Jacques Tourneur's 1947 film noir *Out of the Past*, "now firmly established as an archetypal, indeed quintessential" instance of the genre, a former private detective named Jeff Bailey (Robert Mitchum), now trying to live a wholesome and upright life, finds himself inexorably drawn into a deadly plot in the present that reanimates the passions of his past.[1] One might take this narrative as representative of the way genre texts themselves work: every new genre film always already exists in relation to and gains part of its meaning from the generic texts that preceded it. Every genre film is haunted by earlier work in the genre, just as Bailey is haunted in the present by a past that refuses to go away.

T. S. Eliot made essentially the same observation in his famous essay "Tradition and the Individual Talent" almost a century ago when he observed that because of the importance of what he called the "historical sense," "No poet, no artist of any art, has his complete meaning alone."[2] Of course, when writing these lines in 1919, modernist poet Eliot likely wasn't thinking about cinema, or film genres and genre films,[3] but his observations (which, it needs to be pointed out, he emphasizes apply to all of the arts) certainly make sense in the context of the genre system as much as they do regarding poetic tradition. Indeed, Eliot writes that

> what happens when a new work of art is created is something that happens simultaneously to all the works of art which preceded it. The existing monuments form an ideal order among themselves, which is modified by the introduction of the new (the really new) work of art among them. The existing order is complete before the new work arrives; for order to persist after the supervention of novelty, the *whole* existing order must be, if ever so slightly, altered; and so the relations, proportions, values of each work toward the whole are readjusted.[4]

Here he might well be describing the way film genres themselves form and shift over time. (Even as Eliot was writing his essay, the genre system was already well in process in Hollywood with, for example, several Charlie Chaplin and Harold Lloyd comedies and Hoot Gibson westerns released the same year.) While T. S. Eliot may not be the most likely figure to invoke in relation to film genre, it is in our view not entirely surprising to discover a highbrow modernist writer anticipating questions of popular genre theory at such an early date. Just as genre films necessarily recall those that preceded them, so much of modern genre theory too may be seen to rework issues and questions of earlier criticism.

Peter Hutchings's useful interpretive history of film genre theory and criticism stresses a break between early writing on film genre and later work in the 1970s and after;[5] however, it seems to us, as this collection of early writing on film genre reveals, that this history is marked as much by continuity as rupture, with these earlier writers addressing, however obliquely, similar questions of definition, representation, ideology, audiences, and industry practices despite the attention to methodology that would inform later work on genre. It is, in fact, surprising how much of this writing, despite being originally published decades ago, anticipated the major debates of film genre theory that were to follow.

Hutchings begins his historical account of film genre theory with the contributions of Lawrence Alloway, Robert Warshow, and André Bazin, but we may look even earlier for writing that with the benefit of hindsight we would consider genre criticism. James Agee, for example, brought a traditional humanism to his film reviews but, with the exception of his famous piece on slapstick comedy included in this collection, generally did not explicitly write about movies from the perspective of genre. But in reviewing several war films, including Fritz Lang's *Hangmen Also Die!* (1943), for the *Nation* in May 1943, Agee prefigures Thomas Elsaesser's influential work on melodrama, specifically the notion that the genre's excessive stylistics may be understood in psychoanalytic terms as the hysterical symptomatology of repression, in his remark that "plain melodramas, through their innate artificiality and unpretentiousness, have a good right to exist and may even, within their special formalism, give a remote but decent echo of the truth." Elsewhere, discussing *The Curse of the Cat People* (1944) in the *Nation* in 1944, Agee commented that "the people with whom I saw the film—a regular Times Square horror audience—were sharply on to its faults and virtues."[6] Here Agee anticipates reception and fandom studies in identifying a genre-specific and genre-literate audience and then measuring his judgment in part on the reception of the film. If, as Hutchings claims, early film genre theory tended to exclude the audience, what he calls "the elusive X factor," from the genre equation, it was in fact at least implicitly acknowledged on occasion by critics writing before the rise of film genre theory.[7]

Although he is not typically thought of as such, Siegfried Kracauer, whose work is also included here, may be regarded as the first true film genre theorist. His milestone book, *From Caligari to Hitler: A Psychological Study of the German Film*, published in the United States in 1947, is essentially a genre study, and a rather ambitious one. Kracauer maps the nature of the German "collective soul" by grouping the nation's films into thematic and narrative cycles that he calls tyrant and instinct films. To be sure, Kracauer can be faulted for the single-minded rigidity of his method and his somewhat reductive readings of individual films as he tries to fit them into his categories, but these faults should not obscure Kracauer's pioneering concept of grouping films according to narrative and stylistic patterns and seeing them as both reflecting and constructing a national identity for viewers. As Kracauer observes, "What films reflect are not so much explicit credos as psychological dispositions—those deep layers of collective mentality which extend more or less below the dimension of consciousness." His later writings on American cinema sometimes approached Hollywood movies in terms of genre, as with "Hollywood's Terror Films," subtitled "Do They Reflect an American State of Mind?," published in 1946, and "Silent Film Comedy" from 1951, the one included in this collection. Both of these short essays are informed by the same notion that movies "reflect popular tendencies and inclinations"—a theoretical assumption that informs the overwhelming majority of genre analyses today, despite the now obligatory disclaimers regarding essentialism and the postmodern debunking of the concept of a monolithic national psyche.[8]

Certainly, though, Robert Warshow's essays on the gangster film and the western, first published in the *Partisan Review* in 1948 and 1954, respectively, and André Bazin's pieces on the western in the early 1950s have proved to be the first significant essays of film genre criticism. In his essay on gangster films, included here, Warshow's comment that "the real city . . . produces only criminals; the imaginary city produces the gangster" reveals his understanding of genre as a system of conventions that function as cultural myth. Both Warshow and Bazin may have dodged questions of genre definition, assuming ideal forms for the gangster film and the western—Tom Ryall pointed this out long ago in discussing Bazin's famous comment that John Ford's *Stagecoach* (1939) achieved a position of classical maturity[9]—but Warshow at least was clearly cognizant of the ideological function of genre. In the essay on the gangster film, he echoes the Frankfurt school's views in his observation that works of mass culture tend to endorse the ideological status quo.

Early film genre criticism thus may constitute the beginning of a line of inquiry more than it does a break. Nevertheless, we take 1970 as a convenient year to mark the introduction of theory into the critical discourse on genre with the resultant shift in tone from impressionism to ideology. The publication of Andrew Sarris's famous essay "Notes on the Auteur Theory in 1962," with its attempt (however dubious) to construct a theoretical framework for auteurism, was a clear harbinger of the theorization of film that was to follow in the next decade. Adding the word *theory*, Sarris's provocative gesture ("Henceforth, I will abbreviate *la politique des auteurs* as the *auteur* theory to avoid confusion") opened the door for the importation of grand theory into film studies in the 1970s, with defenses and critiques of auteurism specifically having significant impact on thinking about genre. At the time, the two critical approaches, auteurism and genre, were frequently seen as mutually exclusive rather than enriching. As Lawrence Alloway noted in his hugely influential article "The Iconography of the Movies" in 1963, "Treating movies as personal expression and autographic testament has led to the neglect of the iconographical approach." Andrew Tudor devoted a chapter in his 1973 book *Theories of Film* to establishing the genre and auteur approaches as opposing camps.[10]

In retrospect, this attitude, while characteristic of so much classical film theory, seems somewhat curious nonetheless. Sarris had vaguely defined "interior meaning," the mark of the true auteur, as "extrapolated from the tension between a director's personality and his material," and although he failed to explain what this means, it may be understood, at least within the context of classic Hollywood cinema, as the way a director mobilizes and inflects the elements of genre he was obliged to use. Sarris concludes that the least satisfying film of an auteur is better than the most interesting work by a director who isn't, but, as Alloway points out, "the personal contributions of many directors can only be seen fully after typical iconographical elements have been identified."[11]

The celebrated series of American noir and crime films that Alloway curated in 1969 at New York's Museum of Modern Art (MOMA) is one of the markers of the shift to genre theory in the 1970s. A noted art critic and curator who had been a member of the London-based Independent Group before moving to the United States, Alloway had a strong interest in popular culture. Indeed, he is credited with coining the term *pop art*.[12] Alloway's film series at MOMA, titled *The American Action Movie, 1946–1964*, spanned Robert Siodmak's *The Killers* in 1946 to Don Siegel's *The Killers* in 1964 and included films by usual suspects Anthony Mann, Samuel Fuller, and Robert Aldrich (as well as *Out of the Past*). Two years later, MOMA published Alloway's book based on the series, *Violent America: The Movies, 1946–1964* (1971). The book contained credits and abridged program notes for the films that were screened, as well as five essays on popular cinema, including one on iconography and genre, an expanded version of the aforementioned short essay on iconography that Alloway had published in *Movie* in 1963. In the original essay, Alloway borrowed the iconographical approach from art critic Erwin Panofsky, who wrote that it provides "insight into the manner in which under varying historical traditions, specific themes or concepts were expressed by objects and events." Like Ian Cameron before him, Alloway asserted that the analysis of iconography is revealing in and of itself, apart from the consideration of how individual directors treat it.[13]

By the time Alloway's book appeared, the theoretical interest in genre had clearly intensified. In Great Britain, there was, as Hutchings notes, a push to establish film studies in higher education, largely through the outreach work of the British Film Institute (BFI) and in the journal *Screen*, published by the Society for Education in Film and Television. Colin McArthur authored a discussion paper for the meeting of the British Film Institute's Education Department seminar in March 1969, in which he suggested that the iconographical approach fitted well with the newly developing interest in semiology (McArthur would expand on his interest in iconography and the gangster film in his book *Underworld USA*, published in 1972). A riposte of sorts followed in another BFI seminar discussion paper by Sam Rhodie in 1970. In *Screen* that same year appeared Tom Ryall's essay "The Notion of Genre" and Edward Buscombe's "The Idea of Genre in the American Cinema," both of which reveal an awareness of film genre theory itself as a developing tradition. Buscombe offered a catalog of iconography in the western, which he called the "outer forms" of genre movies, borrowing the term from Austin Warren and René Wellek's influential 1949 book of New Criticism, *Theory of Literature*. Richard Collins's response to Buscombe soon followed, in which Collins argued, along the lines of Vladimir Propp's analysis of Russian folktales, for units of narrative action rather than iconography as the significant defining element of genre.[14] In these essays the term *iconography* appears almost routinely; clearly, the topic of genre was becoming an important part of critical debates about cinema.

The year 1970 also may be seen as marking a major shift for Hollywood following the huge box-office success of *Easy Rider* (1969). The year witnessed the release of a number of movies—*Patton*, *M*A*S*H*, *Catch-22*, *Little Big Man*, *Kelly's Heroes*, *The Ballad of Cable Hogue*, *Two Mules for Sister Sarah*, and *The Private Life of Sherlock Holmes*, among others—many of them box-office hits but at the same time self-conscious, if not cynical, about the genres of which they were a part. It was the beginning of the so-called New Hollywood and the rise of a generation of young directors known as the movie brats, a group that included Steven Spielberg, Martin Scorsese, Brian De Palma, George Lucas, and Francis Coppola. While very different in terms of style and theme, collectively their films offered proof, as Jean-Luc Godard said, that "as soon as you can make films, you can no longer make films like the ones that made you want to make them." Nöel King has noted that New Hollywood was characterized by a combination of "classical Hollywood genre film-making with the stylistic innovations of European art cinema." Thus, the films of the movie brats revealed a self-awareness or self-consciousness of working within established traditions of Hollywood even as they were reinventing them. Many of the important films of these directors were genre movies that reexamined the classic Hollywood genres from a more intellectual and youthful perspective. Coppola's *The Godfather* (1972) and Scorsese's *Mean Streets* (1973) offered fresh approaches to the gangster film, for example, while De Palma concentrated on the horror film with *Sisters* (1973), *Phantom of the Paradise* (1975), and *Carrie* (1976). In a well-known essay titled "*Chinatown* and Generic Transformation in Recent American Films," John G. Cawelti noted the various and dramatic revisionism in genre filmmaking at the time.[15] The very title of the year's biggest-grossing movie, *Love Story*, suggests the general awareness of generic tradition in both movies and other forms of popular culture at the time.

At the same time, there was an explosion of work on genre theory, much of it now from American as well as British scholars. Carlos Clarens's history of the horror film was published in 1967, Jim Kitses's *Horizons West* imported a structuralist methodology to the conceptualization of the western two years later, and also in 1969 *The Crazy Mirror: Hollywood Comedy and the American Image* by British maverick Raymond Durgnat was published in the United Kingdom, a year before it appeared in the United States. By the middle of the 1970s, in addition to the several coffee table-style illustrated genre overviews by authors such as John Baxter and Denis Gifford, there appeared, along with an increasing number of journal articles, Tudor's *Theories of Film* in 1973, with its discussion of genre and auteurism constituting the chapter on "critical methodology"; Stuart Kaminsky's *American Film Genres: Approaches to a Critical Theory of Popular Film* in 1974; Frank McConnell's *The Spoken Seen: Film and the Romantic Imagination*, which contains a chapter on "the problem of film genre," the following year; and Will Wright's *Sixguns and Society: A Structural Study of the Western* the year after that. Barry Keith Grant's anthology *Film Genre: Theory and Criticism*, the first scholarly anthology on film genre, was published in 1977. And in 1980 appeared Steve Neale's BFI monograph *Genre*, and the following year came Thomas Schatz's *Hollywood Genres: Formulas, Filmmaking and the Studio System*, both books seeking to erect theories of the genre system.[16] These books were being published even as film studies programs began to appear in university and college curricula and film studies began to take shape as a discipline with its own theories and methodologies.[17]

Most of this work, as one might expect, focused on Hollywood cinema—the result of "the genius of the system," in Bazin's words. It wasn't until much later that film scholars in the English-speaking world and elsewhere began to write about genre films from Australia, New Zealand, Europe, Asia, and South America. Of course, in the prevideo and -digital world, Hollywood films were more accessible to these scholars than films from other parts of the globe. Still, as Robin Wood has written, one of "the two great contradictory truths" about Hollywood (the other, that it is an industrial model that stifles individual creativity and expression) is that it represents one of the few historical instances of a true communal art, "a great creative workshop, comparable to Elizabethan London or the Vienna of Mozart, where hundreds of talents have come together to evolve a common language."[18] (In yet another instance of critical continuity, Warshow makes the same analogy to Elizabethan drama in his essay on the gangster film.)

Hutchings notes that a consideration of film genre offers the opportunity to discuss cinema as both an industrial and a popular medium and to consider films as texts as well as the audiences and paratexts.[19] The authors in the present collection do consider these various issues, though admittedly not in any sustained or systematic manner. And while generic definition—an issue no contemporary scholar of film genre can avoid addressing—is for the most part assumed by these writers to be unproblematic, these essays do consider the various iconographic, narrative, and stylistic conventions of several of Hollywood's most durable genres, as well as the relations between these generic elements and their relations to the predispositions and values of the culture that produced them.

We have included contributions from film critics, André Bazin the most prominent among them, as well as several important cultural literati, including Agee, Kracauer, Susan Sontag, Dwight Macdonald, and Robert Warshow. There are also contributions from scholars in other academic disciplines such as sociology and theater, indicating the wide interest in popular film genres that existed before the rise of specialist film theory and the institutionalization of film studies as an academic discipline. Unfortunately, apart from Susan Sontag, there are no other women included, just as there are no people of color in this group of white male writers—the result of historical realities rather than any editorial bias. We comment on each of the essays in the introductions to each of the book's four parts, so here we will note only that in all the essays we have silently corrected factual errors, added dates and bibliographical references as endnotes where necessary, and in a few cases added endnotes that are so identified.

In terms of theory, auteurism may have predated genre, but critics were writing about genres from a variety of perspectives long before they were writing about films as the personal expression of their directors. Still today, much of the published work in film studies can be understood as genre criticism, broadly speaking. And although much of it has become, on the one hand, more focused, with scholars examining a particular generic cycle or period, or a specific theme, such as, say, gender or race in one genre, and, on the other hand, broader in scope, focusing on genre in the context of national and global cinema, reception and industry practices, or paratexts, the questions are essentially the same as those raised, albeit less theoretically, in early film genre criticism. Already in his 1970 essay mentioned earlier (and from which we have taken the present volume's title), Tom Ryall sought to define the term *genre* more precisely than it had been before while acknowledging the importance of authorship, audience, and generic awareness, all of which remain central to contemporary genre theory and criticism: "A crucial notion in any definition of genre must be that the genre film is one which exhibits a relationship with other examples of the genre. This also implies a consciousness of this relationship on the part of the man who makes the film, and on the part of the audience who go to see it."[20] It may be true that the writing on film genre before the 1970s, when film studies emerged and took shape as an academic discipline, was often unsystematic, impressionistic, journalistic, and judgmental, but it was often quite insightful nonetheless. These early notions of genre, which appeared in a wide range of academic journals and popular magazines, reveal fascinating attempts to understand genre films and their conventions and how they speak to, for, and about the culture that produces them.

NOTES

1. Jim Hillier and Alastair Phillips, *100 Film Noirs* (London: British Film Institute, 2009), 200.

2. T. S. Eliot, "Tradition and the Individual Talent," in *Selected Essays* (New York: Harcourt, Brace & World, 1950), 4.

3. Or was he? See, for example, David Trotter, "T. S. Eliot and Cinema," *Modernism/Modernity* 13, no. 2 (2006): 237–265, for a discussion of the relationship of Eliot and his work to film.

4. Eliot, "Tradition and the Individual Talent," 5 (emphasis in the original).

5. Peter Hutchings, "Genre Theory and Criticism," in *Approaches to Popular Film*, edited by Joanne Hollows and Mark Jancovich (Manchester: Manchester University Press, 1995), 60–77.

6. James Agee, *Agee on Film: Reviews and Comments* (Boston: Beacon Press, 1964), 35, 86. Elsaesser's essay "Tales of Sound and Fury: Observations on the Family Melodrama" is reprinted in *Film Genre Reader IV*, edited by Barry Keith Grant (Austin: University of Texas Press, 2012), 433–462.

7. Hutchings, "Genre Theory and Criticism," 73.

8. Siegfried Kracauer, *From Caligari to Hitler: A Psychological History of the German Film* (Princeton, NJ: Princeton University Press, 1947), 6–7; Siegfried Kracauer, "Hollywood's Terror Films," in *Siegfried Kracauer's American Writings: Essays on Film and Popular Culture*, edited by Johannes von Moltke and Kristy Rawson (Berkeley: University of California Press, 2012), 45.

9. Tom Ryall, "The Notion of Genre," *Screen* 11, no. 2 (1972): 23.

10. Andrew Sarris, "Notes on the Auteur Theory in 1962," in *Auteurs and Authorship: A Film Reader*, edited by Barry Keith Grant (Malden, MA: Blackwell, 2008), 37; Lawrence Alloway, "The Iconography of the Movies," *Movie* 7 (February–March 1963): 4; Andrew Tudor, *Theories of Film* (New York: Viking, 1974).

11. Sarris, "Auteur Theory in 1962," 43; Lawrence Alloway, *Violent America: The Movies, 1946–1964* (New York: Museum of Modern Art, 1971), 41.

12. For more an Alloway's interest in the cinema, see Peter Stanfield, "Maximum Movies: Lawrence Alloway's Pop Art Film Criticism," *Cinema Journal* 49, no. 2 (2008): 179–193.

13. Erwin Panofsky, "Iconography and Iconology: An Introduction to the Study of Renaissance Art," chapter 1 in *Meaning in the Visual Arts* (Garden City, NY: Doubleday Anchor, 1955), 26–54; Alloway, "Iconography of the Movies," 5; Ian Cameron, "Films, Directors, and Critics," *Movie* 2 (1962): 4–7. Cameron's essay is reprinted in Grant, *Auteurs and Authorship*, 29–34.

14. Hutchings, "Genre Theory and Criticism," 65; Tom Ryall, "The Notion of Genre," 22–32; Edward Buscombe, "The Idea of Genre in the American Cinema," *Screen* 11, no. 2 (1970): 33–45; Richard Collins, "Genre: A Reply to Ed Buscombe," *Screen* 11, nos.

4–5 (1970): 66–75. See also V. Propp, *Morphology of the Folktale*, edited by Louis A. Wagner (Austin: University of Texas Press, 1968). Buscombe's essay is reprinted in Grant, *Film Genre Reader IV*, 12–26.

15. Godard quoted in Pauline Kael, *Kiss Kiss Bang Bang* (New York: Bantam, 1969), 138; Nöel King, "New Hollywood," in *The Cinema Book*, edited by Pam Cook, 3rd ed. (London: British Film Institute, 2007), 60; John G. Cawelti, "*Chinatown* and Generic Transformation in Recent American Films," in *Film Genre Reader IV*, edited by Grant, 279–297.

16. Carlos Clarens, *An Illustrated History of the Horror Film* (New York: Capricorn Books, 1968); Jim Kitses, *Horizons West* (Bloomington: Indiana University Press, 1970); Raymond Durgnat, *The Crazy Mirror: Hollywood Comedy and the American Image* (New York: Delta, 1972); Stuart Kaminsky, *American Film Genres: Approaches to a Critical Theory of Popular Film in 1974* (Dayton, OH: Pflaum, 1974); Frank McConnell, *The Spoken Seen: Film and the Romantic Imagination* (Baltimore: Johns Hopkins University Press, 1975); Will Wright, *Sixguns and Society: A Structural Study of the Western* (Berkeley: University of California Press, 1976); Barry Keith Grant, ed., *Film Genre: Theory and Criticism* (Metuchen, NJ: Scarecrow Press, 1977); Steve Neale, *Genre* (London: British Film Institute, 1980); Thomas Schatz, *Hollywood Genres: Formulas, Filmmaking and the Studio System* (New York: Random House, 1981).

17. For more on the history of film studies as an academic discipline, see, for example, Barry Keith Grant, ed., *Film Study in the Undergraduate Curriculum* (New York: Modern Language Association, 1983); Dana Polan, *Scenes of Instruction: The Beginnings of the U.S. Study of Film* (Berkeley: University of California Press, 2007); and Lee Greveson and Haidee Wasson, eds., *Inventing Film Studies* (Durham, NC: Duke University Press, 2008).

18. Robin Wood, *Howard Hawks*, rev. ed. (Detroit: Wayne State University Press, 2006), 2–3.

19. Hutchings, "Genre Theory and Criticism," 61.

20. Ryall, "The Notion of Genre," 26.

PART I

COMEDY

Part 1 focuses on comedy, which, having strong roots in vaudeville, burlesque, and music hall, had a tradition upon which to build before the invention of cinema. Because slapstick comedy quickly reached a height of inventiveness in Hollywood during the silent era, it was a genre earlier critics were inclined to write about with varying degrees of nostalgia. While comedy is understood today more as a mode than a genre, given that such recognizable forms as screwball comedy, slapstick comedy, romantic comedy, bromance, and parody, among others, all have their own conventions, the achievements of this "golden age" of comedy clearly attracted genre critics early on.

The section opens with James Agee's well-known feature article on silent comedy, "Comedy's Greatest Era," which appeared originally in *Life* in September 1949, followed by Siegfried Kracauer's lesser-known piece "Silent Film Comedy," originally published in the British journal *Sight and Sound* two years later. A screenwriter, poet, and critic who reviewed films for the *Nation* and *Time* through the 1940s, Agee sees the great silent comic filmmakers—Sennett, Chaplin, Keaton, Langdon, Lloyd—as having the imagination to build on physical gags, an ability sadly lacking in the verbal comedians of the day such as Bob Hope, whose film *The Paleface* (1948) pales in comparison to Buster Keaton's *The Navigator* (1924). Both Agee and Kracauer view the introduction of sound as destroying cinematic comedy, but whereas the former focuses on the formal mechanics of the gag, the latter sees slapstick as expressing a sense of alienation from mechanical progress and acknowledging the importance of material reality and its contingencies, qualities Kracauer emphasizes as inherent "affinities" of cinema in his 1960 book, *Theory of Film*.

In turn, British writer Allen Eyles, author of several star studies and histories of British film exhibition and editor of the magazine *Focus on Film* during its run in the 1970s, finds comedy at the time of his writing in 1963 wanting compared to the sound comedies of the 1930s and '40s. In "Uncle Sam's Funny

Bone," from *Films and Filming* in 1963, Eyles provides a wide-ranging overview of contemporary Hollywood comedy and, anticipating later ideological analyses of genre such as those of Judith Hess Wright and Jean-Loup Bourget,[1] emphasizes how the potentially subversive energy of several types of film comedy has become diluted or compromised by industrial and cultural factors.

Next, Dwight Macdonald, a public intellectual who professed progressive politics but took a conservative view on cultural matters, joins the chorus lamenting the current state of film comedy compared to the "golden age."[2] In "Whatever Happened to Hollywood Comedy?," which appeared originally in *Esquire* in 1965, Macdonald seeks to identify a number of structural rules for successful comedy based on the failure of so many recent comic films. Subtlety and sympathetic identification, Macdonald claims, are essential to comedy but sorely lacking in comedies of the time.

The following essay, "The Evolution of the Chase in the Silent Screen Comedy," published in 1964 in *Cinema Journal*, the scholarly journal of the Society for Cinema and Media Studies, by Donald W. McCaffrey, takes an altogether different approach. McCaffrey, a longtime professor of film who taught at the University of North Dakota beginning in 1960 and author of several books on Hollywood comedy, including works on Charlie Chaplin and Bob Hope, is less concerned with aesthetic judgment than with tracing the changes of one specific comic trope, the chase, in relation to the narrative in comedies made during the silent era. In effect, McCaffrey considers what Rick Altman would later call one of comedy's semantic elements and its evolving use in the genre's syntactic structure.[3]

Part 1 concludes with "From Kops to Robbers: Transformation of Archetypal Figures in the American Cinema of the 1920s and '30s," by Carolyn and Harry Geduld. Author of numerous books on film, Harry Geduld taught at Indiana University in Bloomington, where he established its film studies program in 1964 and served as its first director. Like McCaffrey, the Gedulds are interested here in tracing broader patterns in the genre, in this case in the transition from silent to sound comedy. Focusing on the visual dynamic of the conventional "little man" versus the larger villain ("the heavy") in silent comedy, they find fascinating connections to the conventional representations in gangster films while noting the considerably different ideological implications between the two genres and their different responses to changing times.

NOTES

1. Judith Hess Wright, "Genre Films and the Status Quo," and Jean-Loup Bourget, "Social Implications in the Hollywood Genres," both in *Film Genre Reader IV*, edited

by Barry Keith Grant (Austin: University of Texas Press, 2012), 60–68 and 69–77, respectively.

2. See Dwight Macdonald's *Masscult and Midcult: Against the American Grain* (New York: New York Review Book Classics, 2011) for his attacks on the debasing nature of popular culture.

3. Rick Altman, "A Semantic/Syntactic Approach to Film Genre," *Cinema Journal* 23, no. 3 (1984): 6–18, reprinted in Altman's *Film/Genre* (London: British Film Institute, 1999), 216–226, and in *Film Genre Reader IV*, edited by Grant, 27–41.

CHAPTER 1

COMEDY'S GREATEST ERA

JAMES AGEE

IN THE LANGUAGE OF screen comedians four of the main grades of laugh are the titter, the yowl, the belly laugh, and the boffo. The titter is just a titter. The yowl is a runaway titter. Anyone who has ever had the pleasure knows all about a belly laugh. The boffo is the laugh that kills. An ideally good gag, perfectly constructed and played, would bring the victim up this ladder of laughs by cruelly controlled degrees to the top rung, and would then proceed to wobble, shake, wave, and brandish the ladder until he groaned for mercy. Then, after the shortest possible time out for recuperation, he would feel the first wicked tickling of the comedian's whip once more and start up a new ladder.

The reader can get a fair-enough idea of the current state of screen comedy by asking himself how long it has been since he has had that treatment. The best of comedies these days hand out plenty of titters, and once in a while it is possible to achieve a yowl without overstraining. Even those who have never seen anything better must occasionally have the feeling, as they watch the current run or, rather, trickle of screen comedy, that they are having to make a little cause for laughter go an awfully long way. And anyone who has watched screen comedy over the past ten or fifteen years is bound to realize that it has quietly but steadily deteriorated. As for those happy atavists who remember silent comedy in its heyday and the belly laughs and boffos that went with it, they have something close to an absolute standard by which to measure the deterioration.

When a modern comedian gets hit on the head, for example, the most he is apt to do is look sleepy. When a silent comedian got hit on the head, he seldom let it go so flatly. He realized a broad license, and a ruthless discipline within that license. It was his business to be as funny as possible physically, without the help or hindrance of words. So he gave us a figure of speech, or rather of vision, for loss of consciousness. In other words, he gave us a poem, a kind of poem, moreover, that everybody understands. The least he might do was to straighten up stiff as a plank and fall over backward with such skill that his whole length seemed to slap the floor at the same instant. Or he might make a cadenza of it—look vague, smile like an angel, roll up his eyes, lace his fingers, thrust his hands palms downward as far as they would go, hunch his shoulders, rise on tiptoe, prance ecstatically in narrowing circles until, with tallow knees, he sank down the vortex of his dizziness to the floor and there signified nirvana by kicking his heels twice, like a swimming frog.

Startled by a cop, this same comedian might grab his hat brim with both hands and yank it down over his ears, jump high in the air, come to earth in a split violent enough to telescope his spine, spring thence into a coattail-flattening sprint, and dwindle at rocket speed to the size of a gnat along the grand, forlorn perspective of some lazy back boulevard.

Those are fine clichés from the language of silent comedy in its infancy. The man who could handle them properly combined several of the more difficult accomplishments of the acrobat, the dancer, the clown, and the mime. Some very gifted comedians, unforgettably Ben Turpin, had an immense vocabulary of these clichés and were in part so lovable because they were deep conservative classicists and never tried to break away from them. The still more gifted men, of course, simplified and invented, finding out new and much deeper uses for the idiom. They learned to show emotion through it, and comic psychology, more eloquently than most language has ever managed to, and they discovered beauties of comic motion that are hopelessly beyond reach of words.

It is hard to find a theater these days where a comedy is playing; in the days of the silents, it was equally hard to find a theater that was not showing one. The laughs today are pitifully few, far between, shallow, quiet, and short. They almost never build, as they used to, into something combining the jabbering frequency of a machine gun with the delirious momentum of a roller coaster. Saddest of all, there are few comedians now below middle age, and there are none who seem to learn much from picture to picture, or to try anything new.

To put it unkindly, the only thing wrong with screen comedy today is that it takes place on a screen that talks. Because it talks, the only comedians who ever mastered the screen cannot work, for they cannot combine their comic style with talk. Because there is a screen, talking comedians are trapped into a continual exhibition of their inadequacy as screen comedians on a surface as big as the side of a barn.

At the moment, as for many years, the chances to see silent comedy are rare. There is a smattering of it on television—too often treated as something quaintly archaic, to be laughed at, not with. Some two hundred comedies—long and short—can be rented for home projection. And a lucky minority has access to the comedies in the collection of New York's Museum of Modern Art, which is still incomplete but is probably the best in the world. In the near future, however, something of this lost art will return to regular theaters. A thick straw in the wind is the big business now being done by a series of revivals of W. C. Fields's memorable movies, a kind of comedy more akin to the old silent variety than anything that is being made today. Mack Sennett now is preparing a sort of potpourri variety show called *Down Memory Lane* made up out of his old movies, featuring people like Fields and Bing Crosby when they were movie beginners, but including also interludes from silents. Harold Lloyd has rereleased *Movie Crazy* (1932), a talkie, and plans to revive four of his best silent comedies, *Grandma's Boy* (1922), *Safety Last!* (1923), *The Freshman* (1925), and *Speedy* (1928). Buster Keaton hopes to remake at feature length, with a minimum of dialogue, two of the funniest short comedies ever made, one about a porous homemade boat and one about a prefabricated house.

Awaiting these happy events, we will discuss here what has gone wrong with screen comedy and what, if anything, can be done about it. But mainly, we will try to suggest what it was like in its glory in the years from 1912 to 1930, as practiced by the employees of Mack Sennett, the father of American screen comedy, and by the four most eminent masters: Charlie Chaplin, Harold Lloyd, the late Harry Langdon, and Buster Keaton.

Mack Sennett made two kinds of comedy: parody laced with slapstick and plain slapstick. The parodies were the unceremonious burial of a century of hamming, including the new hamming in serious movies, and nobody who has missed Ben Turpin in *A Small Town Idol* (1921), or kidding Erich von Stroheim in *Three Foolish Weeks* (1924), or in *The Shriek of Araby* (1923), can imagine how rough parody can get and still remain subtle and roaringly funny. The plain slapstick, at its best, was even better: a profusion of hearty young women in disconcerting bathing suits, frisking around with a gaggle of insanely incompetent policemen and of equally

FIGURE 1. W. C. Fields with Carol Dempster in D. W. Griffith's *Sally of the Sawdust* (1925).

certifiable male civilians sporting museum-piece mustaches. All these people zipped and caromed about the pristine world of the screen as jazzily as a convention of water bugs. Words can hardly suggest how energetically they collided and bounced apart, meeting in full gallop around the corner of a house; how hard and how often they fell on their backsides; or with what fantastically adroit clumsiness they got themselves fouled up in folding ladders, garden hoses, tethered animals, and each other's headlong cross-purposes. The gestures were ferociously emphatic; not a line or motion of the body was wasted or inarticulate. The reader may remember how splendidly upright wand-like old Ben Turpin could stand for a renunciation scene, with his lampshade mustache twittering and his sparrowy chest stuck out and his head flung back like Paderewski assaulting a climax and the long babyish back hair trying to look lionlike, while his Adam's apple, an orange in a Christmas stocking, pumped with noble emotion. Or huge Mack Swain, who looked like a hairy mushroom, rolling his eyes in a manner patented by French romantics and gasping in some dubious ecstasy. Or Louise Fazenda, the perennial farmer's daughter and the perfect low-comedy housemaid, primping her spit curl and how her hair tightened a good-looking face into the incarnation of rampant gullibility. Or snouty James Finlayson, gleefully foreclosing a mortgage, with

his look of eternally tasting a spoiled pickle. Or Chester Conklin, a myopic and inebriated little walrus stumbling around in outsize pants. Or
Fatty Arbuckle, with his cold eye and his loose, serene smile; his silky
manipulation of his bulk; and his satanic marksmanship with pies (he
was ambidextrous and could simultaneously blind two people in opposite directions).

The intimate tastes and secret hopes of these poor ineligible dunces
were ruthlessly exposed whenever a hot stove, an electric fan, or a bull-
dog took a dislike to their outer garments: agonizingly elaborate drawers,
worked up on some lonely evening out of some godforsaken lace curtain,
or men's underpants with big, round black spots on them. The Sennett
sets—delirious wallpaper, megalomaniacally scrolled iron beds, Grand
Rapids in extremis—outdid even the underwear. It was their business,
after all, to kid the squalid braggadocio that infested the domestic interiors of the period and was almost beyond parody. These comedies told their
stories to the unaided eye, and by every means possible they screamed
to it. That is one reason for the india-ink silhouettes of the cops, and for
convicts and prison bars and their shadows in hard sunlight, and for bare-
footed husbands, in tigerish pajamas, reacting like dervishes to stepped-
on tacks.

The early silent comedians never strove for or consciously thought of
anything that could be called artistic "form," but they achieved it. For Sennett's rival Hal Roach, Leo McCarey once devoted almost the whole of a
Laurel and Hardy two-reeler to pie throwing. The first pies were thrown
thoughtfully, almost philosophically. Then innocent bystanders began to
get caught into the vortex. At full pitch it was Armageddon. But everything was calculated so nicely that until late in the picture, when havoc
took over, every pie made its special kind of point and piled on its special
kind of laugh.

Sennett's comedies were just a shade faster and fizzier than life. According to legend (and according to Sennett), he discovered the tempo
proper to screen comedy when a green cameraman, trying to save money,
cranked too slowly. Realizing the tremendous drumlike power of mere
motion to exhilarate, he gave inanimate objects a mischievous life of their
own, broke every law of nature the tricked camera would serve him for,
and made the screen dance like a witches' Sabbath. The thing one is surest
of all to remember is how toward the end of nearly every Sennett comedy,
a chase (usually called the "rally") built up such a majestic trajectory of
pure anarchic motion that bathing girls, cops, comics, dogs, cats, babies,
automobiles, locomotives, innocent bystanders, sometimes what seemed

like a whole city, an entire civilization, were hauled along head over heels in the wake of that energy like dry leaves following an express train.

"Nice" people, who shunned all movies in the early days, condemned the Sennett comedies as vulgar and naive. But millions of less pretentious people loved their sincerity and sweetness, their wild-animal innocence and glorious vitality. They could not put these feelings into words, but they flocked to the silents. The reader who gets back deep enough into that world will probably even remember the theater: the barefaced honky-tonk and the waltzes by Waldteufel, slammed out on a mechanical piano; the searing redolence of peanuts and demirep perfumery, tobacco, and feet and sweat; the laughter of unrespectable people having a hell of a fine time, laughter as violent and steady and deafening as standing under a waterfall.

Sennett wheedled his first financing out of a couple of ex-bookies to whom he was already in debt. He took his comics out of music halls, burlesque, vaudeville, circuses, and limbo, and through them he tapped in on that great pipeline of horsing and miming that runs back unbroken through the fairs of the Middle Ages at least to ancient Greece. He added all that he himself had learned about the large and spurious gesture, the late decadence of the Grand Manner, as a stagestruck boy in East Berlin, Connecticut, and as a frustrated opera singer and actor. The only thing he claims to have invented is the pie in the face, and he insists, "Anyone who tells you he has discovered something new is a fool or a liar or both."

The silent comedy studio was about the best training school the movies have ever known, and the Sennett studio was about as free and easy and as fecund of talent as they came. All the major comedians we will mention worked there, at least briefly. So did some of the major stars of the twenties and since—notably Gloria Swanson, Phyllis Haver, Wallace Beery, Marie Dressler, and Carole Lombard. Directors Frank Capra, Leo McCarey, and George Stevens also got their start in silent comedy; much that remains most flexible, spontaneous, and visually alive in sound movies can be traced, through them and others, to this silent apprenticeship. Everybody did pretty much as he pleased on the Sennett lot, and everybody's ideas were welcome. Sennett posted no rules, and the only thing he strictly forbade was liquor. A Sennett story conference was a most informal affair. During the early years, at least, only the most important scenario might be jotted on the back of an envelope. Mainly, Sennett's men thrashed out a few primary ideas and carried them in their heads, sure that better stuff would turn up while they were shooting, in the heat of physical action. This put quite a load on the prop man; he had to have the most improbable apparatus on hand—bombs, trick telephones, whatnot—to implement whatever idea might suddenly turn up. All kinds of things did—and were recklessly used. Once a low-comedy auto got out of control and killed the cameraman, but he was not visible in the shot, which was thrilling and undamaged; the audience never knew the difference.

Sennett used to hire a "wild man" to sit in on his gag conferences, whose whole job was to think up "wildies." Usually, he was an all but brainless, speechless man, scarcely able to communicate his idea, but he had a totally uninhibited imagination. He might say nothing for an hour; then he'd mutter, "You take . . . ," and all the relatively rational others would shut up and wait. "You take this cloud . . . ," he would get out, sketching vague shapes in the air. Often he could get no further, but thanks to some kind of thought transference, saner men would take this cloud and make something of it. The wild man seems in fact to have functioned as the group's subconscious mind, the source of all creative energy. His ideas were so weird and amorphous that Sennett can no longer remember a one of them, or even how it turned out after rational processing. But a fair equivalent might be one of the best comic sequences in a Laurel and Hardy picture. It is simple enough—simple and real, in fact, as a nightmare. Laurel and Hardy are trying to move a piano across a narrow suspension bridge. The bridge is slung over a sickening chasm, between a couple of Alps. Midway they meet a gorilla.

Had he done nothing else, Sennett would be remembered for giving a start to three of the four comedians who now began to apply their sharp individual talents to this newborn language. The one whom he did not train (he was on the lot briefly, but Sennett barely remembers seeing him around) wore glasses, smiled a great deal, and looked like the sort of eager young man who might have quit divinity school to hustle brushes. That was Harold Lloyd. The others were grotesque and poetic in their screen characters in degrees that appear to be impossible when the magic of silence is broken. One, who never smiled, carried a face as still and sad as a daguerreotype through some of the most preposterously ingenious and visually satisfying physical comedy ever invented. That was Buster Keaton. One looked like an elderly baby and, at times, a baby dope fiend; he could do more with less than any other comedian. That was Harry Langdon. One looked like Charlie Chaplin, and he was the first man to give the silent language a soul.

When Charlie Chaplin started to work for Sennett, he had chiefly to reckon with Ford Sterling, the reigning comedian. Their first picture together amounted to a duel before the assembled professionals. Sterling, by no means untalented, was a big man with a florid Teutonic style that, under this special pressure, he turned on full blast. Chaplin defeated him within a few minutes with a wink of the mustache, a hitch of the trousers, a quirk of the little finger.

With *Tillie's Punctured Romance*, in 1914, he became a major star. Soon after, he left Sennett when Sennett refused to start a landslide among the other comedians by meeting the raise Chaplin demanded. Sennett is understandably wry about it in retrospect, but he still says, "I was right at the time." Of Chaplin he says simply, "Oh, well, he's just the greatest artist that ever lived." None of Chaplin's former rivals rates him much lower than that; they speak of him no more jealously than they might of God. We will try here only to suggest the essence of his supremacy. Of all comedians, he worked most deeply and most shrewdly within a realization of what a human being is, and is up against. The Tramp is as centrally representative of humanity, as many-sided and as mysterious, as Hamlet, and it seems unlikely that any dancer or actor can ever have excelled him in eloquence, variety, or poignancy of motion. As for pure motion, even if he had never gone on to make his magnificent feature-length comedies, Chaplin would have made his period in movies a great one single-handedly, even if he had made nothing except *The Cure* (1917) or *One A.M.* (1916). In the latter, barring one immobile taxi driver, Chaplin plays alone as a drunk trying to get upstairs and into bed. It is a sort of inspired elaboration on a soft-shoe dance, involving an angry stuffed wildcat; small rugs on slippery floors; a lazy-Susan table; exquisite footwork on a flight of stairs; a contretemps with a huge, ferocious pendulum; and the funniest and most perverse Murphy bed in movie history—and, always made physically lucid, the delicately weird mental processes of a man ethereally sozzled.

Before Chaplin came to pictures, people were content with a couple of gags per comedy; he got some kind of laugh every second. The minute he began to work, he set standards—and continually forced them higher. Anyone who saw Chaplin eating a boiled shoe like brook trout in *The Gold Rush* (1925), or embarrassed by a swallowed whistle in *City Lights* (1931), has seen perfection. Most of the time, however, Chaplin got his laughter less from the gags, or from milking them in any ordinary sense, than through his genius for what may be called inflection—the perfect, changeful shading of his physical and emotional attitudes toward the gag. Funny as his bout with the Murphy bed is, the glances of awe, expostulation, and helpless, almost whimpering desire for vengeance that he darts at this infernal machine are even better.

FIGURE 2. The Tramp (Charlie Chaplin) dines on his shoe in *The Gold Rush* (1925).

A painful and frequent error among tyros is breaking the comic line with a too big laugh, then a letdown, or with a laugh that is out of key or irrelevant. The masters could ornament the main line beautifully; they never addled it. In *A Night Out* (1915), Chaplin, passed out, is hauled along the sidewalk by the scruff of his coat by staggering Ben Turpin. His toes trail; he is as supine as a sled. Turpin himself is so drunk he can hardly drag him. Chaplin comes quietly to, realizes how well he is being served by his struggling pal, and with a royally delicate gesture plucks and savors a flower.

The finest pantomime, the deepest emotion, the richest and most poignant poetry were in Chaplin's work. He could probably pantomime Bryce's *The American Commonwealth* without ever blurring a syllable and make it paralyzingly funny into the bargain. At the end of *City Lights*, the blind girl who has regained her sight, thanks to the Tramp, sees him for the first time. She has imagined and anticipated him as princely, to say the least, and it has never seriously occurred to him that he is inadequate. She recognizes who he must be by his shy, confident, shining joy as he comes silently toward her. And he recognizes himself, for the first time, through the terrible changes in her face. The camera just exchanges a few quiet close-ups of the emotions that shift and intensify in each face. It is enough to shrivel the heart to see, and it is the greatest piece of acting and the highest moment in movies.

Harold Lloyd worked only a little while with Sennett. During most of his career, he acted for another major comedy producer, Hal Roach. He tried at first to offset Chaplin's influence and establish his own individuality by playing Chaplin's exact opposite, a character named Lonesome Luke who wore clothes much too small for him and whose gestures were likewise as un-Chaplinesque as possible. But he soon realized that an opposite in itself was a kind of slavishness. He discovered his own comic identity when he saw a movie about a fighting parson: a hero who wore glasses. He began to think about those glasses day and night. He decided on horn rims because they were youthful, ultravisible on the screen, and on the verge of becoming fashionable (he was to make them so). Around these large lensless horn rims he began to develop a new character, nothing grotesque or eccentric, but a fresh, believable young man who could fit into a wide variety of stories.

Lloyd depended more on story and situation than any of the other major comedians (he kept the best stable of gagmen in Hollywood, at one time hiring six), but unlike most "story" comedians, he was also a very funny man from inside. He had, as he has written, "an unusually large comic vocabulary." More particularly, he had an expertly expressive body and even more expressive teeth, and out of this thesaurus of smiles he could at a moment's notice blend prissiness, breeziness, and asininity and still remain tremendously likable. His movies were more extroverted and closer to ordinary life than any others of the best comedies: the vicissitudes of a New York taxi driver; the unaccepted college boy who, by desperate courage and inspired ineptitude, wins the Big Game. He was especially good at putting a very timid, spoiled, or brassy young fellow through devastating embarrassments. He went through one of his most uproarious Gethsemanes as a shy country youth courting the nicest girl in town in *Grandma's Boy*. He arrived dressed "strictly up to date for the Spring of 1862," as a subtitle observed, and found that the ancient colored butler wore a similar flowered waistcoat and moldering cutaway. He got one wandering, nervous forefinger dreadfully stuck in a fancy little vase. The girl began cheerfully to try to identify that queer smell that dilated from him; Grandpa's best suit was rife with mothballs. A tenacious litter of kittens feasted off the goose grease on his home-shined shoes.

Lloyd was even better at the comedy of thrills. In *Safety Last!*, as a rank amateur, he is forced to substitute for a human fly and to climb a medium-

FIGURE 3. Harold Lloyd climbs the tall building in *Safety Last!* (1923).

size skyscraper. Dozens of awful things happen to him. He gets fouled up in a tennis net. Popcorn falls on him from a window above, and the local pigeons treat him like a cross between a lunch wagon and Saint Francis of Assisi. A mouse runs up his britches leg, and the crowd below salutes his desperate dance on the window ledge with wild applause of the daredevil. A good deal of this full-length picture hangs thus by its eyelashes along the face of a building. Each new floor is like a new stanza in a poem, and the higher and more horrifying it gets, the funnier it gets.

In this movie Lloyd demonstrates beautifully his ability to do more than merely milk a gag, but to top it. (In an old, simple example of topping, an incredible number of tall men get, one by one, out of a small closed auto. After as many have clambered out as the joke will bear, one more steps out: a midget. That tops the gag. Then the auto collapses. That tops the topper.) In *Safety Last!* Lloyd is driven out to the dirty end of a flagpole by a furious dog; the pole breaks and he falls, just managing to grab the minute hand of a huge clock. His weight promptly pulls the hand down from IX to VI. That would be more than enough for any ordinary comedian, but there is further logic in the situation. Now, hideously, the whole clock face pulls loose and slants from its trembling springs above the street. Getting out of difficulty with the clock, he makes still further use of the instrument by getting one foot caught in one of these obstinate springs.

A proper delaying of the ultrapredictable can of course be just as funny as a properly timed explosion of the unexpected. As Lloyd approaches the end of his horrible hegira up the side of the building in *Safety Last!*, it becomes clear to the audience, but not to him, that if he raises his head another couple of inches, he is going to get murderously conked by one of the four arms of a revolving wind gauge. He delays the evil moment almost interminably, with one distraction and another, and every delay is a suspense-tightening laugh; he also gets his foot nicely entangled in a rope, so that when he does get hit, the payoff of one gag sends him careening head downward through the abyss into another. Lloyd was outstanding even among the master craftsmen at setting up a gag clearly, culminating and getting out of it deftly, and linking it smoothly to the next. Harsh experience also taught him a deep and fundamental rule: never try to get "above" the audience.

Lloyd tried it in *The Freshman*. He was to wear an unfinished, basted-together tuxedo to a college party, which would gradually fall apart as he danced. Lloyd decided to skip the pants, a low-comedy cliché, and lose just the coat. His gag men warned him. A preview proved how right they were. Lloyd had to reshoot the whole expensive sequence, build it around defective pants, and climax it with the inevitable. It was one of the funniest things he ever did.

When Lloyd was still a very young man, he lost about half his right hand (and nearly lost his sight) when a comedy bomb exploded prematurely. But in spite of his artificially built-out hand, he continued to do his own dirty work, like all of the best comedians. The side of the building he climbed in *Safety Last!* did not overhang the street, as it appears to. But the nearest landing place was a roof three floors below him, as he approached the top, and he did everything, of course, the hard way, i.e., the comic way, keeping his bottom stuck well out, his shoulders hunched, his hands and feet skidding over perdition.

If great comedy must involve something beyond laughter, Lloyd was not a great comedian. If plain laughter is any criterion—and it is a healthy counterbalance to the other—few people have equaled him, and nobody has ever beaten him.

Chaplin and Keaton and Lloyd were all more like each other, in one important way, than Harry Langdon was like any of them. Whatever else the others might be doing, they all used more or less elaborate physical comedy; Langdon showed how little of that one might use and still be a great silent screen comedian. In his screen character he symbolized something as deeply and centrally human, though by no means as rangily so, as the Tramp. There was, of course, an immense difference in inventiveness and range of virtuosity. It seemed as if Chaplin could do literally anything, on any instrument in the orchestra. Langdon had one queerly toned, unique little reed. But out of it he could get incredible melodies.

Like Chaplin, Langdon wore a coat that buttoned on his wishbone and swung out wide below, but the effect was very different: he seemed like an outsized baby who had begun to outgrow his clothes. The crown of his hat was rounded and the brim was turned up all around, like a little boy's hat, and he looked as if he wore diapers under his pants. His walk was that of a child who has just gotten sure on its feet, and his body and hands fitted that age. His face was kept pale to show off, with the simplicity of a nursery school drawing, the bright, ignorant, gentle eyes and the little twirling mouth. He had big moon cheeks, with dimples, and a Napoleonic forelock of mousy hair; the round, docile head seemed large in ratio to the cream-puff body. Twitchings of his face were signals of tiny discomforts too slowly registered by a tinier brain; quick, squirty little smiles showed his almost prehuman pleasures, his incurably premature trustfulness. He was a virtuoso of hesitations and of delicately indecisive motions, and he was particularly fine in a high wind, rounding a corner with a kind of skittering toddle, both hands nursing his hat brim.

He was as remarkable a master as Chaplin of subtle emotional and mental process and operated much more at leisure. He once got a good three hundred feet of continuously bigger laughs out of rubbing his chest, in a crowded vehicle, with Limburger cheese, under the misapprehension that it was a cold salve. In another long scene, watching a brazen showgirl change her clothes, he sat motionless, back to the camera, and registered the whole lexicon of lost innocence, shock, disapproval, and disgust, with the back of his neck. His scenes with women were nearly always something special. Once a lady spy did everything in her power (under the Hays Office) to seduce him. Harry was polite, willing, even flirtatious in his little way. The only trouble was that he couldn't imagine what in the world she was leering and pawing at him for and that he was terribly ticklish. The Mata Hari wound up foaming at the mouth.

There was also a sinister flicker of depravity about the Langdon character, all the more disturbing because babies are premoral. He had an instinct for bringing his actual adulthood and figurative babyishness into frictions as crawly as a fingernail on a slate blackboard, and he wandered into areas of strangeness that were beyond the other comedians. In a nightmare in one movie he was forced to fight a large, muscular young man; the girl Harry loved was the prize. The young man was a good boxer; Harry could scarcely lift his gloves. The contest took place in a fiercely lighted prize ring, in a prodigious pitch-dark arena. The only spectator was the girl, and she was rooting against Harry. As the fight went on, her eyes glittered ever more brightly with bloodlust, and, with glittering teeth, she tore her big straw hat to shreds.

Langdon came to Sennett from a vaudeville act in which he had fought a losing battle with a recalcitrant automobile. The minute Frank Capra saw him, he begged Sennett to let him work with him. Langdon was almost as childlike as the character he played. He had only a vague idea of his story or even of each scene as he played it; each time he went before the camera, Capra would brief him on the general situation and then, as this finest of intuitive improvisers once tried to explain his work, "I'd go into my routine." The whole tragedy of the coming of dialogue as far as these comedians were concerned—and one reason for the increasing rigidity of comedy ever since—can be epitomized in the mere thought of Harry Langdon confronted with a script.

Langdon's magic was in his innocence, and Capra took beautiful care not to meddle with it. The key to the proper use of Langdon, Capra always knew, was "the principle of the brick." "If there was a rule for writing Langdon material," he explains, "it was this: His only ally was God. Langdon might be saved by the brick falling on the cop, but it was verboten that he in any way motivate the brick's fall."[1] Langdon became quickly and fantastically popular with three pictures, *Tramp, Tramp, Tramp* (1926), *The Strong Man* (1926), and *Long Pants* (1927); from then on he went downhill even faster. "The trouble was," Capra says, "that high-brow critics came around to explain his art to him. Also he developed an interest in dames. It was a pretty high life for such a little fellow." Langdon made two more pictures with highbrow writers, one of which (*Three's a Crowd* [1927]) had some wonderful passages in it, including the prize-ring nightmare; then First National canceled his contract. He was reduced to mediocre roles and two-reelers that were more rehashes of his old gags; this time around they no longer seemed funny. "He never did really understand what hit him," says Capra. "He died broke [in 1944]. And he died of a broken heart. He was the most tragic figure I ever came across in show business."

Buster Keaton started work at the age of three and a half with his parents in one of the roughest acts in vaudeville ("The Three Keatons");

Harry Houdini gave the child the name Buster in admiration for a fall he took down a flight of stairs. In his first movies Keaton teamed with Fatty Arbuckle under Sennett. He went on to become one of Metro's biggest stars and earners; a Keaton feature cost about $200,000 to make and reliably grossed $2 million. Very early in his movie career, friends asked him why he never smiled on the screen. He didn't realize he didn't. He had got the deadpan habit in variety; on the screen he had merely been so hard at work, it had never occurred to him there was anything to smile about. Now he tried it just once and never again. He was by his whole style and nature so much the most deeply "silent" of the silent comedians that even a smile was as deafeningly out of key as a yell. In a way his pictures are like a transcendent juggling act in which it seems that the whole universe is in exquisite flying motion and the one point of repose is the juggler's effortless, uninterested face.

Keaton's face ranked almost with Lincoln's as an early American archetype; it was haunting, handsome, almost beautiful, yet it was irreducibly funny; he improved matters by topping it off with a deadly horizontal hat, as flat and thin as a phonograph record. One can never forget Keaton wearing it, standing erect at the prow as his little boat is being launched. The boat goes grandly down the skids and, just as grandly, straight on to the bottom. Keaton never budges. The last you see of him, the water lifts the hat off the stoic head, and it floats away.

No other comedian could do as much with the deadpan. He used this great, sad, motionless face to suggest various related things: a one-track mind near the track's end of pure insanity; mulish imperturbability under the wildest of circumstances; how dead a human being can get and still be alive; an awe-inspiring sort of patience and power to endure, proper to granite but uncanny in flesh and blood. Everything that he was and did bore out this rigid face and played laughs against it. When he moved his eyes, it was like seeing them move in a statue. His short-legged body was all sudden, machinelike angles, governed by a daft aplomb. When he swept a semaphore-like arm to point, you could almost hear the electrical impulse in the signal block. When he ran from a cop, his transitions from accelerating walk to easy jog trot to brisk canter to headlong gallop to flogged-piston sprint—always floating, above this frenzy, the untroubled, untouchable face—were as distinct and as soberly in order as an automatic gearshift.

Keaton was a wonderfully resourceful inventor of mechanistic gags (he still spends much of his time fooling with Erector sets); as he ran afoul of locomotives, steamships, prefabricated and overelectrified houses, he put

himself through some of the hardest and cleverest punishment ever designed for laughs. In *Sherlock Jr.* (1924), boiling along on the handlebars
of a motorcycle quite unaware that he has lost his driver, Keaton whips
through city traffic, breaks up a tug-of-war, gets a shovelful of dirt in the
face from each of a long line of Rockette-timed ditchdiggers, approaches
at high speed a log that is hinged open by dynamite precisely soon enough
to let him through, and, hitting an obstruction, leaves the handlebars like
an arrow leaving a bow, whams through the window of a shack in which
the heroine is about to be violated, and hits the heavy feet first, knocking
him through the opposite wall. The whole sequence is as clean in motion
as the trajectory of a bullet.

Much of the charm and edge of Keaton's comedy, however, lay in the
subtle leverages of expression he could work against his nominal deadpan.
Trapped in the side-wheel of a ferryboat, saving himself from drowning
only by walking, then desperately running, inside the accelerating wheel
like a squirrel in a cage, his only real concern was, obviously, to keep his
hat on. Confronted by Love, he was not as deadpan as he was cracked up
to be, either; there was an odd, abrupt motion of his head that suggested
a horse nipping after a sugar lump.

Keaton worked strictly for laughs, but his work came from so far inside
a curious and original spirit that he achieved a great deal besides, especially in his feature-length comedies. (For plain hard laughter, his nine-
teen short comedies—the negatives of which have been lost—were even
better.) He was the only major comedian who kept sentiment almost entirely out of his work, and he brought pure physical comedy to its greatest
heights. Beneath his lack of emotion he was also uninsistently sardonic;
deep below that, giving a disturbing tension and grandeur to the foolishness, for those who sensed it, there was in his comedy a freezing whisper
not of pathos but of melancholia. With the humor, the craftsmanship, and
the action, there was often, besides, a fine, still, and sometimes dreamlike
beauty. Much of his Civil War picture *The General* (1926) is within hailing
distance of Mathew Brady. And there is a ghostly, unforgettable moment
in *The Navigator* (1924) when, on a deserted, softly rolling ship, all the pale
doors along a deck swing open as one behind Keaton and, as one, slam
shut, in a hair-raising illusion of noise.

Perhaps because "dry" comedy is so much more rare and odd than
"dry" wit, there are people who never much cared for Keaton. Those who
do cannot care mildly.

As soon as the screen began to talk, silent comedy was pretty well fin-
ished. The hardy and prolific Mack Sennett made the transfer; he was the

FIGURE 4. Buster Keaton's expressive deadpan in *The Navigator* (1924).

first man to put Bing Crosby and W. C. Fields on the screen. But he was essentially a silent picture man, and by the time the Academy awarded him a special Oscar for his "lasting contribution to the comedy technique of the screen" (in 1938), he was no longer active. As for the comedians we have spoken of in particular, they were as badly off as fine dancers suddenly required to appear in plays.

Harold Lloyd, whose work was most nearly realistic, naturally coped least unhappily with the added realism of speech; he made several talking comedies. But good as the best were, they were not so good as his silent work, and by the late thirties he quit acting. A few years ago he returned to play the lead (and play it beautifully) in Preston Sturges's *The Sin of Harold Diddlebock* (1947), but this exceptional picture—which opened, brilliantly, with the closing reel of Lloyd's *The Freshman*—has not yet been generally released.

Like Chaplin, Lloyd was careful with his money; he is still rich and active. Last June, in the presence of President Truman, he became imperial potentate of the AAONMS (Shriners). Harry Langdon, as we have said, was a broken man when sound came in.

Up to the middle thirties Buster Keaton made several feature-length pictures (with such players as Jimmy Durante, Wallace Beery, and Robert Montgomery); he also made a couple dozen talking shorts. Now and again he managed to get loose into motion, without having to talk, and for a moment or so the screen would start singing again. But his dark, dead voice, though it was in keeping with the visual character, tore his intensely silent style to bits and destroyed the illusion within which he worked. He gallantly and correctly refuses to regard himself as "retired." Besides occasional bits, spots, and minor roles in Hollywood pictures, he has worked on summer stages, made talking comedies in France and Mexico, and clowned in a French circus. This summer he has played the straw hats in *Three Men on a Horse*. He is planning a television program. He also has a working agreement with Metro. One of his jobs there is to construct comedy sequences for Red Skelton.

The only man who really survived the flood was Chaplin, the only one who was rich, proud, and popular enough to afford to stay silent. He brought out two of his greatest nontalking comedies, *City Lights* and *Modern Times* (1936), in the middle of an avalanche of talk, spoke gibberish and, in the closing moments, plain English in *The Great Dictator* (1940), and at last made an all-talking picture, *Monsieur Verdoux* (1947), creating for that purpose an entirely new character who might properly talk a blue streak. *Verdoux* is the greatest of talking comedies, though so cold and savage that it had to find its public in grimly experienced Europe.

Good comedy, and some that was better than good, outlived silence, but there has been less and less of it. The talkies brought one great comedian, the late, majestically lethargic W. C. Fields, who could not possibly have worked as well in silence; he was the toughest and the most warmly human of all screen comedians, and *It's a Gift* (1934) and *The Bank Dick* (1940), fiendishly funny and incisive white-collar comedies, rank high among the best comedies (and best movies) ever made. Laurel and Hardy, the only comedians who managed to preserve much of the large, low style of silence and who began to explore the comedy of sound, have made nothing since 1945. Walt Disney, at his best an inspired comic inventor and teller of fairy stories, lost his stride during the war and has since regained it only at moments. Preston Sturges has made brilliant, satirical comedies, but his pictures are smart, nervous comedy-dramas merely italicized with slapstick. The Marx Brothers were sidesplitters, but they made their best comedies years ago. Jimmy Durante is mainly a nightclub genius; Abbott and Costello are semiskilled laborers, at best; Bob Hope is a good radio comedian with a pleasing presence, but not much more, on the screen.

There is no hope that screen comedy will get much better than it is without new, gifted young comedians who really belong in movies and without freedom for their experiments. For everyone who may appear, we have one last invidious comparison to offer as a guidepost.

One of the most popular recent comedies is Bob Hope's *The Paleface* (1948). We take no pleasure in blackening *The Paleface*; we single it out, rather, because it is as good as we've got. Anything that is said of it here could be said, with interest, of other comedies of our time. Most of the laughs in *The Paleface* are verbal. Bob Hope is very adroit with his lines, and now and then, when the words don't get in the way, he makes a good beginning as a visual comedian. But only the beginning, never the middle or the end. He is funny, for instance, reacting to a shot of violent whiskey. But he does not know how to get still funnier (i.e., how to build and milk) or how to be funniest last (i.e., how to top or cap his gag). The camera has to fade out on the same old face he started with.

One sequence is promisingly set up for visual comedy. In it, Hope and a lethal local boy stalk each other all over a cow town through streets that have been emptied in fear of their duel. The gag here is that through accident and stupidity, they keep just failing to find each other. Some of it is quite funny. But the fun slackens between laughs like a weak clothesline, and by all the logic of humor (which is ruthlessly logical) the biggest laugh should come at the moment, and through the way, they finally spot each other. The sequence is so weakly thought out that at that crucial moment, the camera can't afford to watch them; it switches to Jane Russell.

Now we turn to a masterpiece. In *The Navigator* Buster Keaton works with practically the same gag as Hope's duel. Adrift on a ship that he believes is otherwise empty, he drops a lighted cigarette. A girl finds it. She calls out and he hears her; each then tries to find the other. First each walks purposefully down the long, vacant starboard deck, the girl, then Keaton, turning the corner just in time not to see each other. Next time around each of them is trotting briskly, very much in earnest; going at the same pace, they miss each other just the same. Next time around each of them is going like a bat out of hell. Again they miss. Then the camera withdraws to a point of vantage at the stern, leans its chin in its hand, and just watches the whole intricate superstructure of the ship as the protagonists stroll, steal, and scuttle from level to level, up, down, and sidewise, always managing to miss each other by hairbreadths, in an enchantingly neat and elaborate piece of timing. There are no subsidiary gags to get laughs in this sequence, and there is little loud laughter, merely a quiet and steadily increasing kind of delight. When Keaton has got all he can out of this fine modification of the movie chase, he invents a fine device to bring the two together: the girl, thoroughly winded, sits down for a breather, indoors, on a plank that workmen have left across sawhorses. Keaton pauses on an upper deck, equally winded and puzzled. What follows happens in a couple of seconds at most: air suction whips his silk topper backward down a ventilator; grabbing frantically for it, he backs against the lip of the ventilator, jackknifes, and falls in backward. Instantly, the camera cuts back to the girl. A topper falls through the ceiling and lands tidily, right side up, on the plank beside her. Before she can look more than startled, its owner follows, head between his knees, crushes the topper, breaks the plank with the point of his spine, and proceeds to the floor. The breaking of the plank smacks Boy and Girl together.

It is only fair to remember that the silent comedians would have as hard a time playing a talking scene as Hope has playing his visual ones and that writing and directing are as accountable for the failure as Hope himself. But not even the humblest journeymen of the silent years would have let themselves off so easily. Like the masters, they knew, and sweated to obey, the laws of their craft.

NOTE

1. Frank Capra remembers telling the author this story in preparation for this article in his book *The Name above the Title: An Autobiography* (New York: Macmillan, 1971), but recounts it slightly differently: "The key to the proper use of Langdon is the 'principle of the brick.' Langdon might be saved by the brick falling on the cop, but it was *verboten* that he in any way motivate the brick's fall" (62). [Editors' note.]

CHAPTER 2

SILENT FILM COMEDY

SIEGFRIED KRACAUER

SILENT FILM COMEDY, which reached its apogee in America during the twenties, originated in France, where its essential traits were developed long before World War I. At a time when the art of storytelling was still unknown—D. W. Griffith had not yet entered upon the scene—this genre had attained near perfection. It was rooted in the traditions of the music hall, the circus, the burlesque, and the fair, spectacles drawing in varying degrees on the eternal fascination that catastrophe, dangers, and physical shocks exert on civilized man. From its outset film comedy piled up these kinds of thrills in ever-new combinations, with the understanding, of course, that at the very last minute, the characters involved could manage to escape to safety. The purpose was fun, after all. A boy tampering with a garden hose inundates the apartments of a nearby house, people on a pleasure stroll fall smack into a lake, itch powder in the fish does things to the dinner guests, a bride who gets stuck somewhere appears at the wedding party in her underwear—such gags were common in France between 1905 and 1910. Some motifs migrated to America and there became institutions. For instance, the gendarmes, standing figures of the early French farce, reemerged as the Keystone cops and, surviving the Sennett era, continued to the last to play their double role as the pompous pursuers and the chickenhearted pursued, the former mainly for the purpose of collapsing all the more drastically. There is no short Chaplin comedy in which the Tramp would not alternately dread and outwit some bulky policeman—the mouse playing with the cat. Crumbling pillars of order, these gendarmes or cops were visibly intended to deepen the impression of a topsy-turvy world. Similarly, the nightmarish motif of being stripped of one's clothes in front of normally dressed people threaded slapstick from beginning to end; Harold Lloyd losing his pants was just another version of the bride in her underwear.

Film comedy evoked material life at its crudest. And since in those archaic days of the immobile camera life on the screen was synonymous with life in motion, the comedy makers did their utmost to exaggerate all natural movements. With the aid of a single camera trick, they set humanity racing and reveled in games of speed. In *Onesime horloger* (1908), a very charming French one-reeler, Paris runs wild, the Avenue de l'Opéra turns into an agitated ant heap, and wallpaper flies onto walls that have mushroomed a second before. It was cinema; it was fun; it was as if you sat in a roller coaster driving ahead at full blast, with your stomach all upside down. The dizziness happily added to the shock effects from disasters and seeming collisions. To frame these space-devouring adventures, the chase offered itself as an invaluable pretext. Gendarmes chased a dog who eventually turned the tables on them (*La course des sergents de ville* [1907]); pumpkins gliding from a cart were chased by the grocer, his donkey, and passersby through sewers and over roofs (*La course des potirons* [*The Pumpkin Race*] [1907]). For any Keystone comedy to omit the chase would have been an unpardonable crime. It was the climax of the whole, its orgiastic finale—a pandemonium, with onrushing trains telescoping into automobiles and narrow escapes down ropes that dangled above a lion's den.

As should by now be clear, these chases and states of extremity involved not only cops and robbers but pieces of furniture and highways as well. Comedy was cinematic also in that it extended its range to include the whole of physical reality that could be reached by the camera eye. The rule was that inanimate objects held important positions and developed preferences of their own. More often than not, they were filled with a certain malice toward anything human. When the pumpkins rolled down or up a slope, it was indeed as if they wanted to play a practical joke on their pursuers. And who would not remember Chaplin's heroic scraps with the escalator, the beach chair, and the unruly Murphy bed? Among the scheming objects those devised for our comfort were in fact particularly vicious. Instead of serving man, these progressive gadgets turned out to be on the best of terms with the very elements they were supposed to harness; instead of making us independent of the whims of matter, they actually were the shock troops of unconquered nature and inflicted upon us defeat after defeat. They conspired against their masters, they gave the lie to the alleged blessings of mechanization. Their conspiracy was so powerful that it nipped Buster Keaton's smile in the bud. How could he possibly smile in a mechanized world? His unalterable impassivity was an admission that in such a world, the machines and contrivances laid down the law and that he had better adjust himself to their exigencies. Yet at the same time, this impassivity, human though it was, made him appear touchingly human, for it was inseparable from sadness, and you felt that, had he ever smiled while pushing the buttons or declaring his love, he would have betrayed his sadness and endorsed a state of affairs that caused him to behave like a gadget.

Of course, it was all comedy and the threats never came true. Whenever destructive natural forces, hostile objects, or human brutes seemed to win the day, the balance shifted abruptly in favor of their sympathetic victims. The pumpkins returned to the cart, the pursued escaped through a loophole, and the weak reached a provisional haven. Frequently, such minor triumphs were due to feats of acrobatic skill. Yet unlike most circus productions, film comedy did not highlight the performer's proficiency in braving death and surmounting impossible difficulties; rather, it minimized his accomplishments in a constant effort to present successful rescues as the outcome of sheer chance. Accidents superseded destiny; unpredictable circumstances now foreshadowed doom, now jelled into propitious constellations for no visible reason. Take Harold Lloyd on the skyscraper; what protected him from falling to death was not his prowess but a random combination of external and completely incoherent events that, without being intended to come to his help, dovetailed so perfectly that he could not have fallen even had he wanted to. Accidents were the very soul of slapstick. This too was intrinsically cinematic, for it conformed to the spirit of a medium predestined to capture the fortuitous aspects of physical life. Since there were so many happy endings, the spectator was led to believe that the innate malice of objects yielded to benevolence in certain cases. Harry Langdon, for instance, belonged among nature's favorites. A somnambulist fairy-tale prince, he waddled safely through a world of mortal dangers, not in the least aware that he was safe only because the elements succumbed to his babyish candor and sweet idiocy. Was it not even possible to influence chance and assuage spite? When attacked by a tough, Chaplin's Tramp in his anguish invoked the magic power of rhythm to avert the worst; he performed a few delicate dance steps and choice gestures and, with the aid of these emergency rites, hypnotized the tough into a state of incredulous wonder that paralyzed him just long enough to enable the cunning Tramp to take to his heels.

FIGURE 5. The Marx Brothers' *Go West* (1940): dialogue changed the nature of film comedy.

Any such gag was a small unit complete in itself, and any comedy was a package of gags that, in music hall fashion, were autonomous entities rather than parts of a story. As a rule, there was a story of a sort, but it had merely the function of stringing these monad-like units together. What counted was that they succeeded each other uninterruptedly, not that their succession implemented some plot. To be sure, they often happened to build up a halfway consistent intrigue, yet that intrigue was never of so exacting a nature that its significance would have encroached on that of the units composing it. Even though *The Gold Rush* (1925) and *City Lights* (1930) transcended the genre, they culminated in such episodes as the dance with the fork or the misdemeanor of the swallowed whistle, gag clusters that, for meaning and effect, depended so little upon the narrative in which they appeared that they could easily be isolated without being mutilated. Film comedy was an ack-ack of gags. For the rest, it indulged in absurdity, as if to make it unmistakably clear that no catastrophe was meant to be real nor any action to be of consequence. The nonsensical frolics of Sennett's bathing girls smothered the tender beginnings of comprehensible plots, and the many false mustaches on display bespoke a joyous zest for unaccountable foolishness. Absurdity stripped events of their possible meanings. And since it thus cut short the implications they might otherwise have conveyed to us, we were all the more obliged to absorb them for their own sake. It is true that comedy presented acts of violence and extreme situations only to disavow their seriousness a moment later, yet as long as they persisted they communicated nothing but themselves. They were as they were, and the shots rendering them had no function other than to make us watch spectacles too crude to be perceived with detachment in real life. It was genuine cinema, with the emphasis on the pranks of objects and the sallies of nature. This explains why from early slapstick to Chaplin's full-length films, the visuals in a measure retained the character of snapshots. They were matter-of-fact records rather than expressive photographs. But would not art photography have introduced all the meanings that the comedy makers instinctively wanted to avoid? Their concern was alienated physical existence.

Film comedy died with silent film. Perhaps the Depression precipitated its death. But it did not die from the change of social conditions, however unfortunate; rather, it was killed by a change in the medium itself—the addition of dialogue. Those nightmarish tangles, games of speed, and plays with inarticulate matter, which were inseparable from comedy, occurred in depths of material life that words do not penetrate; speech with all that it involves in articulate thoughts and emotions was therefore bound to obscure the very essence of the genre. Comedy ceased to be comedy when the admixture of dialogue blurred our visual experience of speechless events, when the necessity of following more or less intelligible talk lured us from the material dimension, in which everything just happened, to the dimension of discursive reasoning in which everything was, somehow, labeled and digested verbally. It was inevitable indeed that the spoken word should put an end to a genre that was allergic to it. Harpo alone survives from the silent era. Like the gods of antiquity who after their downfall lived on as puppets, bugbears, and other minor ghosts, haunting centuries that no longer believed in them, Harpo is a residue of the past, an exiled comedy god condemned or permitted to act the part of a mischievous hobgoblin. Yet the world in which he appears is so crowded with dialogue that he would long since have vanished were it not for Groucho, who supports the specter's irresponsible doings by destroying dialogue from within. As dizzying as any silent collision, Groucho's word cataclysms wreak havoc on language, and among the resultant debris Harpo continues to feel at ease.

CHAPTER 3

UNCLE SAM'S FUNNY BONE

ALLEN EYLES

THE HOLLYWOOD COMEDY isn't what it used to be. It is easy to illustrate a thesis on the film city's decline by asking where the comedies of style, pace, and unity have gone. The recent survey on the decade in America could single out only *Some Like It Hot* (1959) and *Love in the Afternoon* (1957) as "decent examples." But a question that must be answered is whether present circumstances, economic or sociological, have done no more than dictate a change in form and approach. Perhaps the humorous basis of American comedies is as valid and penetrating as ever, while the form is an adjustment to the modern audience's preoccupations.

However, the feeling is widespread in the United States that humor has declined since the Depression days when Capra, W. C. Fields, Lubitsch, and the brothers Marx were active. One reason is the ready market for the second rate; the cinema and, even more, television offer the writer no incentive to better himself. Nor has the writer often seen much control over his material in either of these media. Behind all the enduring comedies of the thirties lies a notable writer, often in continual partnership with a director or comedian, Robert Riskin in the Capra films and S. J. Perelman with the Marx Brothers, for example. In a wider field the phenomenal success of Harold Ross's *New Yorker* created a precise formula of sophistication that the prestige-seeking humorous writer was invariably tempted to meet, especially after so many of the competing outlets vanished under the new magazine's impact. When so many contributors migrated to Hollywood, between them and the hacks and the Second

Allen Eyles, "Uncle Sam's Funny Bone," *Films and Filming* 9, no. 6 (1963): 45–49. Copyright © 1963 by Hansom Books. Used with permission of the author.

World War there may have been insufficient space for new approaches to squeeze in and make their mark.

The worst barrier to face the new writer is the change in world politics, making a lot of things no longer as funny as they were. Since comedy is essentially of a rebellious if not a revolutionary nature, it is easily labeled subversive in a country so conscious of its preeminent role in the free world. The post-McCarthy climate was not one in which screen satire flourished, and the more courageous writers were often too embittered to conceal their scorn under a veil of comedy. This may well have been an error considering how deep went the satirical jabs Budd Schulberg wrote into *A Face in the Crowd* (1957) compared to the crude histrionics of the rest. Lonesome Rhodes's audition for Vitajex was the best and most savage of them. But only Chaplin's *A King in New York* (1957) (filmed at Shepperton) really continued a line of political satire so richly explored in earlier years by films such as *The Senator Was Indiscreet* (1947), which reached television only recently in an adulterated form.

National solidarity and associated institutions, apart from the armed forces, have to be mocked with caution. The rookie is too familiar a butt to be dropped very quickly. Characters in any way representative of the national spirit have generally to receive soft treatment, in the cinema at any rate. For the rise of the sick joke and more topical humor to a thriving state in nightclubs, small-circulation magazines, and the occasional theatrical production was realized with a small capital outlay and aimed at a small segment of the public. The filming of *One, Two, Three* (1961) with the Berlin situation as the core of the humor has been Hollywood's most extreme response to the new look in the topicality line, and that was encased in a very old form (*Ninotchka*'s [1939] in fact, to seize on the parallel of the three comic commissars and the fact that Billy Wilder was one of the writers there too).

The emphasis on more expensive, individually handled pictures rather than an extensive multiproduction schedule excludes experiment, except as embroidery on a "safe" main theme. Thus do we get the intramural gags of a Billy Wilder or a Frank Tashlin picture beyond what is sufficient for the general public to grasp, but nothing as philosophical or innovatory as a *Les jeux de l'amour* (1960). Furthermore, the importance of foreign returns in the Hollywood economy encourages the hedging of bets on a proven formula with universally appreciated sight gags preferable to esoteric verbal wit. Aligning the big stars against foreign settings also helps (*Come September* [1961] and the others).

The critic is on the offensive in viewing a comedy, daring the film to make him and his small bunch of confreres laugh at the bleak hour of the press show. The public, out to extract value for money and peace of mind after a hard day's work, is not only less suspicious but very content with the current fare, to judge by box-office results. These films are not as innocuous, lightweight, and forgettable as they look; they communicate in basic and broad terms.

As a couple of characteristics, they never depict healthy eccentrics, and geniuses tend to fall foul of their own intelligence. The academic loses his trousers (*Bachelor Flat* [1962]), the psychiatrist is nuttier than the patient (*No Time for Sergeants* [1958]), and the boffin lured from the bench to the nightclub is pitied for his blatantly out-of-fashion dress (Rock Hudson's masquerade in *Lover Come Back* [1961]). Minorities are happily damned for the majority's amusement. Two examples of this from *That Touch of Mink* (1962): the boss dreamily whisks off his secretary's glasses and is recoiled by the sight beneath, and the clever idea of a psychiatrist picking up stock-market tips from a patient and stealing out midsession to make a killing really serves to introduce some coarse homosexual innuendo.

Note in this film how gently treated is Cary Grant, the businessman who doesn't take to marriage. Doris Day may be on the dole, but you wouldn't know it to look at her or her apartment. New York Automats were never so cozy in my experience, nor did they look so clinically clean behind the service hatches. Against this backcloth of happy, humming, hyperactive commerce, only little matters of romantic misunderstandings cause concern. Millionaires, oil kings, advertising executives, magazine publishers, as well as lesser "organization men" may have their temptations and aberrations but come back to the system (and its morality) in the end. A belief in individual responsibility is rare, so that characterization is as limited and stereotyped as situation.

But the face of comedy has been changing in the sector of least resistance: the romantic comedy. Anything can be implied before the happy ending, and little of it will be censorable at the script stage. Once the tone was light, suggestive, based on the triangle situation. The result was a model of good manners. Joseph Mankiewicz's *A Letter to Three Wives* (1949) was a talk picture full of acute psychological observation that conjured up possibilities without realizing any of them: despite the letter, none of the husbands had run off with the town flame.

Now the treatment has become heavy and sniggering. What Lubitsch would signal by a wink as his scene faded out on a bedroom door is treated in laborious half-measure, with scenes like that in *Lover Come Back* where a woman shows the members of the Advertising Council something or other around her neck as an excuse for them to eye her cleavage. Oddly, comedies set in foreign locales seem to have pregnancies galore (*The Perfect Furlough* [1958], *Jessica* [1962], *The Pigeon That Took Rome* [1962]). But no offense must be given to pressure groups on the home front: retribution via a car accident visits the pregnant Yvette Mimieux of *Where the Boys Are* (1960). Americans don't make mistakes (outside of the tearful high school dramas) and remain, to appearances, pure. The cult of stray underwear stems from the same restraints, with fanfares on the soundtrack at every bra on the washing line. Whereas Jean-Pierre Cassel wipes his paintbrush on a bra because it's handy and suitable, Eva Gabor's panties flutter in the breeze to inspire the fleet at the end of one naval comedy, *Don't Go Near the Water* (1957). In *Operation Petticoat* (1959), where the title is evidence, an American submarine identifies itself by letting the underwear of some nurses (who are improperly aboard) surface in front of the enemy. A nurse's girdle even fixes a difficulty in the engine room: so much for what keeps America on the move.

Li'l Abner (1959), liberated by its comic-strip world, can dispense with such inhibitions even to the extent of a chorus worshipping the dollar and the combine of General Bullmoose (bigger than the government) as well as introducing one Appassionata von Climax, whose relationship to the general is queried by innocent Abner, "Do you get bed an' board, ma'am?" "Yes, very." The mere glamour of appearance (form before function) is presented at full strength in Julie Newmar's "stupefying" female who is healthily dismissed by the practical Dogpatch male.

In fact, the more daring the Hollywood comedy seems to be, the more conformist it actually becomes. In *Boys' Night Out* (1962), Kim Novak poses as a call girl to compile her college thesis on the sex urge of the American male. It turns out, in the fashion of *The Bachelor Party* (1957), that nothing happens except some boasting. She beds none of the syndicate who install her in the luxury flat, and she conveniently falls for the one unmarried member. *All in a Night's Work* (1961) had the exhaustively plugged starting point of Shirley MacLaine emerging in only a towel from an aged millionaire's bedroom: but for us to jump to (and, unlike Dean Martin, enjoy) the obvious conclusion only proves in the outcome what dirty minds we all have.

No subject is ipso facto bad comedy, for it all depends on the treatment. A familiar situation in travel sequences is the man-in-the-woman's-bunk routine. Tony Curtis is merely helping the girl surmount the problem of a window that won't open in *The Perfect Furlough*, but what does this lead other people to think? Yet when Billy Wilder puts just such a scene (only

FIGURE 6. Jack Lemmon and Tony Curtis in drag disguise in *Some Like It Hot* (1959).

with more girls and a fresh angle) into *Some Like It Hot*, its use is perfectly acceptable and funny because Jack Lemmon's masquerade as Daphne justifies his presence; the audience is fully entitled to its vicarious enjoyment of it. Wilder's basic situation in *The Apartment* (1960)—an employee letting out his flat for his bosses to conduct overnight trysts—rebounds on the hero and approving members of the audience (encouraged in number by Jack Lemmon's amiable interpretation of the role) when he discovers that his would-be girlfriend (who is to justify his loot) is one of the visitors. Even when plot mechanics force a rosy ending, and the chorus figure of the man next door accepts hero and girl at last as decent people, the spectator is not deceived and can sense where the real force of the film has lain. In this way, Wilder is really an honest cynic.

A contradiction arises from the liberation of vocabulary (*virginity* and so on, since *The Moon Is Blue* defied the censorship in 1953) but not of ideas—except perhaps in *Breakfast at Tiffany's* (1961), where (adding to the novel) there is a very explicit treatment of the writer's position in relation to an older woman. He is not only being kept. As an artist in New York, this is made to seem his easiest solution to lack of recognition and public patronage.

Marilyn Monroe summed up the scene at an early stage of development: all allure and inaccessibility, a goddess really. Even when she is made a chorus girl in *Let's Make Love* (1960), the millionaire gets nowhere with his wealth. Tom Ewell has daydreams along with his seven-year itch, but little more than that. When audiences tired of the "distancing," Jayne Mansfield was brought in. She is not a romanticization but a blunt statement of male preoccupations and is used as such by Frank Tashlin in *The Girl Can't Help It* (1956) and *Will Success Spoil Rock Hunter?* (1957). The assumption is so basic that it tends to be overlooked.

Tashlin is more in touch with fundamentals than any other director or writer of comedy (he is, of course, both). Significantly a former newspaper cartoonist, he seems to rely on intuition to produce a perfect though broad caricature of American mores. In *The Girl Can't Help It*, it is both a crude and a subtle joke when the milkman eyes Jayne's walk and his reaction causes the milk to bubble out from the bottles he is hugging. Similarly, the unpleasant giggling female who is being agitated by a slimming machine while eating chocolate cake in *Bachelor Flat* is a deft expression of the American belief that one can slim without giving up food. And with Tashlin in general, if you can imagine it, he meant it. Tashlin's world is one bound up with sex, status, tranquilizers, dieting, the mod cons, and the neuroses of our time. He has even introduced some harsher elements into his films, but peripherally—as when Edmond O'Brien recalls a song from prison days called "There's No Lights on the Christmas Tree, Mother, They're Using the Electric Chair Tonight" or when Terry-Thomas imagines the "delinquent" (Lolitaesque?) teenager Tuesday Weld being whipped at the reform school if he sends her back. Yet, like all his references, they remain elements and don't cohere. Perhaps it is just that Tashlin is so prolific a filmmaker that he spreads his talent thin, but I doubt it. However, the five or six ideas in a Tashlin film that really take are better when the slipshod, hit-and-miss setting to which they were attached has been forgotten.

A similar situation prevails in *The Chaplin Revue* (1959): near-intolerable length with a sprinkling of great ideas. Yet one has only to go to the early pictures of the Marx Brothers (*A Night at the Opera* [1935] and before) to discover that a film can be so teeming with ideas that the damp squibs (like, quite often, the puns of Chico) get by because one is still relishing the last good joke (perhaps a Groucho wisecrack) or storing away the sublime pantomime of the manic Harpo. In *Horse Feathers* (1932), probably the most penetrating of their social satires, education, sport, love, and the

FIGURE 7. The iceman cometh upon seeing Jayne Mansfield in *The Girl Can't Help It* (1956).

Depression were all deflated into limp remnants of dramatically respectable institutions. One can watch their films again and again (providing one doesn't want "heart," the heavy hand of sentimentality that MGM obtruded into their later pictures to draw in the women) and there's always more to see, whereas a Tashlin film becomes thinner at each viewing as one's imaginative reception of Tashlin's ideas (which in a cartoon strip could flourish in a realm of detachment from natural logic) is rebuffed by his literal representations.

As it happens, Tashlin was one of the scriptwriters on the Marxes' last film, *Love Happy* (1949). It is one of their worst, and whoever devised the sequence in which a cop searches Harpo as he stands against a wall, extracting an enormous amount of junk from his apparently cavernous inner raincoat pocket, ignores the fact that the audience will not delight in the fantasy involved but go for the obvious and rational solution: that the collection of properties is being accumulated from a hole in the wall of the set hidden by the raincoat. When, in *Horse Feathers*, Harpo answers a tramp's plea for the money to buy a cup of coffee by producing one, steaming hot in a saucer, from the same raincoat pocket, the idea scores:

it is quick, and there are no technical distractions. In this case, too, the gag is not isolated but reinforces Harpo's character, of having an impish control over reality.

Yet Tashlin in his Jerry Lewis comedy *The Geisha Boy* (1958) has a man fall in an indoor swimming pool and create a tidal wave that engulfs the whole neighborhood. The mind becomes involved with cubic capacities and the like; the laughter is choked off. For a rare modern instance of the correct scale being applied, one can turn to *Who Was That Lady?* (1960, scripted by Norman Krasna), which leads smoothly up to a climax that has the heroes amid the basement machinery of the Empire State Building smashing it up under the impression that they are scuttling a Russian submarine. Being (take my word for it) firmly based on plot and situation, this climax is quite sublime when one suddenly appreciates the breadth of absurdity involved.

In fact, a concern for the impact of a film as a whole, a feeling for rhythm and climax, is a major deficiency in most Hollywood productions, let alone comedy. There the work of Billy Wilder stands out conspicuously as an exception—and besides his thirties background, one can point to his continuing collaboration with I. A. L. Diamond on his scripts since *Love in the Afternoon*. Knowing what he is about, Wilder has successfully accommodated such a grim sequence as the St. Valentine's Day Massacre into a comedy (*Some Like It Hot*) without killing his overall mood.

To this point, a technique of abstraction has mainly been illustrated, producing the generalizations and stereotypes that front an implicit ideology. Here *parody* is the word rather than *satire*. The successful comedies of character, however, derive their strength from particularizing human behavior, of showing idiosyncrasies and exposing human foibles. Within a predictable story line (allowing for the fact that leading characters will basically conform), the unpredictable details can win sympathetic laughter and enlarge one's understanding of human nature. Frank Capra's *It's a Wonderful Life* (1946) took this type furthest, demonstrating what life would be without the best of us: an angel (Henry Travers) shows a despairing James Stewart just what his life has meant to other people and gives him the strength to surmount his present misfortune. Leo McCarey's *Good Sam* (1948) did much the same thing: the Salvation Army brings Sam (Gary Cooper) home to his wife and kids when disaster has struck in the wake of his unrestrained generosity. The hymn-singing fade-outs may seem the last gooey touch to outrageously mawkish and sentimental proceedings, but this depends on one's taste. (The more recent Capra film *Pocketful of Miracles* [1961] would be hard to defend against such charges.)

The idea of a utopia on earth at the heart of Capra's work seems quite impractical now. The problems are bigger than just a national slump. Americans are not willing to face the more specific ones attached to living in an economy organized on waste and featherbedding when it cushions their lives so comfortably. Capra's answers were not very deep anyway. One can easily recall Longfellow Deeds (Gary Cooper in *Mr. Deeds Goes to Town* [1936]), who inherits a fortune and ends up in court with "an insane desire to be a public benefactor." Deeds slides down banisters, races after fire engines to see the fire, and gives his money away because . . . he wants to. And clearly, if only the drippy sentiments he writes for publication on Christmas cards could be taken seriously, all would be right with the world. We may not quarrel with this, but Capra's demonstration—the rich giving charity to the most outstretching hands of the poor—is preposterous. What of the reticent rich or the too proud poor? We remember Deeds; we forget the plot. The plot deals with special circumstances without general validity, but Deeds represents values that we can take to heart.

That ideas can be integrated into a film (rather than grafted on by the Capra method) is shown by *Kiss Them for Me* (1957). A note of astonishing rancor dominates this film, which showed how some navy men on wartime leave are so disgusted by civilian opportunism and indifference that they return to their posts early. Cary Grant tells a story about a friend who ducked before an explosion. One waits for the punch line, the cue to laugh. He ends: "We never did find his head." Despite Cary Grant, the film was an enormous flop on release. *A Face in the Crowd* fared similarly, and another Andy Griffith starrer, *Onionhead* (1958), with its curiously sour view of the life of a ship's cook, fared no better with the public. Amid the comedy of *Rally 'Round the Flag, Boys!* (1958) lay a remarkably accurate portrait of the typical housewife (Joanne Woodward) in a small town, an instance, probably unintended, of compromise, juxtaposing farce with a glimpse of reality. More direct ideas have been quickly squashed, as Gore Vidal's *Visit to a Small Planet* (1960) shows by its final appearance as an abysmal Jerry Lewis comedy, propped up by incompetent trick work after being shorn of its disarmament theme.

One quite successful venture with the Capra type of theme was *It Happened to Jane* (1959), which misfired perhaps by selecting as its target a railway line. For those who don't sentimentalize over railways, the film could have been hard going. The townsfolk of Maine in this film are a step ahead of the ignorant hillbillies who appear on the screen from time to time, outwitting the city slickers by luck and natural guile (Elvis Presley's *Follow That Dream* [1962]). Given the obstinacy of the widowed heroine (Doris Day) and a lesson in legal rights by lawyer Jack Lemmon, backwoods democracy can win the day. Doris and the Boy Scout troop blended with the charmingly convincing backgrounds to give substance to the domestic scenes. These were marred only by that overworked device for extracting a laugh from the simple-minded, the addition of an unusual household pet—a lobster. (Quite the worst example was the seagull of *This Happy Feeling* [1958].) The sudden reform of the villainous railroad magnate was as glib as anything Capra drew from a hat. Its director was Richard Quine, but along with his erstwhile associate Blake Edwards, there seems too little style or feeling for comedy to warrant closer examination of their approaches.

An outstanding example of recent character comedy is *Please Don't Eat the Daisies* (1960). Perhaps the title was off-putting (derived from the book and used in the film for one of the songs), but the comedy was not especially popular, nor is it particularly well remembered. Because such a film is so rare and because the merit lies more in the whole than any fragments, a detailed look at the film is justified.

Kids are generally a lovable menace in American cinema. Here they are just menace. Doris Day, courageously playing the mother of four children, has trouble getting into her dress. "Maybe you should have lost ten pounds," chirps all too knowledgeable junior. "I'm not kicking, I'm tapping," one child tells its mother with the literalness of the young on being reprimanded at the table. There is a beautifully timed fade-out on the four children standing innocent-like beside an overly enthusiastic and conscientious babysitter after their mother tells them to be on their best behavior; this is picked up when the parents (David Niven as the father) return and summon the lift but glimpse their brood inside before the doors are whisked shut. The eldest child casually picks his nose at an interview with a prissy headmistress, while Niven makes a memorable onslaught on the parent-participation scheme she is forcing onto him. Another child gets his head trapped in a stool.

But the archcriminal would appear to be the youngest of the bunch, Adam. Actually the dupe of his brothers in their sport of dropping water-filled paper bags onto heads in the street below, he is padlocked in a cage. This is a clear echo of a recurrent theme in comedy (classically depicted in *Bringing Up Baby* [1938]), that of making a monkey out of man, of emphasizing his short lead among the primates. (In *Bachelor Flat*, the skull of ancient man has, like Terry-Thomas, a tooth missing.) Whereas the child (whose name, note, is Adam) gets locked up, it is the dog who gets pampered because of his neuroses and has to be carried everywhere.

There are two examples of living nightmares familiar to many spectators: in the first, Doris Day gets unknowingly separated from her companion entering a lift and gaily chatters on, spellbinding the other occupants; second, she locates a wallpaper she likes at a store and arrives home to find it exactly matches the upholstery.

Then there is the supporting cast: a rare and rich appearance by Richard Haydn as an urbane producer, and a quite unforgettable one by Janis Paige in which there is a literal recognition and even a discussion of her particular talent as a rapacious actress in the film — "wiggling her fanny." This is after years of such innuendo as Monroe, poised on the stairs looking back at Tom Ewell in *The Seven Year Itch* (1955) to declare, "My fan's caught in the door" (and, of course but too late, there *was* mention of an electric fan a few minutes before and now the flex *is* taut). *Please Don't Eat the Daisies* strikes a blow for clear expression, even if director Charles Walters doesn't go so far as to let us judge the "wiggling" in close-up.

Still, he brilliantly establishes a warmth in the relationship of husband and wife in this film that makes them and their actions both believable and important. The audience can feel concerned about them because of little details like Doris Day plucking a stray hair out of her head while on the telephone and because of the intelligence of the plot, which concerns the corruption of a theater critic (Niven) who learns to put a witty joke before an accurate review. It incorporates such twists as a mother who doesn't stick up for her daughter (when she is, in fact, in the right) after the pair squabble; instead, she compliments her son-in-law on his new-found characteristics, thereby prompting him to realize just how shabby they are.

A subplot involving a move to the type of country house Mr. Hobbs recently vacationed in produces predictable situations, but the treatment remains intelligent. A scene opens on David Niven complaining about the noise while he tries to write; he speaks against silence, and then the knocking resumes, proving his point. Actually, the far limit of this joke was in *Les jeux de l'amour*, where Jean-Pierre Cassel yells into a thoroughly peaceful street, but one can't expect Hollywood to go "irrational." To extract another parallel with de Broca's film, both have a telephone ringing somewhere in a roomful of muddle, and both unemphasizingly score with it. Robert Riskin's *Magic Town* (1947) had the brilliant reverse to this sight gag: a vacated office floor with only the telephones left, laid out in neat formation, one of them ringing.

Please Don't Eat the Daisies and *Some Like It Hot* were the most successful of recent comedies in their different ways. Justice cannot be done to the other contenders without mentioning good bits in otherwise disappointing results; this involves recognition of some of the fine array of character actors whose practiced scene stealing puts bite into many a limp script. It is, for instance, almost worth enduring the rest of *The Perfect Furlough* (scripted by the prolific but otherwise hardly distinguished Stanley Shapiro) for the one good line that Keenan Wynn seizes on (and the camera homes in for) as he plays an agent learning that his nubile film star is pregnant. He snaps to his secretary at the scene of discovery, "Miss Smith, I shall hold you personally responsible!" Wynn was also featured in that egregious sequence of Capra's unhappy comeback picture, *A Hole in the Head* (1959), in which Sinatra is encouraged to seek a touch only to be brutally spurned for attempting to disguise his need.

Then there is Fred Clark, "Old Marblehead" of *Don't Go Near the Water*, whose pompous persona has been punctured by about every comedy hero going. What quality he added to the opposition (ably partnered by John Williams) as the crooked company director in *The Solid Gold Cadillac* (1956), and how much more glorious Judy Holliday's final triumph as the persistent smallest shareholder when she topples him in the end. In *The Mating Game* (1959) he put further substance into the already lush target of the Department of Taxes who are bemused and befuddled by simple farm folk out in Maryland. In *It Started with a Kiss* (1959), a film that many find disgusting, the accidental appearance of a nude Debbie Reynolds in his bed on schedule for the visiting congressmen to misread the situation seemed uproarious simply in relation to Fred Clark (who is always Fred Clark before any character the script might give him). Paul Ford (except as the foil to Bilko) is a faint carbon copy of this master, while Ernie Kovacs was also a less substantial comedy actor because (like Peter Sellers, unlike Alec Guinness) he suppressed part of his personality to create superficial impersonations rather than substantial characterizations.

Jerry Lewis is a special case. His early films were most distinguished by his magnificent instant caricatures (the one rewarding moment of *At War with the Army* [1950] is his takeoff of Barry Fitzgerald's old priest of *Going My Way* [1944] to Dean Martin's Crosby). In *The Geisha Boy* one finds them still in evidence, like his Bugs Bunny chewing a carrot to end the film ("That's all, folks!"). But his talent of late (except in the odd and rewarding *The Delicate Delinquent* [1957]) has rarely been harnessed to script or even (much) to life. Where his one-man band is marching to, time will tell.

Writers tend to relieve the frustration of scripting to formula by juggling with the intricacies and technicalities of the medium. *The Girl Can't Help It* opens in black and white on standard screen. Tom Ewell appears and apologetically flicks his finger to summon color while the image trundles out to 'Scope. *Will Success Spoil Rock Hunter?* has a special interval for the TV addict: a small telly-shaped screen lost in a black void of Cinema-Scope proportions that is subjected to all imaginable forms of interference. The treatment of Mickey Shaughnessy's speech in *Don't Go Near the Water* is a fine example: selected by Fred Clark to be the Typical Sailor in a morale-boosting campaign, he is found to work a certain expression into every sentence, and this is loudly suppressed on the soundtrack each time. *Operation Mad Ball* (1957) is the most perverse instance, a case (surely unique) where the trailer was funnier than the film (Ernie Kovacs suavely leaning on a mantelpiece that breaks under his weight as he declares, "I have to tell you about a forthcoming movie, which makes more sense than telling you about one that's been here already"). And in as drab a comedy as *This Happy Feeling*, the happiest moment came when Curt Jurgens, keeping pace with the train to declare his love to the departing, disappears down an excavation at the side of the track.

Then there are the comedies that respect traditions, in fact are traditional, but mock themselves a bit as well. *But Not for Me* (1959) had a merciless treatment of its star, Clark Gable, cast as a would-be romantic hero who is always being reminded of his age (variously stated as forty-four and fifty-six) and of encroaching senility as his wristwatch rings to remind him to take his pills or pictures of his debonair self from the thirties pop up in view. And in *Some Like It Hot* George Raft is shot down at the convention of the Friends of Italian Opera by a hood called Johnny Paradise (actually Edward G. Robinson Jr.), whose coin-spinning mannerism refers back to Raft's early role in *Scarface* (1932). And in *One, Two, Three*, when Cagney has his back to the wall, he gasps, "Mother of Mercy, is this the end of Little Rico?" and the initiated recall Edward G. Robinson's line of expiry as Little Caesar. Don McGuire's *Hear Me Good* (1957) was a brilliant little comedy that relapsed entirely into past traditions and played them for their current laugh value. Hal March was cast as a con man in the familiar situation of farce, living (as the epigram has it) in an apartment overlooking the rent. Joe E. Ross was an amiable stooge to March's inveterate liar, fast talking, self-contradicting, often irrelevant, and quite unquenchable. The story line had a savage twist to the mere rigging of a beauty contest that involved setting the dress of a contestant on fire. Static and uncinematic in style, only a low-budget B-feature, it packed more pleasure than the conventionally angled but above-average *Teacher's Pet* (1958) with which it was released.

Hear Me Good gave a whiff of the genuine thirties spirit. Yet such a regression cannot mark a new path for comedy. The many films where ornamentation shines brighter than the integral elements point to a fundamental failure of subject matter and style derived from a ban on originality or a lack of imagination. The face of comedy could do with an uplift—and quick.

CHAPTER 4

WHATEVER HAPPENED TO HOLLYWOOD COMEDY?

DWIGHT MACDONALD

ONCE UPON A TIME, long, long ago, Hollywood comedies were funny. First there was the classic age of Keaton, Chaplin, Harold Lloyd, Harry Langdon, and some—though not as much as sentimental archaeologists now pretend—of the myriad spawn of Mack Sennett, the Diaghilev of slapstick. The tradition carried over into the talkies with W. C. Fields, Laurel and Hardy, and the Marx Brothers. It was dead by the forties, whether because the form had been worked out or historical change had made it archaic, but dead it was, and is, as recent attempts to revive it have demonstrated. With the coming of sound, another comic style developed, not so pure but funny enough for practical purposes: those fast-moving, tough-minded, jaunty social comedies of the thirties and forties that still bring an unwonted liveliness to our TV screens late at night: *The Front Page* (1931), *Trouble in Paradise* (1932), *Bombshell* (1933), *It Happened One Night* (1934), *The Thin Man* (1934), *Twentieth Century* (1934), *My Man Godfrey* (1936), *Nothing Sacred* (1937), *Bringing Up Baby* (1938), *His Girl Friday* (1940), *The Philadelphia Story* (1940), and such works of the unjustly neglected Preston Sturges as *The Great McGinty* (1940), *Hail the Conquering Hero* (1944), *The Miracle of Morgan's Creek* (1944). They were often called screwball comedies—the Huston-Capote *Beat the Devil* (1953) was a belated example—and there was plenty of english on the ball. Patriotism, romance, motherhood, the mass media, civic virtue, Americanism were all given a satiric twist. Nothing sacred.

But in five years (1960–1965), I recall only two American comedies that made me laugh: Wilder's *One, Two, Three* (1961) and Kubrick's *Dr. Strange-*

Dwight Macdonald, "Whatever Happened to Hollywood Comedy?," *Esquire*, June 1965, 14–20, 25.

love (1964). This is curious because in that period, Hollywood has made an extraordinary number of movies that, in form and intention, must be classified as comedies. They are so relentlessly unamusing as to suggest not chance failures but a system. From five recent specimens—*It's a Mad, Mad, Mad, Mad World* (1963), *Bedtime Story* (1964), *Kiss Me, Stupid* (1964), *What a Way to Go!* (1964), and *How to Murder Your Wife* (1965)—I have deduced three basic rules of comedy they violate, systematically.

Rule 1: Humor is like guerrilla warfare. Success depends on traveling light (a joke too long in the telling fails; the fun leaks out of a comic situation too elaborately set up), striking unexpectedly (the shock of incongruity makes us laugh, but a director who lets us anticipate it produces no shock, merely the expected congruity), and getting away fast (reflection or elaboration may increase enjoyment in other forms of art but not in comedy, where he who lingers is lost).

Stanley Kramer's attempt to revive slapstick in *It's a Mad, Mad, Mad, Mad World* fails for every possible reason, but one is that it is more like the battle of the Somme than a Vietcong raid. To watch on a Cinerama screen in full color a small army of actors—105 speaking roles—inflict mayhem on each other with cars, planes, explosives, and other devices for more than three hours with stereophonic sound effects is simply too much for the human eye and ear to respond to, let alone the funny bone. The permutations and combinations of hard-core slapstick are as severely limited as those of hard-core pornography, and for the same reason: they are entirely physical. Sennett's early comedies lasted one reel, or ten minutes; he thought Chaplin mad when he insisted on trying a two-reeler; both of them were right, for Chaplin, with his pantomime and his creation of a character, the "Little Tramp," was going beyond slapstick. Chaplin eventually went all the way to feature-length comedies—which were, still, only one hundred minutes as against Mr. Kramer's almost two hundred minutes—as did Keaton, Lloyd, and Langdon; they were successful because each invented a comic personality whose imbroglios couldn't help being more varied, and unexpected, than the physics of custard pies and runaway automobiles. More amusing even than Mr. Kramer's grand climactic anticlimactic finale with a dozen "name" stars, male and female, being catapulted one by one from the wildly thrashing tip of a six-story fire ladder to soar through the air and crash-land in comic places like a fountain and a pet shop.

What a Way to Go! and *How to Murder Your Wife* are in the screwball tradition, but the old shack has been redecorated with solid-mahogany furniture, plush drapes, and wall-to-wall carpeting. (The sheer material opulence and comfort of our society since the lean thirties and the nervous war years may be a factor: even a Lubitsch or a Hawks might have found it difficult to keep it fast and light with such massively lavish sets and costumes.) Betty Comden and Adolph Green wrote the script for the former, George Axelrod for the latter; all are highly regarded in Hollywood as purveyors of sophisticated wit, but they smother their comic ideas, none too robust to begin with, under scripts that, like lethargic stagehands, take a long time setting up each situation and a long time dismantling it, spelling out each joke for the slow readers and repeating it for those who can't read at all. The directors, J. Lee Thompson and Richard Quine, respectively, cooperate by drawing out each scene with repetitive business and by encouraging such once-lively performers (now slowed down by too many unfunny comedies) as Jack Lemmon and Shirley MacLaine to take their time with their mugging. One of the many ways Mr. Quine puts across the comic point of *How to Murder Your Wife* (which is that Lemmon, a gay bachelor, is trapped into marrying, while drunk, the beautiful Virna Lisi, who proceeds to domesticate him) is to have Miss Lisi invade not only Mr. Lemmon's club but the steam room of Mr. Lemmon's club; one can imagine the uproar, the scandal, the naked males snatching up towels, the immediate arrival of the house committee, fully clad, the immediate expulsion of Mr. Lemmon, etc. It certainly makes the point, as also do the repeated views, throughout the film, of Mr. Lemmon's expanding paunch (point being Miss Lisi is a good Italian wife who stuffs him with pasta). I prefer the way they suggested, in *Nothing Sacred*, that a Vermont village was hostile to a reporter from the city: as he walked up the street from the station, a small boy ran out of a yard and bit him in the leg.

Rule 2: The tragic or the realistic hero can be unattractive—Hedda Gabler was a bitch, Mother Courage one hardly warms up to, the Macbeths, as Max Beerbohm has noted, were deplorable hosts[1]—and no one will object except those who complain that real life is sad enough without paying money. . . . But comedy is different. It cannot claim the license of either high seriousness or low realism. We sympathize with the situation of the tragic/realistic hero, but it is with the comedian himself that we must sympathize, else it's not funny. He either must be positively attractive—the physical grace of a Chaplin, the social grace of a Cary Grant, the poetic ineptness of a Keaton or a Langdon or a Tati—or his unattractiveness must be so grotesque, so stylized, that he transcends reality and wins our sympathy as a figure of wish fulfillment: W. C. Fields surreptitiously delivering a vicious kick to a bratty child, Groucho Marx flicking his cigar ash into Margaret Dumont's pretentious décolletage.

There are many unattractive comedians in these five movies. How Ray Walston and Cliff Osmond would strike me in more sympathetic parts and with a different director, I don't know, but in *Kiss Me, Stupid* they are as frantically unappealing a comedy team as I've seen since the Ritz Brothers. The people in *It's a Mad, Mad, Mad, Mad World* are unattractive in two ways. They are all greedy, double-crossing crooks and bums; even Spencer Tracy, the honest cop, turns crooked at the end, one of Mr. Kramer's many bad ideas. And they don't look very good, either: there's something depressing about seeing Tracy, Durante, Berle, Ethel Merman, and other aging, or aged, stars—Mickey Rooney has gone from adolescence to puffy middle age with no transition—so wrinkled and flabby, trying to cavort around like Keystone cops; in the Sennett era, they who got slapsticked were younger. The most repulsive of all is Marlon Brando in *Bedtime Story*. He is an American soldier abroad who is a liar, swindler, blackmailer, and—his specialty—ruthless seducer (and impregnator) of women, his technique being to play on their sympathies as a lonely little soldier boy far from home. A better actor might have made this heel amusing—seducers and con men have their comic aspects—but Brando makes us detest him as a slob and bully; the pious smirk he puts on when he goes into the soldier-boy act is unappetizing, as well as being amateurishly "indicative" acting.

Rule 3: Comedy is sadistic, making fun of the misfortunes or miscalculations of others. The joke's on them, not us; we laugh at them. And even when we laugh with Falstaff, so witty at the expense of others, we also laugh at him because he has the misfortune to be fat. His corpulence corresponds to the ill-fitting clothes and grotesquely painted face of the clown—who, like him, is both subject and object, wit and butt. "Men of all sorts take a pride to gird at me," Falstaff explains to his page. "I am not only witty in myself, but the cause that wit is in other men. I do here walk before thee like a sow that hath overwhelmed all her litter but one."[2] But there is more to it. Will Rogers's "Everything is funny as long as it is happening to somebody else" is a half-truth. To make us laugh, the sadism must be disguised, carried beyond reality into a fanciful world where nobody really gets hurt: if the man slipping on a banana peel actually injured his spine, nobody would find it comic—except perhaps the Marquis de Sade, whose works are notably lacking in humor. The other half of the truth is Thomas Carlyle's "The essence of humor is sensibility; warm tender fellow-feeling with all forms of existence."[3] Almost any situation can be treated as comedy—even the threat of nuclear annihilation, as Stanley Kubrick has shown—as long as the director makes clear by a stylized treatment that we are not in the real world. But if the treatment is too realistic, so that the comic situation is blurred by real emotions and the comic victims arouse our sympathy, the result is at best confusing, at worst unpleasant, and in either case unfunny. Only on the plane of fantasy can the sadism inherent in comedy be transmuted into Carlyle's "fellow-feeling," uniting butt and spectator in laughter at the god-awful nature of things that defeats them both.

A good illustration of Rule 3 is the difference between Billy Wilder's *One, Two, Three* and two other recent films of his, *The Apartment* (1960) and *Kiss Me, Stupid*. The first was nothing great as comedy—a rapid-fire succession of gags sustained by James Cagney's vitality—but it was funny because it was deliberately artificial, playing around with the comic aspects of the Cold War without pretending to strike below the surface to any human reality. I have analyzed *The Apartment* at length,[4] here enough to note that its chief defect, trying to have it both ways by presenting a gamy situation as both comic and emotionally serious, also vitiates Mr. Wilder's new film, *Kiss Me, Stupid*. The situation is gamy indeed: an unsuccessful songwriter offers his wife for the night to a womanizing pop singer hoping he will plug his songs. But, this being a Wilder film, it's not as simple, or bold, as that: the songwriter hires a local tart to stand in for his wife; after the singer has amorously mauled the "wife" as the songwriter "husband" looks on complaisantly, she finds herself attracted to the latter and he to her, so they throw out the singer, who goes to the local hot spot looking for a woman and—through the complexities of plot too tedious to explain here—ends up sleeping with the wife, thinking she is the tart. What *she* thinks is extremely complex: hitherto a virtuous wife, she submits to the singer because she is angry at her husband (whom she has reason to believe has shacked up for the night with the tart, as is indeed the case), and also drunk, though not so drunk as, once she realizes who the singer is, not to combine business with pleasure by bringing to his attention, before she gives in, one of hubby's songs. The finale, some days later, has the married couple viewing the singer on TV plugging the song. He says, "But, but how come?" or words to that effect, and she says, "Kiss me, stupid." Gamy? A whole game preserve. Leaving aside the laborious hammering home of the comic points (Rule 1) and the unattractiveness of the husband and his sidekick (Rule 2), *Kiss Me, Stupid* also violates Rule 3 by trying to engage our sympathies for the principals as human beings—the husband and the tart fall in love, for that night anyway, and virtuously unite to repel the singer's advances, while the wife has two excuses for cuckolding her husband: intoxication and a sense of duty.

FIGURE 8. Jack Lemmon in Billy Wilder's seriocomic *The Apartment* (1960).

The only decent member of the quadrangle, oddly enough, is Dean Martin as the lecherous pop singer: his simple, direct sensuality blows like a fresh breeze through the fuggy atmosphere of apologetic prurience in which the other three exist. Mr. Martin is also the only success as a comedian: he has an easy grace—a hillbilly Cary Grant—and the director has spared him those queasy, hypocritical "human feelings" about sex that make the other three angles so unamusing. Under Mr. Wilder's direction, Tartuffe would be not a comic monster but just another mixed-up human being like all of us, much to be said on both sides, nobody's all bad, and who are we to judge the poor fellow? Or to laugh at him?

The last part of *Bedtime Story* has Brando trying to con a girl into surrendering to him her virginity and her bankroll; he wins her sympathy by pretending to be a crippled veteran confined for life to a wheelchair. A comical cuss. In real life, the con man depends on the mark's being greedy, dishonest, and foolish, and in con-game comedies this is the minimum, if we are to laugh. But the girl is presented as decent, generous, and, except for her liking Brando, not foolish. It gets really hilarious at the end when that old cutup fakes recovering the use of his legs because of her inspiring love, heaves his bulk out of the wheelchair and, as she encourages him with proudly shining eyes, totters gamely toward her, saves himself from falling by wrapping his arms around her, and pushes her backward into the bedroom, closing the door behind them. The director passed up the final boff—we don't see him collapsing on top of her on the bed—but the joke's on her all right. The Marquis would have been amused. Everything is taken back five minutes later, of course, the picture ending with Brando, regenerated and a heel no longer, married to the girl. I found this more depressing than the seduction, which at least was temporary, but now that nice girl will have to spend the rest of her life with Brando. Had *Bedtime Story* been done in the high style of the old screwball comedies, in which a heel is never resouled in the last act, the nastiness might have been disinfected. Though I wonder if Molière himself could have made comedy out of the wheelchair seduction. I also wonder how *Bedtime Story* went over in veterans' hospitals, maybe on a double bill with another Brando picture, *The Men* (1950), in which he is most affecting as a paraplegic war veteran. It must have helped him give an authentic performance when he played it for laughs in *Bedtime Story*.

A comparison of the old silent comedies with *It's a Mad, Mad, Mad, Mad World* is interesting in terms of Rule 3. They presented not people but abstractions from people whose physical catastrophes were no more distressing to the spectator than the pulverizations and rebirths of animals in movie cartoons, since this is a magical world where nobody *really* gets hurt. But in Mr. Kramer's imitation, the old magical world has vanished: these comedians are flesh and blood, and their sufferings are subject to the laws of the real world. The result is not amusing. An old man dying by the roadside after an automobile accident is not funny even if he is Jimmy Durante and even if we get many close-ups of his contorted face sweating with pain. A poor couple's pickup truck hurtling down a hillside out of control while the driver and his wife cling on desperately and their modest household goods spill out is not funny either, even if they are Negroes. A young married couple trapped in the burning cellar of a hardware store is not funny even if a stack of cans of paint is about to catch fire and incinerate them and even if they are named Sid Caesar and Edie Adams.

NOTES

1. The actual quotation is "To mankind in general Macbeth and Lady Macbeth stand out as the supreme type of all that a host and hostess should not be." [Editors' note.]

2. *Henry IV, Part 2*, act 1, scene 2.

3. Charles Douglas, *Forty Thousand Quotations* (New York: Sully, 1915), 980.

4. Dwight Macdonald, "*The Apartment*," in *Dwight Macdonald on Movies* (Englewood Cliffs, NJ: Prentice Hall, 1969), 280–283.

CHAPTER 5

THE EVOLUTION OF THE CHASE IN THE SILENT SCREEN COMEDY

DONALD W. MCCAFFREY

OF ALL THE DISTINGUISHING characteristics of the comedy of the silent screen, the "chase" is probably the most fascinating. The medium's capability to create an unusual world of outlandish speed, mayhem, and chaos is fully exploited. All logic of our world is shattered when the motion picture audience observes people, horses, cars, and boats thrown in a whirlwind of activity. If someone is not being pursued in this great rush, there is a scurry from danger or a race to prevent a marriage, a disaster, or to win a coveted prize. The comic "chase," therefore, cannot be said to confine itself to material that is designated by the term itself; *chase* has come to mean not only pursuit, but any activity that involves a race or a rush to or from something. Many changes in the treatment of this type of material may be observed by tracing the chase from its inception in the early films to the height of its development in the silent screen comedy of the twenties.

According to John Montgomery, the comedy "race" or "chase" film originated in France, Italy, and Britain, and not in America. In 1903 short comedy chase skits were an important part of the motion picture programs offered by the Egyptian Hall in London.[1] Evidently, the early films that employed this type of material centered upon the "race" or "chase" with only slight attention to preliminary, motivating actions:

When it was realized that each film should have a theme, and be a sequence of events telling a story or relating action, the comic films began to develop a craziness of their own. A man would be seen run-

Donald W. McCaffrey, "The Evolution of the Chase in the Silent Screen Comedy," *Journal of the Society of Cinematologists* 4 (1964): 1–8. Copyright © 1964 by the University of Texas Press. Reprinted with the permission of the University of Texas Press.

ning wild—perhaps in a nightshirt—dashing downhill on roller skates, through barrels and past dray carts and cabs, miraculously avoiding danger, while the audience gasped a series of "Oooohhs!," knowing that soon he would finish up in a lake, or in a bin of flour, oil, soot, molasses, glue, paint, dough or treacle. These were the "chase comic" films, which are still with us today, with variations.[2]

With a popular one-reel comedy, *Cohen at Coney Island*, Mack Sennett launched into the field of broad slapstick comedy in 1909,[3] and many of the creations that were ground out steadily by his Keystone comedies organization followed in the chase traditions of the European comedies. Using similar situations, Sennett expanded the scope of the chase, and introduced plots with slightly better motivation. Much of the humor, however, was primitive slapstick; it was based on the overstatement of speed and violence. Pratfalls and physical combats between offenders of the law and policemen were repeated with slight variation. While a great deal of credit may be extended Sennett as a pioneer in the comedy film, he was not an effective innovator; his films lacked controlled, organized comic invention. Lewis Jacobs aptly describes the rapid accumulation of improbable gags that constituted the chase sequences of Sennett's early work: "Guns fire hundreds of bullets at dozens of cops who chase a culprit in a flivver which mows down telephone poles, crashes through houses and fences, plunges into the river and out again unharmed, only to explode when the victim is finally caught and being taken to jail."[4]

The scene that Jacobs describes in his history of American films reveals the typical ending of many one- and two-reel works directed by Sennett that featured the famous Keystone cops. In 1914 he produced a six-reel work, *Tillie's Punctured Romance*, the first feature-length comedy film.[5] The high point of the action in the climactic portion of this comedy featured an elaborate chase with the Keystone cops pursuing Tillie and Charlie. This wild, fantastic chase culminated on a pier with the police car knocking Tillie, itself, and the policeman clinging to it into the ocean. Assisting in the chase, another brand of policemen, water police, pursued the offenders in two boats. Accidentally, the boats collided, throwing the occupants into the water. Elaboration in the feature film under Sennett's guiding hand, therefore, was achieved by adding more policemen and an incident with more comic falls by these policemen. Nevertheless, *Tillie's Punctured Romance* used a complete final reel with all the thrills of violent fights and wild chases. It was a forecast of a bright, lively future for the feature-length comedy.

"FOR THE LOVE OF TILLIE"
Formerly
"TILLIE'S PUNCTURED ROMANCE"

FIGURE 9. Mack Sennett's *Tillie's Punctured Romance* (1914): the first comedy feature.

The year following this pioneering effort, comedian Harold Lloyd employed material and patterns of plot similar to those used by Sennett. A review of Lloyd's first one-reel Lonesome Luke work revealed these similarities:

> Lonesome Luke Pathé Written by "Tad" the well-known cartoonist, this split reel comedy, though entirely lacking in originality and utilizing time-worn features still has several amusing parts. A bear escapes from a menagerie and a prisoner in the jail is offered his freedom to don a bear skin and enter a cage with a lion. He enters the cage, but immediately becomes afraid, and escaping into the audience causes consternation, until he is finally captured by an alleged comedy police department.[6]

A clear indication of how frequently this type of chase material was used in the final portions of the film comedy at this time in Lloyd's career was revealed in 1927 to interviewer John B. Kennedy: "Our record week's output was three. Wide, heavy slapstick on the simplest theme—eight hundred feet of so-called plot. Whatever the plot, the picture always ended with two hundred feet of chase."[7]

Further evidence of the frequent use of chase material may be established by looking at Chaplin's comedies that were made while he was working independently for Mutual Films. In a period of two years, 1916–1917, a stage in Chaplin's development that Theodore Huff calls "his most fertile year" with "almost perfect comedies," Chaplin wrote, acted in, and directed twelve two-reel works.[8] Six of these works depend strongly on a climactic chase, two of them on a fight, and one on a rescue.[9]

Even though Chaplin still favored traditional materials in this period of his development, he moved the film chase forward a giant's step. While Sennett had molded his chase material into a stock pattern that he repeated over and over even in his one- and two-reel works in the twenties, Chaplin refined and elaborated the chase. He placed a series of gags in the chase scenes. Heretofore, only a few gags were employed—slapstick gags that were often repeated without significant variation. Chaplin, however, developed chases with an excellent sense of comic invention. In Chaplin's *Easy Street* (1917), for example, a chase pivoted on a desperate game of hide-and-seek. Charlie, the Little Tramp, came out of hiding to kick in the seat of the pants the bully who was chasing him, he slipped down a drain pipe on the outside of a tenement building as if he were a fireman, and, at the climax of his flight, he achieved a temporary victory over his foe by dropping a stove on his head from a second-story building. Each of these comic incidents was carefully worked out in detail. The grotesque, broad comedy of the early Sennett films was still present, but the action was well motivated, and each incident was developed with a series of clear-cut, increasingly laughable gags.

An even greater step forward was achieved when Chaplin, Lloyd, Buster Keaton, and Harry Langdon launched into the creation of feature-length works in the twenties. Chase material was elaborated upon and carefully worked into the plot of films that sustained a comic drama for an hour to an hour and a half. One of the most significant changes was the use of chase material in portions of the film other than the climactic sequence.[10]

Chaplin's first venture into the feature-length field, *The Kid* (1921), revealed a climactic sequence without chase material. His Little Tramp was, however, chased by a policeman and a bully when he innocently offended them in other sequences of the work. Lloyd, Keaton, and Langdon seemed to follow a pattern similar to Chaplin's *The Kid* when they started producing feature works. Affairs of the heart were introduced in the longer films; the more involved plotting of the works seemed to affect the total design of the comedy. Greater variety was employed in the use of material in the climactic sequence. While the importance of the chase sequence seemed

FIGURE 10. Chaplin defeats the bully in *Easy Street* (1917).

to wane in the climactic portion of the work, chase material was still used extensively in many feature films.

Harold Lloyd's debut in feature films with *Grandma's Boy* in 1922 revealed the use of an elaborate chase sequence immediately preceding the climactic sequence—a fight with a rival. Lloyd interestingly developed and capitalized upon chase material, carefully motivating the chase sequence. It was set in a realistic framework and seldom exhibited the fantastic gag incidents that Sennett used when he treated similar material. This sequence proved to be one of the most enjoyable in the film. Movie reviewer Robert E. Sherwood neglected the climactic fight sequence and turned his attention to the chase by describing it "as thrilling and as broadly comic as any in the literature of slap-stick."[11]

The realistic treatment of chase material and the placement of this material in the sequence before the climax also seemed to be a practice that Buster Keaton often followed. His second feature film for Metro Pictures, Inc., *Our Hospitality* (1922), featured an elaborate chase sequence that was blended with a climactic rescue scene. Scott O'Dell analyzed the rescue as an example of melodramatic material used in the comic film. He concluded that "there is no reason why a comedy should not take on a

melodramatic aspect providing the action is the logical outcome of a predetermined cause."[12] In the sophisticated age of the silent screen comedy,
the major comedians tried to develop their plots skillfully and logically.

It should be emphasized that a fresh twist was being given to the traditional chase material. Such novel invention of the film was pointed out by
Bardeche and Brasillach in their history of the movies:

> The automobile chases especially, making use as they did of rapid-motion
> photography, began to take on a grotesque quality which has delighted
> us since in many a Harold Lloyd and Buster Keaton picture. Part of the
> fun consisted in the fact that these films were a parody of the automobile
> chases—grimly serious, of course—in so many screen dramas of the day.
> Then fresh conceits were introduced every few minutes to tickle the audi-
> ence and save the film from its own naivete.[13]

When Harold Lloyd returned to the traditional placement of the chase
sequence at the climax of *Girl Shy* in 1924, he created one of the best extended treatments of the chase.[14] This work reveals strong elaboration
upon stock chase materials that were used in the formative period of the
silent screen comedy; it illustrates the approach to this type of material
that was taken by other comedians during the twenties. Many means of
obtaining a goal (in this case, the race is undertaken to prevent a wedding
of a sweetheart) produce a wealth of comic detail. When the comic hero,
Harold Meadows, is forced to take various types of vehicles in his race to
stop the wedding, gag potentials are increased. A brief account of the basic
actions will reveal many opportunities for comic invention:

1. Harold Meadows runs to catch a train as it leaves the station but misses
   it when a woman's shawl blows from the train and covers his head,
   obscuring his vision.
2. Forced to hitchhike, he is repeatedly turned down by passing
   automobiles. Ingeniously, he blows up a paper bag and pops it. This
   trick stops a driver who thinks he has a flat tire. Harold, however, is
   refused a ride. Desperately, he jumps onto the car and clings to the
   running-board, concealed from the driver's vision. His attempt to steal
   a ride is fruitless, however. The car goes only a few feet and pulls into
   a garage.
3. He tries to thumb a ride from a woman who is receiving driving
   instructions. Since she has so much difficulty with this minor skill,
   she starts and stops several times. Harold believes he is repeatedly

being accepted and then rejected as a rider. He finally grabs onto the rear spare tire of the automobile, only to be brushed against a telephone pole when the novice driver spins around in circles and backs into the pole.

4. In desperation he steals a car from a young man and woman who are picnicking by the side of a road. Forced to travel on a detour that is replete with huge bumps, his car, evidently receiving broken springs from the detour, continues rocking and shaking ludicrously until Harold abandons the vehicle with a gesture of disgust.

5. He jumps into another automobile and is trying to start it when he discovers the car is attached to a tow truck and is being pulled backwards.

6. When two streetcar conductors do not heed Harold's plea to take him to his destination, he absconds with their car and races it wildly down the street, causing many accidents as the streetcar rushes through intersections and around sharp curves. When the trolley's swiveled pole becomes disengaged from the overhead electrified wire, Harold climbs up to replace the pole. The streetcar starts and races wildly on. As the streetcar rounds a bend in the tracks, Harold, still holding onto the pole, swings out from the car and dangles over an automobile. Unable to hold onto the pole, he falls through the roof of the automobile.

7. Harold forces the unwilling driver of the car to go faster by pressing his own foot on the accelerator. The car is stopped for speeding by a police officer on a motorcycle.

8. As the police officer writes out a ticket for the hapless driver, Harold gets out of the car and escapes with the motorcycle. He causes further consternation as he roars madly down the street and through an open air market. He finally runs the motorcycle through a ditch and crashes on top of a pile of dirt.

9. Harold sees a wagon with a team of two horses nearby. He snatches it and drives the horses at furious pace. When a wheel falls off the wagon, he jumps onto one of the horses and continues his mad dash without interruption. He rides up the steps of the estate in which the wedding is taking place.

10. Jumping from the horse, he breaks into the house and dramatically stops the wedding by carrying off the bride.

Such elaboration on traditional comic material was the typical treatment that comedians gave to chase sequences when the silent screen comedy reached the peak of its development in the twenties. The above description has many comic details that have been left out of this limited study for the sake of brevity. Actions numbered 2, 3, 5, 6, 7, and 8 contain many more comic incidents. Gag follows gag in a strong cause-and-effect relationship. Each incident builds to a final more laughable incident. Such an accumulation and variety of comic detail were rare in the early one- and two-reel chase comedies. While *Girl Shy*'s chase sequence relies on accelerated motion in a way similar to that in which the early works used it, this dizzy, fast movement of objects and people is only one means of achieving the comic. In order to obtain a comic effect, the chases of the one- and two-reel comedies depended greatly on this photographic technique; they relied heavily also on the pratfall and fights between the adversaries engaged in the chase. In short, comic invention was slight.

Having developed a lively nine-minute chase sequence in the climactic portion of his 1924 feature, *Sherlock Jr.*, Buster Keaton exploited the chase in *The General* (1927) to the fullest extent by making it the core of his plot development. The inciting incident in the development of this Civil War comedy was the stealing of Buster's locomotive by Northern spies. Engineer Buster's pursuit of the train to the Northern army headquarters and his return of the locomotive named General to the Southern encampment were brilliant. A new high had been reached in the use of chase material. Extensive comic embellishment on the many incidents that result from this chase revealed Keaton using a pattern of development similar to that used in Lloyd's chase sequence of *Girl Shy*. As Joe Franklin pointed out in his *Classics of the Silent Screen*, a lion's share of the film was devoted to a chase. "No movie chase," he wrote, "has ever been sustained so long, so successfully, or with such expert intermingling of genuine thrills and hilarious comic situations."[15]

While Keaton employed the chase as the core of his work, he used a climactic sequence that featured a comic version of a Civil War battle. In the same year, Harry Langdon used an elaborate fight sequence for the climactic portion of *The Strong Man*, with only minor chase sequences in other parts of his comedy. A new, different function for the comic chase had evolved in the feature comic film of the twenties.

One of the reasons the climactic chase was less frequently used in the twenties by Chaplin, Lloyd, Keaton, and Langdon was that these comedians didn't want to continue using a device that was being overused by others. Many one- and two-reel comedies, still being ground out by the Mack Sennett and Hal Roach comedy mills, employed the chase as the high point of the dramatic action. Also, light comedians such as Charles

Ray, Douglas MacLean, and Wallace Reid, seldom noted for their comic inventiveness, used the climactic chase in many of their pictures, and these comedians produced features in abundance. Faced with this deluge of comedy features, Chaplin, Lloyd, Keaton, and Langdon were forced to seek new material and a fresh approach to old material. Keaton stated this problem aptly:

> The best way to get a laugh is to create a genuine thrill and then relieve the tension with comedy. Getting laughs depends on the element of surprise, and surprises are harder and harder to get as audiences, seeing more pictures, become more and more comedy-wise. But when you take a genuine thrill, build up to it, and then turn it into a ridiculous situation, you always get that surprise element.[16]

Lloyd's *Safety Last!* (1923) and Chaplin's *The Gold Rush* (1926) and *The Circus* (1928) employed new climactic material by placing their comic characters in dangerous situations. Lloyd's comic character was shown trying to fulfill the role of a human fly by climbing up the side of a twelve-story building. In *The Gold Rush*, Charlie was caught in a miner's cabin after a storm moved the dwelling to the edge of a precipice. The little cabin teetered on the edge of this cliff so precariously that a sneeze or cough of its occupants would send it into the abyss below them. Forced by love to be daring, Charlie was shown trying to imitate the feats of a tightrope walker in *The Circus*. On the high wire, Charlie performed reckless and dangerous stunts when he was plagued by escaped monkeys who crawled over his face and tore off his trousers while he was trying to maintain his balance. New material such as this was constantly being sought, or old material was being given a fresh twist. In these works by Lloyd and Chaplin, however, the chase still provided the comic spice for other portions of their films.

In its evolution, therefore, the silent comic film did not reject the chase sequence. Some films, such as *Girl Shy* and *Sherlock Jr.*, retained the climactic chase. But a new function was found for this type of material. In the formative age of the film comedy, the chase was frequently the high point of the work, but chases in the twenties were often employed elsewhere in the film. In its evolution, the chase lost many of its fantastic qualities and was established in a more realistic cause-and-effect relationship with the story line of the total film. Greater elaboration on the comic chase was also part of this change and growth. Gag after gag were arranged in a way that would build the comic chase sequence to a high point of the action or help point and build toward the climax of the total film. These chase sequences, moreover, provided exciting, laugh-provoking portions of the film that often displayed some of the best comic invention of the work of the major comedians of the twenties, Chaplin, Lloyd, Keaton, and Langdon.

NOTES

1. John Montgomery, *Comedy Films* (London: George Allen & Unwin, 1954), 22.

2. Ibid.

3. Terry Ramsaye, *A Million and One Nights: A History of the Motion Picture through 1925*, 2 vols. (New York: Simon and Schuster, 1926), 2:583. Reprint, New York: Touchstone, 1986.

4. Lewis Jacobs, *The Rise of the American Film* (New York: Teacher's College Press, 1939), 211.

5. Ramsaye, *Million and One Nights*, 2:648. (Starring comedians in this film were Marie Dressler and Charles Chaplin.)

6. Review of *Lonesome Luke*, *New York Dramatic Mirror*, June 9, 1915, 39.

7. John B. Kennedy, "It Pays to Be Sappy," *Collier's*, June 11, 1927, 12.

8. Theodore Huff, *Charlie Chaplin* (New York: Henry Schuman, 1951), 65. Reprint, New York: Arno Press, 1972.

9. Two of the films in Chaplin's Mutual output are concerned with the love affairs of the "Little Tramp" and are atypical for this period. *The Vagabond* (1916) shows Charlie jilted by the girl he loves in the climax, and *The Immigrant* (1917) shows him winning the hand of the girl. These works reveal characteristics that Chaplin was to employ in his feature works.

10. Sequence refers to a major action that is composed of many incidents. A feature film may be composed of many such units. Allardyce Nicoll uses the term in this way in *Film and Theatre* (New York: Thomas Y. Crowell, 1934), 43–44. The term is also given this same meaning by Frederick Palmer in *Technique of the Photoplay* (New York: Moving Picture World, 1912), 95–97.

11. Robert E. Sherwood, *The Best Moving Pictures of 1922–23* (Boston: Small, Maynard, 1923), 11.

12. Scott O'Dell, *Representative Photoplays Analyzed* (Hollywood: Palmer Institute of Authorship, 1924), 300.

13. Maurice Bardeche and Robert Brasillach, *The History of Motion Pictures* (New York: W. W. Norton, 1938), 83.

14. This sequence is currently being presented at motion picture theaters as one of the basic comedy selections from Lloyd's *Harold Lloyd's World of Comedy*, a potpourri created from many of his works.

15. Joe Franklin, *Classics of the Silent Screen* (New York: Citadel Press, 1959), 90.

16. Montgomery, *Comedy Films*, 155.

CHAPTER 6

FROM KOPS TO ROBBERS: TRANSFORMATION OF ARCHETYPAL FIGURES IN THE AMERICAN CINEMA OF THE 1920S AND '30S

CAROLYN AND HARRY GEDULD

MANY HISTORIANS OF THE motion picture have chronicled the revolutionary impact of the arrival of the sound film in the late twenties. One immediate effect of the new technology of the sound studio was to create a demand for screenplays that were radically different from those employed in the making of the silent pictures. Another related effect was the eclipse—in some instances temporary, in others permanent—of certain genres that had become well established by 1927. Until many technical problems of sound had been mastered, early talkies were forced to be fairly static: at the worst, to cut out extraneous noise, it was sometimes necessary for scenes to be played in stifling, insulated glass-walled boxes, like telephone booths; at best, the action of speaking characters was limited to a small area of the studio set where the dialogue could be picked up by hidden microphones. For several years, such restrictions precluded the making of sound epics to emulate the silent *Ben-Hur: A Tale of the Christ* (1925) and *King of Kings* (1927) and the production of cliffhangers, westerns, and other fast-paced outdoor adventure films.

Yet even after the introduction of the boom microphone and other sound apparatus designed to give the film its freedom of mobility once again, certain genres that had been popular in the silent era failed to recover from the decline into which they had fallen. Probably the most striking of these eclipsed genres was the comedy short film in two or three reels. Significantly, Kalton Lahue's *World of Laughter*, a study of the motion picture comedy short, designates 1930 as the end of the golden age of the two- and three-reel comedy, of the era of John Bunny, the Keystone cops, and the two- and three-reelers of Chaplin, Harold Lloyd, Buster Keaton, Harry Langdon, Larry Semon, et al.[1]

During the silent era, the motion picture comedy short had often depended heavily upon physical caricature for comic effect. Fatty Arbuckle's girth, for instance, and John Bunny's bloated baby face had an instant impact. As types, they were humorous in themselves, even without the added trappings of the comic narrative. The most enduring, indeed archetypal, comic hero of that era, however, was the little man who had appeared on the screen again and again, most memorably in the roles created by Chaplin, Keaton, and Langdon. The figure of the small-man hero, more than any other comic type, was more than simply a funny physical specimen—he was rooted deeply in the American consciousness. The heroic little man, if not an American everyman, at least typified the immigrant or the uprooted rural American arriving in an urbanized society, or the small-town dweller overtaken by the pressures of the big society, or the worker coping with the dehumanizing powers of machinery and automated factories engaged in mass production. The intense popularity of this figure indicates the strength of audience identification with the "little man." As a type, he was too significant to disappear with the conversion to sound. And, in fact, traces of the heroic little man are to be found frequently in the films of the thirties—though not, as we shall see, in any development of the motion picture comedy short.

These traces can be discovered by looking beyond the comedy of the "little man" films to their most essential noncomic elements. Basically, two characteristics seem to be shared by the majority of short films made by Lloyd, Langdon, Chaplin, and Keaton. First, as we have noted, the heroes of these films are undersized—often they are more puny or delicate than the heroines. Second, these short comedies usually involved a chase that was the climax and raison d'être of the film. It is noteworthy that those who chased the little man were often his physical opposites: large men (like Mack Swain) with gross features who were frequently mustachioed, an unmistakable sign of brutality to those accustomed to the conventions of melodrama.

Now, with the conversion to sound, one would have expected a decline in the use of such physical typecasting, for either melodramatic or comic effect. But this was not to be the case. Although dialogue could now have conveyed what only the most unrestrained acting and caricatured appearance were able to express in the twenties, the thirties frequently saw a use

FIGURE 11. Fatty Arbuckle and other silent comedians depended heavily on physical caricature.

of physical excess that was even more extreme than in the earlier silent films. Most striking was the use of the "little man" again — not in the comedy but in the gangster film. The "tough" characters created by such men of pointedly small stature as James Cagney and Edward G. Robinson (who were certainly more enduring in the genre than the larger Paul Muni, whose only memorable triumph as a gangster was in *Scarface* [1932]) seem physically to have more in common with their predecessors in the silent short comedy than with the beefy "Bull" Weed, the hearty gangster-hero of Sternberg's *Underworld* (1927).

Moreover, the situations in which the gang leaders of *Little Caesar* (1931), *The Public Enemy* (1931), and *The Roaring Twenties* (1939) frequently found themselves had also been anticipated in the silent comedy shorts—for what is the story of the little gangster being chased by big tough cops (or by big tough rivals) but a noncomic variation on the story of the little man being chased by big tough guys?

By contrast, the villains of silent comedy had their counterparts in the comedians of the early sound era. The most memorable and popular villains of silent comedy were tall, fat men, while the popular film comedians of the early thirties were portly or plump (W. C. Fields, Mae West) or formed of a large number of small men (e.g., the Marx Brothers). Behind their facade of comedy, the comedians of the sound era were as brutal as their villainous antecedents. The Dadaism of Fields has been particularly noted by film critics—and it is notable that he was especially cruel to children and animals, groups with whom the "little man" once identified. Significantly, those early sound comedians who did not exploit physical brutality usually exploited a kind of verbal brutality or "hardness" of manner (as did Groucho Marx and Mae West).

Such comedy teams as Laurel and Hardy were, on the other hand, transitional figures who pointed back to the silent comedies while reaching forward to the sound film. However, one member of the team, Laurel, clearly functioned as a "little man" hero. He was much smaller than his would-be-tough colleague and spoke infrequently, usually depending on silent comedy gags for his best effects. He may be contrasted with a comedian like Groucho Marx, who was undeniably a product of the sound film and whose humor depended upon wisecracks, though his mustache, thick eyebrows, and cigar also gave him an obvious physical resemblance to his earlier archetype—the silent comedy villain.

Similar correspondences exist between the heroines of silent comedies and gangster films. In both, the relatively harmless Pickfordian Dear One was a tangible reward for the gangster or comic hero. But the nice girl in these films also had a more threatening counterpart: the henpecking wife and the vamp in the silent two-reelers and their continuation as the screen moll of the thirties. These dangerous women were characterized by dissatisfaction—they wanted more money or more virility than their "little men" could provide or aspire to, and it was to escape from or to satisfy them that the crime that justified the chase was committed. The big cops, in this sense, merely externalized the secret danger of the often physically large women who pursued the little tramps and the little gangsters.

Big cop, large woman, little man—it is not impossible to see in this triangle common to films of the twenties and thirties a re-creation of an archetypal family situation, at least as it appears in the nightmares of children. Certainly, Robinson's grotesque infant face and Keaton's big-eyed baby face were consciously meant to be associated with the child, as was the dwarfed size of all our small heroes. These boy-men "ran" from their cruel "mothers" (in the form of moll, vamp, or henpecking wife) and their menacing "fathers" (in the form of syndicate rivals or cops) into—if they were comic figures or reformable gangsters—the arms of the kindly mother-wife (the Dear One or sweetheart), who gave comfort when "bad dreams" came to an end.

In spite of their similarity, it would be an oversimplification to say that the silent comic hero was merely a "funny" sound gangster. While both participated in a horrific vision of childhood, the Chaplin type was clearly an innocent, or, at worst, a "naughty" boy, who nevertheless provoked extreme punishment, while the Cagney type was a "juvenile delinquent," whose flouting of authority was nothing less than pathological. In short, there seems to have been a difference in the direction and intensity of aggression (comic elements aside) between these sound and silent types.

In the silent comedies, the aggression or menace was directed from the environment (parental figures: the cops, the vamps, the henpecking wife, the boss) to the unfortunate hero. But in the gangster film, the aggression—which was not mitigated by comedy—was directed, primarily, from the gangster himself to the environment (the cops, banks, the rich, the Crime Commission—all obvious figures of or representatives of authority). Often, it must be noted, the gangster's aggression was a form of retaliation for what he believed the environment originally did to him or for what it failed to provide him as a child. Whether his accusations were justified or not, he was invariably punished in the end, unlike the silent comic hero, who was usually, or at least often, able to outwit his environment. In essence, these differences seem to have sprung from sociohistoric sources rather than from filmic ones.

America's easy identification with the child, at least in the early centuries of its history, is discovered in the very words formerly used to describe its land: *innocent, young, unspoiled, rebel,* etc. This sense of immaturity was to remain a part of the American unconscious long after it had surpassed its European "elders," technologically, in the twentieth century. Even in the most recent decades, America has continued to be fascinated, culturally and in literature, with the adolescent typified by Salinger's Holden Caulfield, James Dean's performance in *Rebel without a Cause* (1955), the immense vogue of beach-party movies displaying the talents and bodies of teenagers, and, currently, by the flower children and "under-twenty-five generation." But the great American "child" has always had to cope with omnipresent "parental" elements representing a threat to innocence. In the nineteenth century and before, the "child" felt menaced by the uncontrollable forces of nature and in the first two decades of the twentieth by the increasing automation and mechanization of the environment.

The silent two-reel comedies were made at a time when the still enduring rural innocence of America was receiving its greatest challenge from a fast-growing urbanization of American society. This innocence still coexisted with optimism—the American "child" knew that his nightmare was only a dream—and so, in the silent two-reeler, when the little man was hounded by the not-so-evil representatives of society, he usually escaped without receiving any critical wounds. Notably, the comic hero seldom "grew up" in the last episode of the film; usually, he retained his unspoiled innocence and charm, refusing to play "adult" or responsible citizen.

By the thirties, however, all the underlying fears of the child-Americans had been spectacularly realized by the Depression. Suddenly, the nightmare was real; the child could not wake up! Now there was drama—"proof" of the malicious intent of society, which, like evil parents, chose to neglect its "children" and let them starve. Thus, in the gangster film, the embittered "boy" tried, however feebly in a larger context, to strike back at a society that was now represented by such abstract and untouchable institutions as banks and the Federal Bureau of Investigation. If he thumbed his nose, like the silent comics, he would not even be noticed; instead, he had to resort to the most drastic crimes, and even those proved futile, resulting ultimately only in his personal annihilation.

The aggression of the gangster, then, arose when the historical threat of the environment became fact: the little man took a beating after all, and this "unjustified" punishment killed optimism, humor, and finally—in the gangster film—the little man himself.

The comedians of the thirties, who, as we have noted, are associated with the villains of the twenties, participated in a similar reversal of archetypal roles. They were not psychic infants, like their silent comic predecessors, but parental types who poked barbed fun at innocence as well as at the institutions of society. Mae West was the new vamp who subtly snared her little men. W. C. Fields's humor often depended on brutality to children, animals, and "trapped" little men in dentists' or barbers' chairs. And the Marx Brothers, playing it both ways, deflated the matronly Margaret Dumont while simultaneously adopting all other "normal" people to their own brand of lunacy. Typically for the thirties, there was little attempt to disguise the aggression that was used to attack not only elements in the environment, but even the audience watching the movie. The razor edge of their humor "punished" both the embittered child and the menacing institutions represented by the American filmgoer of the Depression era.

In their purest form, the silent two-reel comedies are now continued most faithfully in *Tom and Jerry*–type cartoons, in which cat chases undefeatable little mouse. Significantly, these cartoons are intended ostensibly for viewing by children, who might still retain a sense of innocent humor, perhaps because their "cruel" parents are kind enough, at least, to let them attend the movies. For the adult audience, the identification with the innocent small-town boy was lost long ago in the misery of the Depression, when the films that best dramatized their secret nightmares were those involving the boy-gangster who died before he could grow up.

NOTE

1. Kalton C. Lahue, *World of Laughter: The Motion Picture Comedy Short, 1910–30* (Norman: University of Oklahoma Press, 1972).

PART II

THE WESTERN

Part 2 is devoted to writing about the western, the genre famously referred to as the "American cinema par excellence" by André Bazin. Remarkably, as Edward Buscombe has noted, "From around 1910 until the beginning of the 1960s, films in the Western genre made up at least a fifth of all titles released. No other genre has ever occupied anything like such a dominant position."[1] Even as film critics were looking at the western, literary scholars were also moving toward an interest in the cultural myths embodied in the western and its literary antecedents, from James Fenimore Cooper through the dime novels to contemporary pulps. Henry Nash Smith's *Virgin Land: The American West as Symbol and Myth* (referenced by George Bluestone in his essay) was published in 1950, Leslie Fiedler's *Love and Death in the American Novel* in 1960, Leo Marx's *The Machine in the Garden: Technology and the Pastoral Ideal in America* in 1964, and Fiedler's *The Return of the Vanishing American* in 1968. It is no surprise that a film genre as rich in tradition and so vital throughout the studio era as the western would be a primary focus of early writers on film genre as well.

The section opens with Frederick Elkin's essay "The Psychological Appeal of the Hollywood Western." Elkin was a professor of sociology at McGill University in Montreal and York University in Toronto, with a particular interest in the family. In his essay, originally published in the *Journal of Educational Sociology* in 1950, Elkin argues that the conventions of the western may be understood as speaking to the fantasies of children for negotiating the more complex moral and social dynamics of the real world. Elkin explicitly compares the psychological work of the western to that of the fairy tale, anticipating Bruno Bettelheim's influential *The Uses of Enchantment: The Meaning and Importance of Fairy Tales* (1976) by a quarter century. In delineating the broad patterns of the conventional western while mentioning none specifically, Elkin's brief reference to more nuanced examples of the genre such as *Duel in the Sun* (1946) as "super-westerns" reveals a conceptual essentialism that aligns his view with that of Bazin.

One of the founding editors of *Cahiers du Cinéma* (along with Jacques Doniol-Valcroze and Lo Duca), Bazin was an influential voice in French film culture and a major theorist of realism in the cinema. In his essay included here, "The Western, or the American Film Par Excellence" from *Cahiers du Cinéma* in 1952, originally written as the preface for Jean-Louis Rieupeyrout's book *La grande adventure du western, 1894–1964* (1964), Bazin similarly argues that the western functions as a cultural myth, but he also stresses the significance of style in the genre, seeing its penchant for long shots and landscape as an expression of its epic function and as a quality that makes it the very "essence of cinema."

Next, Harry Schein, too, sees the western as a mythic form, stressing its function as quasi-religious social ritual. An important figure in Swedish film culture, as the founder and the first managing director of the Swedish Film Institute from 1963 to 1978 Schein was instrumental in bringing the work of several directors, including Ingmar Bergman, Bo Widerberg, and Jan Troell, to international attention. Prior to assuming this administrative role, between 1948 and 1956 Schein wrote film reviews for *Litterära Magasin*, the period from which his essay "The Olympian Cowboy" comes. While Schein's view of the western's function as cultural myth is generally consistent with Bazin's, he connects westerns explicitly to topical politics and accepts the genre's move toward greater realism, even as he wonders how it will ultimately affect that mythic function.

As the title of George Bluestone's essay "The Changing Cowboy: From Dime Novel to Dollar Film" suggests, this evolution is already regarded as a fait accompli that is itself of interest. Bluestone was a professor of English and a producer of several films, including *The Walking Stick* (1970), starring David Hemmings and Samantha Eggar. His book *Novels into Film: The Metamorphosis of Fiction into Cinema*, published in 1957, regarded as one of the foundational works of film adaptation studies, begins with a comparative discussion of film and literary aesthetics before moving on to detailed analyses of six films, including one western, *The Ox-Bow Incident* (1943). In his essay included here from *Western Humanities Review* in 1960, Bluestone, after quickly recounting the common mythic view of the classic western, goes on to trace the development of the "adult western" from Tom Mix through then-recent westerns such as Arthur Penn's *The Left-Handed Gun* (1958), concluding that this change allows for greater artistic potential.

In "Sociological Symbolism of the 'Adult Western,'" published in the journal *Social Forces* in 1960–1961, sociologist Martin Nussbaum considers the popularity of the television western at the time. Picking up on Schein's observation about the phallic implications of the gun in westerns, Nussbaum offers a rationale for the genre that, remarkably, precedes the currently fashionable view of postwar America's "crisis in masculinity" by decades.

Closing part 2 is Peter Homans's contribution, "Puritanism Revisited: An Analysis of the Contemporary Screen-Image Western," originally published in the journal *Studies in Public Communication* in 1961. Homans taught psychology and religious studies at the University of Chicago, where his research focused on the relationship between religion and psychology, especially as concerns the processes of mourning and healing. His interest in the evolution of religious symbolism and precepts in contemporary culture is clear in his essay, which describes the conventions of the classic western (like Elkin, without mentioning specific titles), particularly around gunplay and violence, and interprets them as constituting a narrative equivalent to a puritan allegory of temptation and sin.

NOTE

1. Edward Buscombe, *100 Westerns* (London: British Film Institute, 2006), ix.

CHAPTER 7

THE PSYCHOLOGICAL APPEAL OF
THE HOLLYWOOD WESTERN

FREDERICK ELKIN

THE MASS MEDIA OF COMMUNICATION—the press, radio, motion pictures, magazines, books, and television—may be viewed from either a social or a psychological perspective. Socially, the mass media may be viewed
as they relate to the development of modern urban and industrial life, as
means of communication that in part substitute for the body of custom,
tradition, established rules, and ritual that bound together our grandpar-
ents. Psychologically, the mass media may be viewed as they relate to the
more anonymous isolated individual of the modern world, as they affect
him or her or as they meet his or her personal needs and dispositions.

In these mass media of America, certain popular patterns have developed and have apparently been satisfying some of the needs and dispositions of the general public for several years. In fiction, for example,
are found such standardized story plots as the crime-investigator story,
the "whodunit" mystery, the historical romance, the soap-opera drama,
and the western. We shall take one of these story forms—the western—
describe it as it appears in motion pictures, and discuss it in relation to the
psychological dispositions of its audience, primarily its child audience.

Although our data are derived from the Hollywood westerns—which
constitute almost 25 percent of the motion picture features produced—
the western is not solely a Hollywood development. The western, as a
story form with relatively standardized plots and character types, has been
popular in America for several decades, having gained early prominence
in the Bret Harte stories and in the Buffalo Bill and Deadwood Dick dime
novels. Currently, the western commands a worldwide weekly audience

Frederick Elkin, "The Psychological Appeal of the Hollywood Western," *Journal of
Educational Sociology* 24, no. 2 (1950): 72–86.

of millions through magazines, novels, comic strips, radio programs, and television, as well as movies.

WHAT ARE THE CHARACTERISTICS and values of the Hollywood western? The western, with a few exceptions, deals with the development of the American West in the late 1800s. The action takes place in a small western town in which law and order have never been firmly established. It is a town with one central street, a hitching post, a combination sheriff's office and jail, a saloon, and perhaps a barbershop, livery stable, and stagecoach office. The characters of the western are ordinarily ranchers or miners plus a miscellaneous assortment of townsfolk, of whom few if any are women and children.

There are two basic characteristics to all westerns: action and simplicity. The standard western story is a continual series of chases, daring rescues, galloping horses, gun battles, and fistfights. And there are few complications—no changes of clothing; no variations in settings; no intrusions of traffic, mothers, schools, or economic hardship; no complex characters; no mistaking the good men from the bad; and no serious doubt about the story's outcome.

The moral values are those of our Christian society. In the conflict of Good and Evil, the Good is invariably held up as right. On the side of Good are honesty, loyalty, sympathy for the oppressed, respect for just law, and, if it is occasioned in the story, love of children and respect for religion. On the side of Evil are treachery, callousness, ruthlessness, contempt for the underdog, and disdain for civil rights. It is suggested that justice and morality are worth fighting for and are worthy of great risks. Those who fight to achieve them are honored and respected, while those who seek other aims at their expense are denounced and despised. Only in that human life is not always held up as sacred is the western unchristian.

It is also suggested in the western, as in numerous other story types, that circumstantial evidence is likely to lead honest men astray and incriminate innocent persons. Thus, there is often a conflict between law and justice. In such cases justice is always considered the more worthy. So the heroes will, if necessary, commit burglaries, jailbreaks, and other illegal actions to thwart the criminals, protect the innocent, and see that justice is done.

The criminals are always motivated by a desire for wealth or power, although wealth and power in themselves are not considered evil. In fact, to seek them within the law and within a moral code is praiseworthy. However, even when honestly sought, they are not the most worthy of western goals, being attributes of the good folk, but not of the western heroes. The heroes, if they willed it, could always have positions of wealth and prestige, but they choose to continue their unattached, more heroic way of life.

Another group of values emphasized in the western are derived more directly from frontier history and suggest that America has a rich and exciting heritage. These values focus on rugged individualism, frontier folk equality, and other characteristics of the western way of life. The value of individualism is evidenced primarily in that the protagonist is invariably one single independent adult, without family, hometown, or any responsibility to others save that of fighting for justice. Ordinarily, he is not even a representative of the law. It is further suggested, as it is in most western European and American stories, that problems do not have social or economic causes, but result from the machinations of evil men. Were there no such evil men, the West would develop naturally and democratically.

The value of ruggedness is expressed primarily by the cowboy hero who roams the frontier, struggles against odds, and achieves victory because he is more fit. It is suggested that it is praiseworthy to be aggressive against dishonest men and that those who are strongest, bravest, and cleverest will be victorious. Victories are achieved not by magical strokes of luck, but by actual struggle and merit.[1]

It is further implied that the American West is beautiful and spacious and that the life of the frontier represents a free and admirable way of life. Not only are there few restrictions imposed on the individual, but there is also a friendly folk equality. No one is superior because he has more head of cattle, speaks better English, or has ancestors who were old Massachusetts or Virginia settlers. In American frontier tradition it is affirmed that characters are judged only by their personalities and their abilities.

According to western movies of a few decades past, western life was one of constant action. Now, however, in a large percentage of the western features, the action is interspersed with casual leisure, a leisure in which men ride along, strum their guitars, and sing western songs. It is suggested that we in America have a musical heritage and that life among the wide-open spaces is a peaceful, contented life when there are no villains to disturb it.

Some of the current westerns have veered from the traditional pattern by becoming more modern. The Roy Rogers and Gene Autry westerns, for example, take place in present-day America and introduce radio stations, airplanes, and even World War II veterans. By so doing, these westerns lose some of their folklore and fairy-tale quality. However, they still have

FIGURE 12. Gene Autry strumming his guitar.

the standardized plots, values, and other features of the traditional western and must be considered only as modern offshoots.

This description of the characteristics and values of the standard Hollywood western does not cover super-westerns like *South of St. Louis* (1949), *Duel in the Sun* (1946), *Silver River* (1948), or *Fort Apache* (1948), which in dramatizing the West may also introduce noisy mobs, red-satined ladies, big-time gambling halls, dashing cavalry troops, or just plain sex. However, these super-westerns constitute just a handful of the western pictures and are not the type that the child will regularly see, let alone read about or hear on the radio.

It is also to be noted finally that a positive emphasis on certain values implies the devaluation of others. Thus, for example, a stress on rugged individualism suggests a devaluation of cooperative and family movements, emphasis on activity and practical accomplishments devalues intellectuality and a contemplative life, and a primary focus on the solution of a crime devalues romantic relationships.

ALSO OF IMPORTANCE in understanding the content of the western are the character ideals, for a character—be he hero, heroine, villain, or comic—by his very personality symbolizes values either positive or negative. Certain personality characteristics are suggested to be worthy of respect and emulation; others deserve only disparagement and disdain.

All westerns revolve about the hero. In the earliest of westerns, these heroes were men who lusted for vengeance and killed at the slightest provocation. It was not long, however, before the western stars developed more respectable Anglo-Saxon qualities. Now they are trim, neat, and never lose their tempers; they do not smoke, drink, or gamble; they do not express deep emotion; they fight fairly. They have nicknames, such as Johnny, Jimmy, Rocky, and Gene, suggesting that they are friendly democratic folk. And as always, they are dauntless, confident, quick on the draw, excellent horsemen, and adept with a lariat. All of these characteristics, of course, are held up as positive values.

Most of the western heroes, following the old movie tradition, are serious, manly, rugged, and grim, and they have no romantic inclinations. Such, for example, are Johnny Mack Brown, Charles Starrett, Tim Holt, and Allan "Rocky" Lane. However, it has been a development of the past years to star a new type of western hero, men like Gene Autry or Roy Rogers. This newer western hero not only sings but also smiles more freely and charmingly, wears theatrical costumes, acts more neighborly, and becomes involved quite personally with girls, be that relationship one of antagonism, "palliness," or just embarrassment.

Accompanying these two general types of heroes are two types of heroines. There is, first, the traditional simple, gentle girl who accepts without question her role as a ranch housekeeper and, second, the more recent development of the independent heroine. The latter is likely to have a job and is just as much at ease with a man as with a woman. She participates confidently in his activities and his jokes. In one recent picture, such a heroine even operated an airline with men employees. This trend toward the independent heroine reflects a correspondent trend in the American milieu. The western heroine, like the modern woman, is no longer content with a recessive home-centered role and has proclaimed her equality and identity with man.

This newer development in heroine type complements the development in hero type. In the old-style western that took place in a "man's world," it was enough for a hero to be brave and rugged. These alone were sufficient to win love and respect. But in this more recent western development, in a world in which both men and women are prominent, the western hero must not only be brave and rugged; he must also have a certain charm, glamour, popularity, and willingness to accept the independent woman as his partner. Instead of dominant man and complementary recessive woman, this type of western sets up an ideal of a companionate relationship, a relationship in which the man and woman participate in the same activities.

The other prominent character roles of the western are the villain and the comic. The villains are of two types—the white-collar city slicker wearing a suit coat, vest, and watch chain and the crude drinking, gambling, heavy-set brute—both types, of course, representing distinctly negative personality values. The white-collar villain is generally the gang leader and, although dishonest, sinister, and ruthless, invariably poses as a respectable and honorable citizen. This gang leader is an autocratic dictator who stands in sharp contrast to the friendly, moral, clean-cut hero. However, these villains too, it is to be noted, are rugged individualists who are persevering, courageous, and clever.

In a few recent westerns, although as yet certainly no trend is indicated, the villain leader has been a woman with all the characteristics of the male villain except that men do her fighting and her dirty work. Being a villain, like being a pal, is another reflection of the social trend toward sex equality. The woman is affirming her right to compete with man and be his equal.

The comics of the western are of two types—the fat, simple buffoon, such as Smiley Burnette or Andy Devine, and the grizzly, perhaps bearded, westerner, most notable of whom is George "Gabby" Hayes. The comics, always honorable and loyal to the hero, represent the simplest type of humor—that of the clown. They are comic not only in appearance, but also in action; for example, they might clumsily mount a horse facing backward, be extremely embarrassed when a grateful girl kisses them, have nightmares or talk in their sleep, invent new gadgets that backfire, or continually do "double takes."

The sneering villains have only contempt for these comic characters and play ill-natured jokes on them, while the heroes, on the contrary, are friendly and sympathetic and enlist their aid. The comic characters are not held up as ideals worthy of emulation, but it is suggested that one should be sympathetic to characters who appear ludicrous but are basically good.

THE WESTERN HAS BEEN described with regard to its characteristics and its positive and negative values. The next step logically concerns the relationship between such characteristics and values and the members of the audience. Our concern here is not, however, with the possible influence of the western on its audience, but with the psychological bases for its popularity.

The western, with its standard plots, values, and character types, is essentially fairy tale and folklore, and the actors have skills completely at variance with those that we of the audience might possess. That such fanciful elements make up the western and that it has been so universally and consistently popular suggest that it appeals to our psychological predispositions. In this section we should like to indicate some of the predispositions to which these westerns appeal, with special emphasis on children.

Our focus is primarily on children partly because the psychological data about them are more reliable and partly because they are in many respects the most significant part of the western audience. Children constitute less than half of this audience but, being immature, presumably are most affected. Also, a child does not just see a western; he or she vividly and emotionally participates in it.[2]

We shall discuss first those general psychological factors that might apply to any dramatic hero stories, for, as has been suggested, the westerns are similar to hero stories of all peoples and all times, and second the more specific psychological satisfactions relevant to the western itself.

There is little doubt that a child, as well as many an adult, finds the world to be a complex and confusing place. There is so much that the child does not understand and that, especially when it involves human behavior, he cannot predict. In the western—as, of course, in most hero stories—the child can imagine himself in a world that is simple, clear-cut, and well ordered. There are no unnecessary characters, no irrelevant intrusions, no complex personalities, and no problems left unresolved. For the child who as yet makes no artistic demands, surely it is psychologically satisfying to identify with a world he can readily understand.

It is also generally agreed by child psychologists that a child has certain feelings of inferiority and insecurity. Not only does the child find it difficult to understand the big, confusing world, but the world and its members can be very threatening. The child is smaller and necessarily weaker than others who can enforce their will over him or her. Symbolizing these threats in the western are the dangerous situations of the hero. The hero is invariably threatened by powerful groups of outlaws or dishonest citizens. In identifying with the confident hero of the western story, the child is reassured. No matter what the odds or the dangers, the child in his imagination can, without the slightest fear or hesitation, overcome his adversaries and affirm his own strength and importance.

It is another characteristic of normal children that they demand some kind of imaginative activity. The child is restricted and hemmed in by the conditions of his actual life—by the smallness of his apartment, the constant demands of the school and the family, and his own weakness. In the western, the child can imaginatively escape from the enclosures and the demands and give rein to his desire for freedom. Like the hero, he becomes free to roam amid the wide-open spaces of the West, to choose his own direction and his own course of action.

The child also has aggressive feelings, feelings that, according to most psychologists, are primarily a reaction to frustration. Certainly, the frustrating forces are many. The child, of necessity, cannot freely express his impulses. He must, at different ages, undergo toilet training, refrain from playing with matches or pulling his sister's hair, remain quiet when he wishes to cry out, and the like. This being the case, it is psychologically satisfying for the child to have outlets for the blocked energies and impulses, and one outlet is the expression of aggression. Such aggression appears in the western in numerous chases, gun battles, and slugfests. The hero too, with whom the child identifies, is a man capable of vigorous aggressive action, such action being condoned, of course, only when he is fighting for justice. In this way, the western relieves a child's tension.

It is another important aspect of these western stories that the hero is fighting for right and justice. Thus, when the child imaginatively does these heroic and aggressive deeds, he is winning sanction from those very forces of society that make demands on him and from whom he seeks approval. In fighting for justice and in winning moral victories, the child symbolically wins the love and admiration of his parents, teachers, and religious leaders.

Related to this type of satisfaction is the approval the child might also get from his own conscience. Having been taught a moral code of behavior that he does not completely live up to, the child may develop guilty feelings. In fighting for justice, the child can, to some degree, salve his conscience and atone for his guilty actions and thoughts.

And finally, the western serves a psychological function in offering the child a choice of heroes. At a certain stage in his development, the normal child will stop idealizing his onetime all-powerful parents and substitute other heroes, these heroes in turn being replaced later by others. The westerns, as well as numerous other sources, add to the choice of heroes from which the child may select.

IN ADDITION TO THESE more basic gratifications offered by the western and most hero stories, a child may derive satisfactions from certain specific details of the western.

One such detail is the prominence of the horse. It has often been observed that the individual who controls a horse—a big, live, active, strong, responding animal—feels a deep sense of his own power. That a child who feels small and inferior should get such satisfaction out of a fantasy in which he owns and rides a horse seems very plausible. We leave aside any possible phallic significance.

Also, this horse in many westerns is more than just a symbol of strength. The horse, being named, glorified, and exhibited, becomes something of a personal pet. Roy Rogers's horse, for example, is "Trigger, the Smartest Horse in the Movies," and Gene Autry's is "Champion, the Wonder Horse," and both of these horses often have roles in the plot. So imaginatively, the child might also have the satisfactions of the pet, the pet of whom he is proud, to whom he gives love, and from whom he can always be sure of receiving love.

Another such specific element in the western that offers psychological satisfaction is the role of the comic. First, because the hero is a close friend of the comic character, it is suggested that he, the hero, is a fine and sympathetic person. Then too, this comic is generally a flunkey who never questions the hero's authority or hesitates to obey his commands. To the child who feels that demands are always being made on him, this can be an important satisfaction, for imaginatively he can now completely dominate another human being.

The comic expresses a very simple humor, and the child can also feel satisfactions similar to those of watching a circus clown. These may include the satisfactions of relieving emotional tension, of feeling superior to an adult, and of expressing aggression.

Another minor satisfaction of the western derives from the fact that the villain leader always poses as an honorable citizen. Thus, imaginatively, the scoundrel can symbolize a person one knows, dislikes, and perhaps envies, an individual whom others consider respectable. Thus, to the child, the villain may symbolically represent the teacher's pet or the boy next door who dutifully practices his musical instrument. In the western,

FIGURE 13. Roy Rogers and his horse Trigger.

the child, identifying with the hero, always gets the satisfaction of exposing and thrashing this villain.

There are also several miscellaneous characteristics of the western that emphasize the star's heroics. The hero, for example, always fights fairly, while the villains whom he defeats do not. Further, the hero is often offered positions of wealth and prestige, or in these modern westerns the love of a beautiful woman, but the hero proudly refuses these offers, choosing to remain an independent hero of the frontier. In stressing the heroic qualities of the hero, such details build up the psychological satisfaction for the child who identifies with him.

It is another possible minor satisfaction for the American child—one that appeals to his pride—to know that it is the history of his own country that is being portrayed. Each type of western, although following the standard pattern, does have its own peculiar characteristics, and these characteristics do suggest different psychological satisfactions. Thus, Charles Starrett, like Superman of the comic strips, plays a dual role. On the one hand, he is an ordinary cowboy, symbolizing what the child of the audience really is, while, on the other, he is the respected, mysterious Durango Kid, clothed in black, wearing a mask, riding a white horse, and appearing in the nick of time—symbolizing what the child would like to be.

Some westerns, especially those of Bill Boyd, alias Hopalong Cassidy, and Rocky Lane, often have a mystery angle, and the suspense satisfactions of the "whodunit" become part and parcel of the western. In some westerns, the hero might be framed and the crowds turn against him. In the end, of course, his true motives are recognized and he is more than vindicated. Others have musical comedy teams; others, romances between minor characters; others, heroes who stand out because they are bullwhip experts; other, singing stars; and so on. Each type of western varies slightly in the characteristics and thereby in its potential psychological appeals.

WE HAVE BEEN DISCUSSING primarily the characteristics of the western as they apply to the psychological needs of children. However, almost two-thirds of the western audience, say the producers, is composed not of children but of adults—mostly rural adults. Many of the psychological gratifications discussed apply to any group that regularly attends the western movie or reads western stories. However, there is another particular reason for the popularity among rural audiences.

The rural folk are often quite aware that they are rural. Not only are they familiar with the jokes about "hicks," but they are likely to feel ill at ease in a metropolitan city, with its crowds, anonymity, bright lights, and sharp characters. To these folk, the westerns have a special appeal. The westerns take place in a country setting, and there are no difficult problems of identification. Also, most of the characters, including the stars, with their drawls, group singing, and casual friendliness, are distinctly rural types. The only city-type characters in the standard western are the villain gang leader, whom the hero always defeats, and the fat and sympathetic, but inferior, comic.

FIGURE 14. The westerns of Hopalong Cassidy (William Boyd) often had a mystery angle.

Thus, the rural folk can bolster their own sense of pride. It is suggested not only that they need feel no inferiority or backwardness, but also that western life can be just as dramatic and exciting as anything that occurs in the city.

THE FOREGOING DISCUSSION should be tempered by a few qualifications. The division and listing of the various psychological appeals are entirely arbitrary and serve only an analytic function. Each individual, of course, is an organic unity and responds as such. Also, this discussion has intended to suggest only possible psychological satisfactions and does not presume to apply to all individuals or all children. The personality variations among individuals are without limit, and probably no two will ever see exactly the same things or respond in exactly the same manner. Each, according to his own orientation, perspective, and unique personality, will select out those elements of the western that are most meaningful to him and will appropriately interpret them.

Nor have we touched on the problem of the possible influence of the western on the child. Exactly what the influence of the western, or any mass media, might be is a very complex problem about which specialists do not agree. We might only note here, first, that the impact of the western depends more on what the child already is than on the characteristics of the western itself and, second, that the impact must be seen in the perspective of the total environment—an environment that includes the school, the neighborhood, the gang, the church, the newspaper, the comic booklets, the radio programs, other movies, and, above all, the family.

NOTES

1. These values manifested by the heroic leader who struggles and succeeds against odds really have their origins in the far-distant past. Such hero glorification occurs, for example, in Bible stories and in Greek and Teutonic legends. Further, certain aspects of rugged individualism were reinforced by the Renaissance, the Reformation, and the development of European capitalism. Only certain unique characteristics of the western can be directly explained by American frontier history. Instead of idealizing the daring explorer who cuts through jungles, the zealous missionary who civilizes the heathen, or the venturesome trader who sails the oceans, we came, because of our frontier, to glorify the rugged cowboy who rides a horse, carries a six-shooter, and tracks down cattle rustlers and stagecoach robbers.

2. We are assuming throughout that the normal child identifies with the western hero. Considering that the hero is by far the most prominent of the characters in the western and that the child in the theater cheers the hero, feels tense when he is in danger and relieved when he is safe, this seems a justifiable assumption.

CHAPTER 8

THE WESTERN, OR THE AMERICAN FILM PAR EXCELLENCE

ANDRÉ BAZIN

THE WESTERN IS THE ONLY genre whose origins are almost identical with those of the cinema itself and that is as alive as ever after almost a half century of uninterrupted success. Even if one disputes the quality of its inspiration and of its style since the thirties, one is amazed at the steady commercial success that is the measure of its health. Doubtless, the western has not entirely escaped the evolution of cinema taste—or indeed taste, period. It has been and will again be subjected to influences from the outside—for instance, the crime novel, the detective story, or the social problems of the day—and its simplicity and strict form have suffered as a result. We may be entitled to regret this but not to see in it a state of decay. These influences are felt in only a few productions of relatively high standing and do not affect the low-budget films aimed principally at the home market. Furthermore, it is as important for us to marvel at the western's capacity to resist them as to deplore these passing moments of contamination. Every influence acts on them like a vaccine. The microbe, on contact, loses its deadly virulence. In the course of fifteen years, the American comedy has exhausted its resources. If it survives in an occasional success, it is only to the extent that, in some way, it abandons the rules that before the war made for successful comedy. From *Underworld* (1927) to *Scarface* (1932), the gangster film had already completed the cycle of its growth. The scenarios of detective stories have developed rapidly, and if it is still possible to rediscover an aesthetic of violence within the framework of the criminal adventure that they share with *Scarface*, we would be hard put to see in the private eye, the journalist, or the G-man the reflection of the original hero. Furthermore, if there is such a genre as the American detective film, one cannot attribute to it the independent identity of the western; the literature that preceded it has continued to influence it, and the latest interesting variants of the crime film derive directly from it.

On the contrary, the durability of the western heroes and plots has been demonstrated recently by the fabulous success on television of the old Hopalong Cassidy films. The western does not age.

Its worldwide appeal is even more astonishing than its historical survival. What can there possibly be to interest Arabs, Hindus, Latins, Germans, or Anglo-Saxons, among whom the western has had an uninterrupted success, about evocations of the birth of the United States of America, the struggle between Buffalo Bill and the Indians, the laying down of the railroad, or the Civil War?

The western must possess some greater secret than simply the secret of youthfulness. It must be a secret that somehow identifies it with the essence of cinema.

It is easy to say that because the cinema is movement, the western is cinema par excellence. It is true that galloping horses and fights are its usual ingredients. But in that case the western would simply be one variety of adventure story. Again, the continuous movement of the characters, carried almost to a pitch of frenzy, is inseparable from its geographical setting, and one might just as well define the western by its set (the frontier town and its landscapes), but other genres and schools of filmmaking have made use of the dramatic poetry of the landscape (for example, the silent Swedish film), but although it contributed to their greatness it did not ensure their survival. Better still, sometimes, as in *The Overlanders* (1946), a western theme is borrowed—in this case the traditional cattle drive—and set in a landscape, central Australia, reasonably like the American West. The result, as we know, was excellent. But fortunately, no attempt was made to follow up this paradoxical achievement, whose success was due to an unusual combination of circumstances. If in fact westerns have been shot in France against the landscapes of the Camargue, one can only see in this an additional proof of the popularity and healthiness of a genre that can survive counterfeiting, pastiche, or even parody.

It would be hopeless to try to reduce the essence of the western to one or another of these manifest components. The same ingredients are to be found elsewhere but not the same benefits that appear to go with them. Therefore, the western must be something else again than its form. Galloping horses, fights, and strong and brave men in a wildly austere landscape could not add up to a definition of the genre or encompass its charms.

Those formal attributes by which one normally recognizes the western are simply signs or symbols of its profound reality, namely, the myth. The western was born of an encounter between a mythology and a means of expression: the saga of the West existed before the cinema in literary or folklore form, and the multiplication of western films has not killed off western literature, which still retains its public and continues to provide screenwriters with their best material. But there is no common measure between the limited and national audience for western stories and the worldwide audience for the films that they inspire. Just as the miniatures of the *Books of Hours* served as models for the statuary and the stained-glass windows of the cathedrals, this western literature, freed from the bonds of language, finds a distribution on the screen in keeping with its size—almost as if the dimensions of the image had become one with those of the imagination.

This book will emphasize a little-known aspect of the western: its faithfulness to history.[1] This is not generally recognized—primarily, doubtless, because of our ignorance, but still more because of the deeply rooted prejudice according to which the western can tell only extremely puerile stories, fruits of a naive power of invention that does not concern itself with psychological, historical, or even material verisimilitude. True, few westerns are explicitly concerned with historical accuracy. True, too, these are not the only ones of any value. It would be absurd to judge the characters of Tom Mix—still more of his magic white horse—or even of William Hart or Douglas Fairbanks, all of whom made lovely films in the great primitive period of the western, by the yardstick of archaeology.

After all, many current westerns of honorable standing—I am thinking of *Across the Great Divide* (1941), *Yellow Sky* (1948), or *High Noon* (1952)—have only a tenuous relation to historical fact. They are primarily works of imagination. But one would be as much in error not to recognize the historical references in the western as to deny the unabashed freedom of its screenplays. J.-L. Rieupeyrout gives a complete account of the birth of its epic-like idealization, based on comparatively recent history, yet it could be that his study, concerned to recall to us what is ordinarily forgotten, or even not known, and confining itself to films that justify his thesis, discards by implication the other side of the aesthetic reality. Still, this would show him to be doubly right, for the relations between the facts of history and the western are not immediate and direct, but dialectic. Tom Mix is the opposite of Abraham Lincoln, but after his own fashion he perpetuates Lincoln's cult and his memory. In its most romantic or most naive form, the western is the opposite of a historical reconstruction. There is no difference between Hopalong Cassidy and Tarzan except for their costume and the arena in which they demonstrate their prowess. However, if one wanted to take the trouble to compare these delightful but unlikely stories and to superimpose on them, as is done in modern physiognomy, a number of negatives of faces, an ideal western would come through, composed of all the constants common to one and to the other: a western made up solely of unalloyed myth. Let us take one example, that of the woman.

In the first third of the film, the good cowboy meets the pure young woman—the good and strong virgin, let us call her—with whom he falls in love. Despite his chasteness, we are able to guess this love is shared. However, virtually insurmountable obstacles stand in its way. One of the most significant and most frequent comes from the family of the beloved—for example, her brother is a sinister scoundrel, and the good cowboy is forced to rid society of him, man to man. A modern Chimène,[2] our heroine refuses to see in her brother's assassin any sort of a fine fellow. In order to redeem himself in his charmer's eyes and merit forgiveness, our knight must now pass through a series of fabulous trials. He ends by saving his elected bride from a danger that could be fatal to her person, her virtue, her fortune, or all three at once. Following this, since we are now near the end of the film, the damsel would indeed be ungrateful if she did not feel that her suitor had repaid his debt and allow him to start dreaming of a lot of children.

Up to this point, this outline into which one can weave a thousand variants—for example, by substituting the Civil War for the Indian threat, cattle rustlers—comes close to reminding us of the medieval courtly romances by virtue of the preeminence given to the woman and the trials that the finest of heroes must undergo in order to qualify for her love.

But the story is often complicated by a paradoxical character—the saloon B-girl—who as a rule is also in love with the cowboy. So there would be one woman too many if the god of the screenwriter was not keeping watch. A few minutes before the end, the prostitute with the heart of gold rescues the man she loves from some danger or another, sacrificing her life and her hopeless love for the happiness of her cowboy. This also serves to redeem her in the eyes of the spectators.

There is food for thought here. Note, first of all, that the distinction between good and bad applies only to the men. Women, all up and down the social scale, are in every case worthy of love or at least of esteem or pity. The least little prostitute is redeemed by love and death—although she is spared the latter in *Stagecoach* (1939), with its resemblance to de Maupassant's "Boule de suif" (1880). It is true that the good cowboy is more or less a reformed offender so that henceforth the most moral of marriages with his heroine becomes possible.

Furthermore, in the world of the western, it is the women who are good and the men who are bad, so bad that the best of them must redeem themselves from the original sin of their sex by undergoing various trials. In the Garden of Eden, Eve led Adam into temptation. Paradoxically, Anglo-Saxon puritanism, under the pressure of historical circumstances, reverses the biblical situation. The downfall of the woman comes about only as a result of the concupiscence of men.

Clearly, this theory derives from the actual sociological conditions obtaining in primitive western society that, because of the scarcity of women and the perils of a too harsh existence in this burgeoning world, make it imperative to safeguard its female members and its horses. Hanging was considered enough punishment for stealing a horse. To engender respect for women, more was needed than the fear of a risk as trifling as the loss of one's life, namely, the positive power of a myth. The myth of the western illustrates and both initiates and confirms woman in her role as vestal of the social virtues, of which this chaotic world is so greatly in need. Within her is concealed the physical future and, by way of the institution of the family to which she aspires as the root is drawn to the earth, its moral foundation.

These myths, of which we have just examined what is perhaps the most significant example (the next is the myth of the horse), may themselves doubtless be reduced to an even more essential principle. Basically, each of these particularize, by way of an already specific dramatic plot, the great epic Manichaeanism that sets the forces of evil over against the knights of the true cause. These immense stretches of prairie, of deserts, of rocks to which the little wooden town clings precariously (a primitive amoeba of a civilization) are exposed to all manner of possible things. The Indian, who lived in this world, was incapable of imposing on it man's order. He mastered it only by identifying himself with its pagan savagery. The white Christian, on the contrary, is truly the conqueror of a new world. The grass sprouts where his horse has passed. He imposes simultaneously his moral and his technical order, the one linked to the other and the former guaranteeing the latter. The physical safety of the stagecoaches, the protection given by the federal troops, the building of the great railroads are less important perhaps than the establishment of justice and respect for the law. The relations between morality and law, which in our ancient civilization are just a subject for an undergraduate paper, were a half century ago the most vital thing confronting the youthful United States. Only strong, rough, and courageous men could tame these virgin lands. Everyone knows that familiarity with death does not keep alive the fear of hell, nor do scruples or moral debate. Policemen and judges are of most help to the weak. It was the force of this conquering humanity that constituted its weakness. Where individual morality is precarious, it is only law that can impose the order of the good and the good of order.

But the law is unjust to the extent that it pretends to guarantee a moral society but ignores the individual merits of those who constitute that society. If it is to be effective, this justice must be dispensed by men who are just as strong and just as daring as the criminals. These virtues, as we have said, are in no way compatible with virtue in the absolute sense. The sheriff is not always a better person than the man he hangs. This begets and establishes an inevitable and necessary contradiction. There is often little moral difference between the outlaw and the man who operates within the law. Still, the sheriff's star must be seen as constituting a sacrament of justice, whose worth does not depend on the worthiness of the man who administers it. To this first contradiction a second must be added, the administration of justice, which, if it is to be effective, must be drastic and speedy—short of lynching, however—and thus must ignore extenuating circumstances, such as alibis that would take too long to verify. In protecting society, such a form of justice runs the risk of unkindness to the most turbulent though not perhaps the least useful or even the least deserving of its children.

Although the need for law was never more clearly allied to the need for morality, at the same time never was their antagonism more concrete and more evident. It is this which provides a basis, within a slapstick framework, for Charlie Chaplin's *The Pilgrim* (1923), at the conclusion of which we see our hero riding his horse along the borderline between good and evil, which also happens to be the Mexican border.

John Ford's *Stagecoach*, which is a fine dramatic illustration of the parable of the Pharisee and the Publican, demonstrates that a prostitute can be more respectable than the narrow-minded people who drove her out of town and just as respectable as an officer's wife, that a dissolute gambler knows how to die with all the dignity of an aristocrat, that an alcoholic doc-

FIGURE 15. Charlie Chaplin's *The Pilgrim* (1923) explores the tension between law and morality.

tor can practice his profession with competence and devotion, and that an outlaw who is being sought for the payment of past and possibly future debts can show loyalty, generosity, courage, and refinement, whereas a banker of considerable standing and reputation runs off with the cash box.

So we find at the source of the western the ethics of the epic and even of tragedy. The western is in the epic category because of the superhuman level of its heroes and the legendary magnitude of their feats of valor. Billy

FIGURE 16. Social and moral distinctions are examined in John Ford's
Stagecoach (1939).

the Kid is as invulnerable as Achilles, and his revolver is infallible. The
cowboy is a knight-at-arms. The style of the mise-en-scène is in keeping
with the character of the hero. A transformation into an epic is evident
in the setups of the shots, with their predilection for vast horizons, all-
encompassing shots that constantly bring to mind the conflict between
man and nature. The western has virtually no use for the close-up, even
for the medium shot, preferring by contrast the traveling shot and the
pan, which refuse to be limited by the frameline and restore to space its
fullness.

True enough. But this epic style derives its real meaning only from
the morality that underlies and justifies it. It is the morality of a world in
which social good and evil, in their simplicity and necessity, exist like two
primary and basic elements. But good in its natal state engenders law in
all its primitive rigor; epic becomes tragedy on the appearance of the first
conflict between the transcendence of social justice and the individual
character of moral justice, between the categorical imperative of the law
that guarantees the order of the future city and the no less unshakable
order of the individual conscience.

The Corneille-like simplicity of western scripts has often been a subject for parody. It is easy to see the analogy between them and the text of *Le Cid*: there is the same conflict between love and duty, the same knightly ordeals on the completion of which the wise virgin will consent to forget the insult to her family, and the same chaste sentiments that are based on a concept of love subordinated to respect for the laws of society and morality. But this comparison is double-edged: to make fun of the western by comparing it to Corneille is also to draw attention to its greatness, a greatness near perhaps to the childlike, just as childhood is near to poetry.

Let there be no doubt about it. This naive greatness is recognized in westerns by simple men in every clime—together with the children—despite differences of language, landscape, customs, and dress. The epic and tragic hero is a universal character. The Civil War is part of nineteenth-century history; the western has turned it into the Trojan War of the most modern of epics. The migration to the West is our *Odyssey*.

Not only is the historicity of the western not at odds with the no less evident penchant of the genre for outlandish situations, exaggerations of fact, and the use of the deus ex machina (in short, everything that makes for improbability); it is, on the contrary, the foundation of its aesthetic and its psychology. The history of film has only known one other epic cinema, and that too is a historical cinema. Our purpose here is not to compare epic form in the Russian and in the American film, yet an analysis of their styles would shed an unexpected light on the historical meaning of the events reconstructed in the two of them. Our only purpose is to point out that it is not their closeness to the facts that has given them their styles. There are legends that come into being almost instantaneously, that half a generation suffices to ripen into an epic. Like the conquest of the West, the Soviet revolution is a collection of historical events that signal the birth of a new order and a new civilization. Both have begotten the myths necessary for the confirmation of history, both had to reinvent a morality to rediscover at their living source and before mixture or pollution took place the foundation of the law that would make order out of chaos, separate heaven from earth. But perhaps the cinema was the only language capable of expressing this, above all of giving it its true aesthetic dimension. Without the cinema the conquest of the West would have left behind, in the shape of the western story, only a minor literature, and it is neither by its paintings nor by its novels that Soviet art has given the world a picture of its grandeur. The fact is that henceforth the cinema is the specifically epic art.

NOTES

1. Jean-Louis Rieupeyrout's *La grande adventure du western, 1894–1964* (Paris: Editions du Cerf, 1964), for which Bazin was here writing the preface. [Editors' note.]

2. Chimène is a character in the French opera *Chimène; ou, Le Cid* by Antonio Sacchini. [Editors' note.]

CHAPTER 9

THE OLYMPIAN COWBOY

HARRY SCHEIN

TRANSLATED FROM THE SWEDISH BY IDA M. ALCOCK

WHEN MIDDLEBROW PEOPLE want to express their utter contempt for films, they often cite the "western" as typical of the idiocy they wish to deprecate. Actually, the western is the backbone, not the tail, of the art of the film.

The western, for that matter, is much more than a film. It offers us the opportunity to experience the creation of folklore, to see how it grows and takes form. The roots of the mythology of Europe and the Far East are hidden in the past, and today can be only imperfectly reconstructed. But the white man's America is no older than the Gutenberg Bible. It attained economic independence and, therewith, cultural independence about the time the novel achieved its artistic and popular success. It is no accident that James Fenimore Cooper's work stands as America's first significant contribution to literature. It is just as natural that the film, at its very beginning, seized upon the western motif. In the life span of less than one generation, it has developed from an apparently innocent, meaningless form into a rigidly patterned and conventional mythology, into one body of young America's folklore.

Of course, most of the westerns of silent films were substantially side-shows performed by puppets. But somewhere between William S. Hart and Hopalong Cassidy, a change occurred. The simple, upright, and faithful cowboy became more and more decked out with silver spurs and guitars; he sang much and drank little; he never worried about women even while protecting them. Almost imperceptibly, he was changing into an

Harry Schein, "The Olympian Cowboy," *American Scholar* 24, no. 3 (1955): 309–320. Copyright © 1955 by the Phi Beta Kappa Society. Reprinted with the permission of the *American Scholar*.

omnipotent father symbol whose young attendants consistently avoided heterosexual and other traps of an unmanly nature.

The child is father to the man. The western of the days of the silent film already contained the material and the tendencies that, little by little, as the element of sound consolidated the form of the film, were deepened and rigidified. Folklore demands a rigid form. If one is to feel the power of the gods, repetition is required. It is precisely the rigid form of the western that gives the contents mythological weight and significance. This requires a ritualistic handling, with a rigid cast of characters similar to that of the commedia dell'arte and a strict orthodoxy like that of the Japanese Kabuki theater.

Several years ago, when the Swedish state film censorship bureau wished to demonstrate the justification for its existence by showing what erotic and brutal shocks we escaped because of the intervention of the censor, it was found that these consisted to a great extent of saloon fights in westerns. The similarities among these fights, taken from perhaps ten different films, were astounding: the same bar counter, the same supernumeraries, the same groupings, the same choreography in the fights themselves. And when the Czech puppet-film director Jiri Trnka decided to produce a satire on American films, it was natural that he chose the western. It was simple enough to use puppets instead of human beings to make the rigid form and strict convention appear grotesque.

The movement in a stereotype is as obvious as the ticking of a clock in an otherwise absolute silence. The postwar shifts in perspective that the western underwent did not disturb the mythological stability but gave it a profound meaning aside from its aesthetic value. The genre has produced several good and many bad films, but even the stuttering priest can speak about God. Naturally, the western does not lack aesthetic interest. Even in its role of nursery for American film directors, it has a certain aesthetic significance. Moreover, the rigid form requires speed, action, and movement and, in propitious circumstances, can contribute to a dramatic conclusion. In addition, it creates an enormous demand for freshness within the limitations of the stereotype, an aesthetic stimulus as good as any.

Also characteristic of the western is the public's relationship to it. The desire to experience the same thing time after time implies on the part of the public a ritualistic passivity similar to that which one finds in a congregation at divine service. It cannot be curiosity that drives the public to the western; there is no wish for something different and unfamiliar, but a need for something old and well known. One can scarcely talk about escape from reality in the usual sense; it is a hypnotic condition rather than a complicated process of identification. The western has the same bewitching strength as an incantation: the magic of repetition.

THE HERO AND WOMEN

In the center stands the hero. He is always alone in the little community. He often lacks family and, not infrequently, is one of those exceptional human beings who seem never to have had a mother. Opposed to him are the bandits (there are always several) and their leader, an older, rich, often to all appearances respectable man in league with corrupt political bosses. The bandit, too, usually lacks a wife, and only now and then does he have an unfortunate daughter. Finally, there is the little community itself— respectable, timid, and neutral in action.

The action often takes place in the period immediately after the Civil War. In such cases, the hero is often a Southern officer, and his opponents are Northerners. The struggle between these two elements is an epilogue to the war, often with a reversed outcome. Uncle Sam is like a father figure, powerful and hateful, but at the same time filled with guilt feelings toward the ravished Southerners. Although the western apparently takes revenge for the defeat of the South, the revenge is still illusory, a rebellious gesture that culminates in loyal submission and father identification.

The hero is surrounded by a good woman and several bad saloon girls, who later either sing about love or dance the cancan. The good woman is usually a blonde and a specialist in making apple pie. The bad women are the kind one goes to bed with. Although the beds rarely appear in western interiors, there is reason to assume that the saloon ladies are supposed to suggest those prostitutes who, during the enormous woman shortage of the 1800s, were imported into the West and, through their kind actions, saw to it that not all the men shot one another to death. Of course, in more advanced films, the typical mixed figure appears—an apparently bad woman who seems to be on the side of the bandits but who gradually shows herself to be innocent and finally helpful in their destruction.

The hero's relationship to women is very subtle. He shields them without actually being involved. In more and more westerns, a direct enmity toward women is displayed. Sadism is directed most often toward the bad women but now and then even toward the mixed type. *Duel in the Sun* (1946) offers the best example of this. Often a triangle drama appears (a woman and two men), which ends with the men becoming good friends and arriving at the realization that the woman is not worth having. In

FIGURE 17. Jennifer Jones (Pearl Chavez) and Gregory Peck (Lewt McCanles) in *Duel in the Sun* (1946).

The Outlaw (1943), the young man, after prolonged abuse, humiliates the woman by choosing, in a toss-up between her and a fine horse, the horse. In a priceless homosexual castration fantasy, the father figure of the film shoots off the earlobes of the young man when he dares to defend himself. The pistol in westerns is by now accepted as a phallic symbol.

In a series of films, the weapon stands in the center of the action—a bowie knife, a Winchester rifle, a Colt revolver. He who owns the weapon is unconquerable. The good men are rightful owners from whom the bad men are trying to steal potency. To own the weapon is much more important than to own the woman. It is important how one draws the weapon. Bad men draw it too often but too slowly. Like Casanova, they shoot in all directions without finding their mark. The hero, who defends home—as an institution—draws his weapon quickly. He shoots seldom, but never misses. As protector of the community, he cannot afford to be promiscuous. There must be an outcome of the shooting. A strong man is able to fire six shots without reloading.

So much for the rigid western pattern, familiar even to the more occasional moviegoers. It may be of interest to determine what variations this pattern displays and particularly those tendencies that have been most pronounced since World War II. The question, in other words, is this: is there a relation between America's politically dominant situation in the postwar period and a new arrangement of luminaries in its mythology?

THE THREE MODERN VARIANTS

Accepting the usual risks of generalization, one may speak of three basic elements in the western: the symbolic, the psychological, and the moral. If one bears in mind the fact that the western is usually a mixture of these elements, it will not be too gross a simplification to discuss each of these factors separately.

It is said that Chaplin never had any inkling of his profundity until he began to read what various intellectuals wrote about him. Then he himself became intellectual. That is, of course, sheer nonsense. If, however, this kind of reasoning is applied to the symbolism of the western, it probably has a certain correctness. In other words, the western seems to have becomes conscious of its symbolic purport and, as a result of this consciousness, has become quite dreadfully symbolic.

That unconscious enmity toward women, formerly expressed with lip service paid to chivalry while actions denoted inner indifference (placing on a pedestal always implies humiliation), now finds stronger and more direct expression. The hatred of women has become so obvious that it must give rise to speculation. Their ill treatment in a physical and often purely sadistic sense is an increasingly common element not only in the western but also in other American films such as *Gilda* (1946). *Winchester '73* (1950) is an outstanding example. *Colt .45* (1950) is a symbolic parody of this motif. Not only must the pistol be regarded from a symbolic point of view—it goes off with a louder bang than the rifle—but the villain in the film has a favorite position, teetering on a chair, half sprawling, with his hands on his hips and the pistol profile following a naturalistic line. Even if this conscious smuggling in of symbols can never take in an artistically interested customs officer, it indicates an ambition to make more than a classical spectacle of the western.

This ambition is made even clearer through the psychological element. Though westerns are undoubtedly unpsychological for the most part, they have a predilection for dealing with the psychology of the villain. Even this is refreshing to an eye that yearns for some gray oases in the black-and-white desert.

Through trying to clarify the villain's behavior, the films muster a certain sympathy for him. He becomes a product of unfortunate circumstances, orphaned at an early age and brought up in a loveless milieu. He has, as a rule, suffered injustice and seeks revenge in a certain criminal but, in the deepest sense, forgivable way. Often, as stated before, he is a Southern officer whose home was devastated. The villain, of course, must die, but as a rule he dies happy, in a redeeming self-sacrifice through which the blessedness of the final kiss acquires a charmingly melancholy background.

These psychological efforts can give rise to important thematic rearrangements. A few years ago two films were made about Jesse James—a legendary western figure who is well on the way to becoming America's Robin Hood. In one of these films, *The Great Missouri Raid* (1951), the James brothers are formidable enemies but chivalrous supermen of steel, dutiful toward their mother. They are, of course, Southerners, and their enemy is a Northern general modeled after a hateful Gestapo type. The film is very well made and belongs to the classical western pattern. The other film, *I Shot Jesse James* (1949), seems more unpretentious. It concerns a man who shot his best—and oldest—friend in the back in order to obtain amnesty for himself and to be able to marry a saloon girl (cf. Freud). The victim is the bandit sought by the law, the murderer the one who is protected by the law. The psychological complications caused by this rearrangement of boundaries between the territory of the villain and the hero are dealt with in two sections. The murderer is certainly free, but he is detested by public opinion. Even the girl is unkind enough not to trouble herself with him after the treachery that has been committed for her sake. The murderer, desiring to defy public opinion, accepts an offer from a traveling theatrical troupe to appear on the stage and show how he shot James in the back. In another part of the film, he forces a singer to render the ballad of the murder of Jesse James. Thus, as his crime is repeated again and again, the murderer returns to the mental scene of the crime and suffers an inner decay that leads to a new crime, this time unprotected by the law.

I Shot Jesse James is not the only western that sets friend against friend. Very often the motif is family; now and then brother stands against brother, father against son. As a rule it is a woman who divides them. Something like biblically elemental conflicts are deftly extracted from, or themselves extract, a taken moral stand. When form and conclusion are rigid, a fundamental moral problem can have some of the simple, prime-

FIGURE 18. The young challenger (Skip Homeier, *right*) confronts Jimmy Ringo (Gregory Peck) in *The Gunfighter* (1950).

val strength of the drama of fate and thus prevent the repetitions from becoming mechanical.

These moral conflicts are undoubtedly the most interesting elements in the modern western. They are evident in *The Gunfighter* (1950), a very fine film with far from ordinary psychological creativity, and in *High Noon* (1952), until now the genre's most outstanding artistic success.

The Gunfighter deals with a middle-aged and unglamorized gunman. No one in the entire West can handle a gun as he does. He is, therefore, challenged by all the young fighting cocks who wish to take over his reputation for being invincible. He is forced to kill them in self-defense. He flees from his home, but his reputation is swifter than his flight; he is always recognized, and the killing is repeated time after time. Though he is fed up to the gills with it, there is always someone who will not leave him in peace. Finally, there comes a man who draws the gun a fraction of a second more quickly than he. The gunfighter dies with what is almost relief, but at the same time he is filled with pity for his murderer: now it is *his* turn to take over this reputation as the foremost gunman of the West, his fate to kill and never to be able to flee from killing until he himself is killed.

The western's moral problem revolves around the fifth commandment. One can understand that a country traditionally pacifist but suddenly transformed into the strongest military in the history of the world must begin to consider, how with good conscience, it can take life. In somewhat awkward situations it is always good to take shelter behind the lofty example of the mythologies' gods.

I see *High Noon* as having an urgent political message. The little community seems to be crippled with fear before the approaching villains; seems to be timid, neutral, and halfhearted, like the United Nations before the Soviet Union, China, and North Korea; moral courage is apparent only in the very American sheriff. He is newly married; he wants to have peace and quiet. But duty and the sense of justice come first, in spite of the fact that he must suddenly stand completely alone. Even his wife, who is a Quaker and opposed on principle to killing, wishes to leave him, and only at the last moment does she understand that her duty to justice is greater than her duty to God. The point is, of course, that pacifism is certainly a good thing, but that war in certain situations can be both moral and unavoidable.

High Noon, artistically, is the most convincing and likewise certainly the most honest explanation of American foreign policy. The mythological gods of the western, who used to shoot unconcernedly, without any moral complications worth mentioning, are now grappling with moral problems and an ethical melancholy that could be called existentialist if they were not shared by Mr. Dulles.[1]

THE SUFFERING GOD

This conscious symbolism, these psychological ambitions and moral statements of account, give both color and relief to the mythological substratum. The anchorage in realism, for example, in historical characters like Billy the Kid and Jesse James, or in the more ambitious and thoroughly worked-out description of milieus, contributes to the creation of an impressive space before the footlights of the mythological scene. The native strength and possibilities of the western are developed in the counterplay between American film production and American film critics. As witness thereof, take that farfetched but characteristic comparison between *High Noon* and "That Old Game about Everyman," of which Howard A. Burton is guilty in a recent number of the *Quarterly Review of Film, Radio, and Television*.[2] His puzzle certainly does not fit together, but one still discerns an Olympian landscape model, the Rocky Mountains—saturated with divine morality. Even satires on the western, such as Bob Hope's *The Paleface* (1948), indicate a growing consciousness of the genre's true function.

An awareness of the mythological element is thus found not only among talentless writers, but also among talented directors like George Stevens. According to a statement in the English film magazine *Sight and Sound*, he is reported to have expressed his desire to "enlarge" the western legend and to have said that the pioneers presented in the western fill the same role for the Americans as King Arthur and his knights hold in English mythology.[3] In Stevens's film *Shane* (1953), that ambition is entirely realized. As a matter of fact, the film incorporates the complete historical development of the western, including the protest against the father and the identification with the father. It is, to be sure, an imperfect attempt—but still an attempt—at synthesis of the classical pattern enriched with the three modern variations: symbolic, psychological, moral.

A large and fertile valley in the West is ruled by a powerful and greedy cattleman. With the help of his myrmidons, he carries on a private war of attrition against a handful of farmers who are struggling to bring the grazing lands under cultivation. To one of these small farms Shane comes, dressed in romantic garb of leather, cartridge belt, and gun. He takes a job there and becomes good friends with the farmer, his wife, and their twelve-year-old boy, Joey. Shane has a mysterious past; he has been a gunman who now is trying to begin a new and peaceful life. He manages, for the longest time, to avoid being provoked by the cattleman's hirelings, but the terror of the farmers becomes unbearable. When one of them is shot down by an imported murderer, the others are willing to give up and move away. No one dares to meet terror with terror. Then Shane takes off his blue work clothes and puts on his old leather outfit. He gets out the gun that he hoped he had laid down forever, rides forth to the saloon, and kills the murderer. He has tried to begin a new life, but he has not succeeded. He has killed again and must ride away to the unknown from which he came.

Shane cannot, from an artistic point of view, be compared with *High Noon*, possibly because it has not an equally emphasized main point. It deals, as a matter of fact, with two motifs: Shane and the little family and Shane and the community versus the dictatorial cattleman and his band. But the film is obviously strongly influenced by *High Noon*. The tempo is equally slow and heavy with fate, the portrayal of the milieu equally

FIGURE 19. *Shane* (1953): a western aware of its own mythic implications.

penetrating. The action is one unbroken loading of a charge up to the climax. This is unusual for a western, with its generally very rapid changes
of scene.

Like the gunman in *The Gunfighter*, Shane is the man marked by fate,
he whom the gods set out to kill. The distance between him and Mr. Bab-
bitt, the farmer, and the small-town dweller in *High Noon* is as great as the
distance between Brooklyn and Korea. Only the woman lacks perception
of the hovering air of fatefulness. She sees only what she can touch. Be-

tween Shane and her the atmosphere is tense with fear and eroticism, but only her husband can give her security.

The really original element in *Shane* is the relationship between Shane and the little boy, Joey. Joey cherishes a boundless, completely hysterical admiration for Shane, for his skill with the pistol. He himself is still not permitted to play with loaded weapons, but they occupy his imagination. He smacks his lips to imitate the sound of shooting; he catches sight of game without being able to press after it; he shoots imaginary enemies with imaginary bullets. His confidence in Shane is upset a trifle when Shane knocks his father unconscious. However, when the boy understands that Shane has not robbed his father of life but only of potency (Shane wants to prevent him, less experienced in the art of shooting, from risking his life and takes away his pistol), the boy identifies himself completely with Shane. He follows him to the saloon, witnesses the battle, and afterward takes leave of Shane, prepared to become his heir.

Shane, more than any other western hero, is a mythological figure. This is partly because the film sees him so much through the eyes of Joey, looking upward. Shane's entry is as godlike as his exit; it is a higher being who comes, driven by fate-impregnated compulsion, to fulfill his mission. Shane is more than Robin Hood, more than Cinderella's prince. He is a suffering god, whose noble and bitter fate it is to sacrifice himself for others.

Shane is distinguished by a realism seldom worked out so thoroughly in westerns. The film takes the time to portray the people in the valley, their everyday lives, their little festivities. A series of impressionistically bold details gives the production a sensitive and fine-grained texture. Its world is familiar and close to reality. Only Shane is alien. He is not Zeus who, disguised as a human being, visits the earth to cavort with its women, but an American saint, the cowboy who died in the Civil War and sits at God's right hand. He is a leather-bound angel with a gun, a mythological Boy Scout, always ready to keep the hands of true believers and the community unsullied by blood.

A BLOODY FUTURE

As a rule, of course, it is meaningless to discuss the degree of individual vision behind a work of art or a film with a mythological purport. Mythology rests on a collective foundation that also includes the creative artist.

When creative vision is expressed in the form of satire, it has quite obviously freed itself from the mythological substratum, but at the same time it strengthens the existence of that substratum—a puppet show that does not concern itself with the obvious is a paradox. As far as the western is concerned, Bob Hope and the Marx Brothers demonstrate a blasphemous emancipation. Large sections of the American public, through television's mechanization of the western, have become surfeited with the genre. Since *Shane* is neither mechanical nor satirical, it ought to be reckoned as the first offspring, and, through Stevens's statement, the first "documented" offspring, of the new vision.

The question remains: is this newly awakened mythological vision going to sabotage mythology itself by dispelling the cloud that carefully used to conceal the summit of Olympus? It is not altogether certain, since vision in and of itself does not preclude piety. Probably, however, these films are going to have a more strongly motivated central idea, whereby the distance between the hero of the western and the rest of its cast is going to increase in proportion to the square of its consciousness. Most interesting, though, will be the future attempts to cram more and more current morality into the mythological pattern. When Shane's little Joey grows up and gets ammunition, he is not going to lack a target worth shooting at.

NOTES

1. John Foster Dulles was secretary of state under Republican President Dwight D. Eisenhower from 1953–1959.

2. Howard A. Burton, "*High Noon*: Everyman Rides Again," *Quarterly Review of Film, Radio, and Television* 8, no. 1 (1953): 80–86.

3. Penelope Houston, "*Shane* and George Stevens," *Sight and Sound* 23, no. 2 (1953): 76.

CHAPTER 10

THE CHANGING COWBOY:
FROM DIME NOVEL TO DOLLAR FILM

GEORGE BLUESTONE

THE PROGRESSION FROM dime novel to dollar western is a progression from innocence to experience, a gradual erosion of the simplistic myth toward complexity and ambiguity. If the cowboy hero of the dime novel has relevance to the America of the open range, the new hero of the serious western has something to say to us.

In recent years, thanks to Merle Curti, Henry Nash Smith, Marshall Fishwick, and others who have had the courage to assault formidable collections of dime novels, we have begun to see the cowboy in clearer outline.[1] From 1860, when Erastus Beadle unleashed his torrential series of orange-backed books, to 1902, when Owen Wister published *The Virginian*, we can trace the emergence of the cowboy and his cousins—the sheriff, the outlaw, and the hired gun. Looking back to Leatherstocking, we see his origins in the hunters, trappers, and woodsmen of earlier paperbacks. By the time Edward Ellis published *Seth Jones* in 1860, and Edward Wheeler began his Deadwood Dick series in the 1870s, the main conventions, iron-clad and fixed, had been prepared for dime-novel cowboys like Prentiss Ingraham's Buck Taylor, Ned Buntline's Buffalo Bill, and Edward O'Reilly's Pecos Bill as late as 1923. The development of the open range in the 1870s merely offered a new and substantial setting, as well as a new attractive figure in the personage of the rancher. Combining the myth of the paradisiac garden with the practicality of the industrial baron, the pastoral, half-nomadic cowboy became a perfect hero for

George Bluestone, "The Changing Cowboy: From Dime Novel to Dollar Film," *Western Humanities Review* 14 (1960): 331–337. Copyright © 1960 by the Estate of George Bluestone.

repressed urban readers. The terminal point of all those Texas cattle, after all, was the old Chicago slaughterhouse.

Qualifications must be attended to, of course. Smith tells us that the cowboy in literature has little to do with cattle at first. Rather, "The professional duty of the Beadle cowboys is to fight Indians, Mexicans and outlaws."[2] And we are reminded that as late as 1881, the pejorative connotations of the term *cowboy* were still operative. Chester A. Arthur's first annual message to Congress mentions a disturbance of public tranquility by a band of "armed desperadoes known as 'Cowboys,' probably numbering from fifty to one hundred men," who had for months been committing acts of lawlessness in the territory of Arizona across the border into Mexico. But in the main we can observe the hardening of the cowboy's legendary arteries, the disparity, from the beginning, between his actual life as described in Douglas Branch's *The Cowboy and His Interpreters* and his fictional life as described, say, in Ned Buntline's vigorous machine-made stories.[3] Fishwick's summary of the cowboy ethic, "Everyone knows what he is supposed to do, and does it," is merely a restatement of an earlier prescription by the editor of *Ranch Romances*: "We aim," he said, "to lead our readers away from the complexities of civilization into a world of simple feeling and direct emotion."[4] As a summary statement, it is accurate enough.

Since the dime-novel western, with few exceptions, has existed as a subliterary form, refusing to submit to serious criticism, we have been driven back to cultural and psychological analysis. To make the cowboy comprehensible at all, we speak of him as an extraliterary figure, as a public dream, more interesting to anthropology than to fiction. Tristram P. Coffin has connected this public image to the pressures of historical development in the last half of the nineteenth century. The cowboy, Coffin writes, "is a direct result of the combined forces of western local color and nationalism on one side and the urge toward individual law and violence on the other."[5] Hence, he sees the cowboy not only as a representative of the natural or common man derived from Rousseau, but also as a figure of menace, at times indistinguishable from his bad-man quarry (the sinner who constitutes a law unto himself), a figure looking back to Robespierre and ahead to Mickey Spillane.

In general, however, we have been willing to subscribe to the more benevolent face of the public dream. Speaking for the present generation of cultural historians, Smith points out that the dime novel, in spite of its subliterary status, "tends to become an objectified mass dream like the moving pictures, soap operas, or the comic books that are the present-day equivalent of the Beadles stories. . . . [I]t is the presumably close fidelity of the Beadle stories to the dream life of a vast inarticulate public that renders them valuable to the social historian and the historian of ideas."[6] Factual tales about real cowboys, coupled with the shrewd chicanery of an Ingraham or a Buntline, who knew how to parlay a good thing into a vast and lucrative market, were enough to hurl the cowboy, full-bodied and ir-refrangible, into the twentieth century. It only remained for Zane Grey, Max Brand, and Ernest Haycox to finish the job. The cowboy appears with such force that the momentum has carried him right down to the nearest television set.

The cowboy myth was, of course, made to order for motion pictures. And just as the movies, once they discovered narrative and editing, took over melodrama and stage spectacle, as Nicholas Vardac has shown us, so they appropriated the cowboy story virtually intact.[7] The style could be easily transferred to a medium where objects assume the efficacy of actors and where movement becomes expressive form. The appropriate settings, the horses, the mountains and mesas and rivers, were readily supplied by America's natural terrain. The melodramatic conventions were all there: the aristocratic hero in rustic disguise, a hero who is never defeated by the ravages of nature or of man; the black craftiness of the bad men; the res-cue of Anglo-Saxon damsels in distress; the assumption of Aryan superi-ority for the hero and of manifest destiny for the nation; the covert racism; the suspicion of easterners and foreigners alike; the studious sexlessness coupled with an excess of violence; the cool professionalism that operates best with a maximum of mobility burdened by a minimum of thought. All these were fixed before the cowboy ever appeared on the screen. All the actor had to do was don the proper costume and mount the proper horse, and he was ready to head for the nearest hills.

With the emergence of William S. Hart, however, the movie cowboy be-comes a slightly ambiguous figure. His fictional life becomes so merged with his private life that his sense of reality becomes fuzzy and blurred. The actor becomes a poseur in real life, and the imaginary cowboy is pre-sented realistically. Where the dime-novel cowboy, to support claims to authenticity, frequently took off from a real-life model, the movie cowboy took off from a real-life actor who was expected to appear as resourceful and taciturn as his filmic counterpart. William Hart, like William Cody before him, becomes a painful case of nature imitating art. It is true that Hart brought a kind of grainy realism to the western, that he avoided silk shirts and immaculate horses, that his celebrated steely eyes and rocklike jaw transmitted a sort of photographic honesty, indicating that life in the

West was serious, hard, and above all strictly virtuous. But that he was telling anything but the truth about the West never seems to have occurred to Hart. If the surfaces were right, then the psychology was, too, an illusion that Hollywood has been at pains to foster right down to the present day.

After Hart, Tom Mix, and Hoot Gibson, the portrait of the cowboy splits in two. The first image floods the juvenile market with a milky, bland, commercially stylized cowboy who reverts to the type of Deadwood Dick and Buck Taylor and becomes more concerned with fighting outlaws than with raising cattle. This cowboy is a singer who slings his guitar along with his six-shooter, appears at rodeos and on cereal packages, assumes a foppish kind of dress, and rides a horse named Trigger who is more tricky than fierce. Today, Roy Rogers, Gene Autry, and Hopalong Cassidy firmly dominate this juvenile market.

The second image, on the other hand, looks ahead to that curious coinage of television, the "adult" western. The term itself is a tacit admission that the cowboy formula, or at least what it has become, can no longer be taken seriously by sophisticated grown-ups, who, having abandoned the farm and the small town, now inhabit those bleak, bright, and pennymatching suburbs. To a generation that has suffered a major depression and one or two major wars, the milkweed cowboy is bound to seem foolish and even absurd.

The direction of the serious western, however, is a different story and one that deserves our critical attention. Even today *The Ox-Bow Incident* (1943), the first important film in this western cycle after John Ford's *Stagecoach* (1939), can create the shock of novelty. Though frequently revived, it has never been a financial success, but it has, at least, been accorded the rare privilege of a succès d'estime that has influenced all subsequent experimentation. It is easy to see why. By questioning the root relationship between lynching and the law, and, incidentally, the relationship between illusion and reality, *The Ox-Bow Incident* prepared the way for similar deviations from hitherto airtight formulas. One by one, almost every convention that had been hardened through one hundred years of accretion has been challenged, questioned, and strangely varied.

In *The Big Country* (1958) we see a blatant sadism behind the rationalizations of courage and honor. We see an increasing ambiguity in the claims of good and evil. In *The Fastest Gun Alive* (1956) and *Johnny Concho* (1956) we see fear and cowardice behind the smooth style of the central character. It is true, in these instances, that the westerner ultimately finds his courage and becomes a killer of men, usually bad men, but some-

FIGURE 20. *The Ox-Bow Incident* (1943): an important example of the serious western.

times good men, too—but to an earlier generation even the possibility of a coward-hero would have been unthinkable. In *Red River* (1948) and *Yellow Sky* (1948) we see a total disenchantment with the glamour of western living. A cattle drive is pictured as an ordeal, a hardship, a lonely and sometimes desperate fight against grieving plains, gorging rivers, blistering heat, and gagging dust. And when, in *Yellow Sky*, Anne Baxter snarls at Gregory Peck, "You stink—worse than Apaches," the olfactory detail has the stunning sting of the actual. In *High Noon* (1952) we see a social framework that ultimately betrays the hero, again reminiscent of *The Ox-Bow Incident*. It is significant, I think, that one can no longer discuss the cowboy without discussing his social perimeter—his women, his handymen, his sheriffs, his judges, his tradesmen.

In many of these westerns we see a kind of complex dialogue between innocence and experience. In *Red River* and *The Tin Star* (1957) the young novices, possessing more courage than skill, must be taught that courage without skill is not only foolhardy but dangerous. The novice must be taught that the style of the hero, his uncanny rightness, his instinctive professionalism, must be learned, slowly, painfully—but learned. Heroes do

FIGURE 21. Anne Baxter and Gregory Peck in *Yellow Sky* (1948).

not spring full grown from Minerva's ear. Along with moral complexity, the notion of process and the hardship of responsibility have invaded the western. It will never be easy again.

In *The Tin Star* and *The Gunfighter* (1950) we see a hero who is tired, exhausted, grimly determined to exist without the gratuitous violence of old-fashioned heroics. In *The Tin Star* Henry Fonda is a bounty hunter, a complete cynic about human motivations. This is a total reversal of the old chivalric code. The bounty hunter is a professional who uses his skill not to rescue the virtuous, or even to do the good, gratuitously, but simply to make a living. This completely frank mercenary somehow manages to engage our sympathies, however, probably *because* of his frankness and his honest disenchantment. Clearly, the mood is closer to our own.

In *The Gunfighter*, the best and most neglected of the postwar westerns, Gregory Peck is an ex-outlaw who is trying to live down his past as a skillful killer of men. His stark old hat and grim mustache attest to his utter abnegation. When a young killer insists on challenging him, in the time-honored tradition of the gun duel, and is bitterly refused, the youth resorts to the coward's trick of shooting Jimmie Ringo in the back. When the gunfighter's friend wants to retaliate, Ringo restrains him. Now the punk will be hounded by every trigger-happy kid in the West who is out to test the mettle of Jimmie Ringo's killer. "Let him live—let him find out what it's like," Ringo says before he dies, a death from exhaustion more than from defeat. It is a startling indictment of the western myth, indicating a growing concern with violence, a concern that borders on outright pacifism. It is true that in these films the pacifist hero must still learn,

FIGURE 22. *Red River* (1948): a complex dialogue between innocence and experience.

however reluctantly, the necessity of violence in a world he never made, but that the question has been posed at all indicates the distance we have come in revising the conventions. In George Stevens's *Shane* (1953) a good part of our response is due to the ending, where the boy is seen calling to his hero, who has meanwhile disappeared, as in a dream, among those blue mysterious hills. It is as if the duel between the black villain and the noble wanderer, repeated through a century of variations, has been after all the figment of a child's imagination.

Finally, in *The Left-Handed Gun* (1958), produced by Fred Coe and directed by Arthur Penn from a script by Gore Vidal, so many of these alien strains converge that we get a weird amalgam, an almost surrealist, avant-garde, highbrow kind of movie in which Billy the Kid is merely the occasion for a bitter indictment of all our stock conventions. Instead of an aristocrat masquerading as a hunter, we have the intellectual assuming the persona of the cowboy. The thin veneer of myth and psychoanalysis that has nosed around these westerns in the past few years, turning pistols into phalluses, brushes rather deeply here. Paul Newman as Billy the Kid is at once a victim, a hero, a hipster of the beat generation, a repressed or actual homosexual, and a suffering Christ. He is allowed to do what no pre-war westerner was ever allowed to do—i.e., virtually to commit suicide. The symbolism is quite explicit. Newman's face several times breaks into lines of anguish and suffering, wholly inconsistent with the conventional mask of repose, reserve, and self-confidence. And at least twice, instead of giving himself up in the immemorial, vertical gesture of surrender, he yields with his arms horizontal, the classic gesture of crucifixion. The conscious artiness of the film, derived from the intimate drama of television, the "method" of the Actors Studio, and a strident southern literary symbolism (Catherine wheels, burning, tiny flutes), produces a strange effect, like superimposing negatives of Freud and Natty Bumppo. It reveals the sly excursions of the intellectual, trapped in the journey work of the mass media, scorning his own dilemma.

In these recent westerns even the scenery undergoes a change, as Robert Warshow has pointed out in an illuminating essay. When the western shifts from innocence to experience, from a sense of possibility to a sense of limitation, not only does the action slow down, but even the landscape "ceases to be quite the arena of free movement it once was, but becomes instead a great empty waste, cutting down more often than it exaggerates the stature of the horseman who rides across it."[8] Instead of making man free, nature merely makes him seem absurd.

Another impressive fact about these dollar westerns is how slight the

FIGURE 23. *The Left-Handed Gun* (1958): Billy the Kid (Paul Newman, *right*) as victim, hero, hipster, repressed homosexual, suffering Christ.

deviations really are. As John Steinbeck reminds us in a charming essay, "How to Tell the Good Guys from the Bad Guys," the villains of *High Noon* and *Shane* still tend to be spiritually if not sartorially black.[9] Yet to experience even these slight deviations is to feel our universe rock, which should indicate, I think, that further and more serious metamorphoses are possible.

Warshow argues that "since it is not violence at all which is the 'point' of the western movie, but a certain image of man, a style which expresses itself most clearly *in* violence," it follows that "when the impulse toward realism is extended into a 'reinterpretation' of the West as a developed society, drawing our eyes away from the hero if only to the extent of showing him as the one dominant figure in a complex social order, then the pattern is broken and the West itself begins to be uninteresting."[10] But it seems to me that the response of adult audiences to the dollar western indicates that Warshow is at least mistaken in his emphasis. As the cowboy has come within the purview of serious films, precisely *because* President Arthur was right about his being, at times, an armed desperado outside the pale of society, he has become more, not less, interesting and probably never more interesting than he seems right now. We are beginning to see in him not an idyllic image of a man who never was but a human being not at all unlike ourselves. It is no accident that the modifications in the myth have coincided with the emergence of America as an undisputed world power that must live down its onus of innocence as well as its new and terrible responsibilities.

About two years ago, I attended a film series at a cinema club in Florence, Italy. The series included a dozen westerns, from John Ford's *Stagecoach* to Fred Zinneman's *High Noon*. The title of the series was "Paradiso Perduto"— Lost Paradise. It was an apt description, suggesting both the compulsive power of the myth as well as its recent erosion. Only lost paradises have proved interesting to our poets. Likewise, when the cowboy loses his innocence, he becomes a fit subject for epic or tragedy. Rather than destroying the purity of the myth, the new western has redeemed the cowboy from the crude anonymity of the potboiler for the sharper contours of possible art. Only the compromising pressures of a commercial industry now prevent him from becoming truly first-rate.

NOTES

1. Merle Curti, "Dime Novels and the American Tradition," *Yale Review* (June 1937): 761; Henry Nash Smith, *Virgin Land: The American West as Symbol and Myth* (Cambridge, MA: Harvard University Press, 1950); Marshall Fishwick, "The Cowboy: America's Contribution to the World's Mythology," *Western Folklore* 11, no. 2 (1952): 77–92.

2. Smith, *Virgin Land*, 125.

3. Douglas Branch, *The Cowboy and His Interpreters* (New York: Appleton, 1926).

4. Fishwick, "The Cowboy," 91.

5. Tristram P. Coffin, "The Cowboy and Mythology," *Western Folklore* 12, no. 4 (1953): 290.

6. Smith, *Virgin Land*, 101.

7. Nicholas Vardac, *Stage to Screen: Theatrical Origins of Early Film: David Garrick to D. W. Griffith* (Cambridge, MA: Harvard University Press, 1949).

8. Robert Warshow, "Movie Chronicle: The Westerner," in *The Immediate Experience: Movies, Comics, Theatre and Other Aspects of Popular Culture* (New York: Atheneum, 1971), 144.

9. John Steinbeck, "How to Tell Good Guys from Bad Guys," *Reporter* 12, no. 5 (1955): 43.

10. Warshow, "Movie Chronicle: The Westerner," 153, 147.

CHAPTER 11

SOCIOLOGICAL SYMBOLISM OF
THE "ADULT WESTERN"

MARTIN NUSSBAUM

EVERY CULTURE HAS AT SOME precise time in its growth created a folk-type art form in response to its inner turmoils and strivings to satisfy its need for expression of its character. Thus, various art forms such as the Elizabethan theater, Grecian sculpture, Arthurian legends, impressionistic painting, classical ballet, ethnic folk singing, flamenco dancing, and so forth arose as the answer to a need for expression of the culture.

For example, the Elizabethan theater arose in greater part to articulate intense feelings of nationalism, to provide an outlet for the craving for romantic adventure, to resonate the thoughts of a people just throwing off the shackles of feudalism and searching for knowledge, and to contribute to the enthusiasm and passion for the newly formulated language. The Spanish Armada had been decisively defeated by an all-English navy, English explorers were planting the flag throughout the world and carrying back exotic stories of foreign lands, the Renaissance had liberated the soul and endowed it with a great questioning attitude toward its environment, and the advent of printing had stabilized and focused attention on the nascent language.

In such a manner, the "adult western" has evolved at this precise time in our culture as a new art form delineating our motivations and psychoses and permitting their vicarious catharsis. It must be understood that we are speaking of art not in the classical sense, but rather in its secondary meaning as the systematic application of knowledge or skill in effect-

Martin Nussbaum, "Sociological Symbolism of the 'Adult Western,'" *Social Forces* 39 (October 1960–May 1961): 25–28. Copyright © 1960 Oxford University Press. Reprinted by permission of Oxford University Press.

ing a desired result by the adaptation of ideas or emotions to a form of expression.

What, then, are these recurring ideas or emotions that influence and produce the adult western and make it so enjoyable to all segments of our society? First, the western contains the spirit of foreign adventure, of new and exciting places, the same element that made the operettas of the twenties and thirties so popular, the locale that is foreign to ours and gives us a chance to escape our everyday environment and visit someplace exotic. Shakespeare used this element successfully in his tales of the kings and the histories that all used foreign locales in the plot. Hollywood used this element in the thirties with a raft of pictures about tropical islands in the prewar South Pacific. Remember, although the western takes place in the United States, the locale is still exotic and foreign, because this locale is not in evidence today and few people have a living memory of it.

Coupled with this spirit of foreign adventure is the inherent romance of the West. As the Greeks were concerned with their Trojan Wars, the Spaniards with their New World conquests, and the English with their colonization, so the American is preoccupied with the West of the beautiful landscapes, with the wide-open spaces, the valleys, canyons, mountains, and other scenery. The very landscape breathes heroism between not men but giants. To exist in this land you need heroic will. To the average city dweller, confined to a neighborhood of row houses, a stretch of prairie or mountain range extending as far as the eye can see offers a transcending exhilaration.

A second feature lending form and direction to the western format is the unique western hero, for with the western, America has developed its first universal-type hero. America has always been hero shy; all its heroes are either modern, like movie stars or sports figures, or men of a limited locality, such as Paul Bunyan or Rip Van Winkle. Americans have never made a fetish of their navy and army heroes as the British or as the Russians of their Cossacks. America has no mythology as the Europeans, it has no ties with the land or the past as the Israelis, and it has had no kings or conquerors leading its armies. The closest America has to heroes are its frontier scout hunter or Indian fighter and its Babe Ruths and Lou Gehrigs.

Western man is the true heroic man whose characteristics have never varied, from Joshua, Ulysses, and Lancelot on through the lineage. He is a man with a mission, a faceless man, a universal man of mystery, a loner. And he is a soft-spoken man, for like Joshua, Ulysses, and Lancelot, he never raises his voice needlessly. But when the action demands, he cries out in anger and righteousness. For example, the westerner hates guns and killing, but he is quick on the trigger when he is compelled to fight. An example of the unvarying quality of the heroic type is Paladin, who is the true knight-errant of the Arthurian Idylls. His name means "royal guard," or a knight of the round table. He has a picture of a chess knight on his holster, the most versatile piece of the chess board that can move in eight different directions. Like the true knight, he upholds the principles of law and order, he sets out on knight-like adventures, he is able to cope with all emergencies, in the midst of trouble he remains relaxed, and finally, he is always expecting the worst. And if and when it occurs, he is not shaken, for he knows that life is deadly serious and there is no way to avoid it.

The format of the western is shaped further by a third and fourth feature, which by their nature are closely linked: the protagonist's independence and individualism and his primitive and uncomplicated contact with nature. The western hero is characterized by his restlessness and freedom of action. He can "pick himself up" whenever he desires and, like the wind, drift on, because he is not troubled with family ties or attachment to a permanent home. He is a drifter, a vanishing symbol of individualism in an age of togetherness and conformity. The westerner can do what we can't; when the pressures and monotony of life become depressing and wearisome, he can "saddle up" and vanish into the setting sun. For us, who lead lives of stifled routine, identification with the westerner, via television, affords us a temporary escape.

To go a step further, the western hero can go out on horseback and live off the earth for months, making his own way and not worrying about where he will obtain his food and shelter. This primitive contact offers him a fundamental appreciation of the life processes. We, on the other hand, were we to be transplanted to a western environment, would probably starve to death in the midst of plenty. We do not know how to hunt, trap, or live off the land. We don't even know how to bed down out-of-doors. If the inconvenience wouldn't overwhelm us, the elements would. We are so removed from nature that it has become foreign to us. It takes strong persuasion to convince a city child that the fresh, white milk that is delivered in clean bottles comes from an animal called a cow, or that eggs are not manufactured, or that the steak he ate for dinner was stripped from a steer who was butchered by bashing in his head.

Another recurring theme, our fifth, is the old Aristotelian concept of good and evil in modern dress. For centuries man has been guided by the logic that any object (including man) must be either good or evil. By its nature, this concept, known as the law of the excluded middle, allowed for no middle ground. It proposed, for example, that a man is either all good or all evil. In the thirties and forties this concept permeated every class-B cowboy movie, giving rise to a generation who could think only in terms of "goodies" and "baddies." We identified both groups in the first reel, and they remained consistent. We never undertook to discover why each was its own way.

It became apparent that these concepts of black and white, with no shades of gray interspersed, would seem ridiculous to the sophisticated postwar audiences who were becoming exposed to theories of psychology and philosophy and more significantly to a world where there were millions of shades of gray between good and evil, a world where each of us was a combination of good and evil. So the authors of the adult westerns set about to humanize their characters. They explained why Blackie was bad and that he wasn't all bad. They showed that the hero wasn't all good (for example, Paladin works for a fee, Maverick gambles, Dillon drinks hard liquor, Randall works mostly for reward money, and so forth) and that he was capable of some costly mistakes. What they accomplished, in effect, was to graft on to the western characters the emotions, fears, inadequacies, and psychoses of modern man. But problems that remain unsolved in life must be solved in stories, so they salvaged the old good-evil concept and converted it to a concept of judicial right and wrong. Thus, the western espouses that all men are a combination of good and evil, but some, by their own volition or circumstances beyond their power, have placed themselves on the wrong side of the law, a law that transcends man's law and has overtones of moralistic law. It falls to the western hero, then, to judge the rightness and wrongness of an act and to satisfy the law if it has been violated. Today, when all our problems are so complicated that there is really no right and wrong but rather many shades of gray, it is gratifying to see complex problems reduced to an either-or proposition, adjudicated and resolved by a single action.

We now come to the sixth and final of the main features of the adult western, the most singular, fascinating, satisfying, and symbolic of all the features, the use of the gun. The gun, in whatever form it appears (six-shooter, Buntline special, sawed-off carbine, hopped-up rifle, and so forth), coupled with the fast draw, symbolizes maleness, individualism, and the Greek deus ex machina. To treat the last first, the deus ex machina (literally god from a machine) was a mechanical stage contrivance similar to a platform raised by a block and tackle. Whenever, in the Grecian theater, any of the characters were inextricably involved, whenever the problems became really insurmountable, the apparatus would bear one of the Olympian gods to earth and he, with but one stroke of his hand, would resolve all the difficulties.

The adult western makes use of the gun in this manner. Innumerable times, we have seen the western hero strap on his gun and attempt to resolve a difficult situation in the only way possible, after all other methods have failed. The western hero may have his back to the wall and be facing an overpowering adversary, but when, lightning-like, he draws his gun from its holster, we see the god leaping to earth and fusing with the hero into an overpowering force. How many times have we wished that all our problems could be settled with such a definite action?

Much has been made of the gun as a symbol of masculinity. Swedish critic Harry Schein, writing in the *American Scholar,* goes so far as to say, "The pistol in westerns is by now accepted as a phallic symbol."[1] Schein is probably not overstating the truth. The western hero looks deficient or inadequate without his gun belt on, but with his gun strapped to his side he is a complete man. It is a symbol of masculine authority and respect. Possibly the most degrading spectacle we can witness is when the western hero, taken by surprise (e.g., when someone else has gotten the "drop" on him), is told to unbuckle his gun belt and let it fall to the ground. At a time when men are concerned with the loss of their masculinity (and not necessarily to or because of a woman), they can sublimate by identifying with the western hero. In essence, the western hero exercises his masculinity symbolically as he employs his gun, uninhibited, decisive, fearless, and noble.

Perhaps the most symbolic of all its features, the gun has helped produce the individualism of the westerner. With its aid, both implied and actual, the westerner can champion whatever cause he desires. Few of his enemies are inclined to get him to conform or change his mind when they realize they face not only him but his gun as well. And for us watching the action, by identification, we are literally ten feet tall, for here we see ourselves, small, insignificant, in many cases unappreciated, hemmed in by the mundane oppression of conformity and the vicissitudes of everyday life, finally being able to stand up and shout to the world, "Look at me, I'm Charlie Brown, and I'm as good as you are, maybe even better, and I intend to live my own life."

If we shift our point of view to our present world, we can see this symbolism of individuality appear in the form of the automobile. Many psychiatrists and sociologists are convinced that in a majority of cases, when the ordinary American gets behind the wheel of his car he undergoes a transformation of personality. He becomes more aggressive, more assertive, and more prone to take a risk. He identifies himself with the capabilities of his car and attempts to make an individual of himself by attaching all sorts of multihued ornaments and accessories to the car. He takes better care of his car than of himself. For example, he will take his car to a garage at the slightest symptom of malfunctioning, but may not visit his physician or dentist for years. To return to the western, we will find an almost identical identification between the western and the gun. The gun is treated with reverence and respect and as a transformer of personality. To conclude, perhaps the reason the gun has become such an important feature of the adult western is because it is such a quick and potent agent of death or sustainer of life.

And so, we have shown that by the skillful use of recurrent features, we have adapted ideas and emotions symbolically to a form of expression, the adult western. Of course, just as not all attempts at creativity within an art form are successful, so not all westerns are successful "adult westerns." Many of the newer western shows, striving to create a new format, fall short of their more successful counterparts, and they are nothing more than reincarnations of the old class-B cowboy movies or good dramatic shows with western backgrounds. It is our opinion that the shows that consistently adhere to the adult western format and are the classics of the form are *Gunsmoke* (1955–1975), *Have Gun, Will Travel* (1957–1963), and *Cheyenne* (1955–1963). Though all three utilize good scripts, top actors, and fine production, *Gunsmoke* must be singled out for the best stories, Paladin (Richard Boone) in *Have Gun, Will Travel* as the best actor, and *Cheyenne* for the best overall adherence to the adult western format.

Why has the adult western appeared at this precise time? We believe the western has arisen as a revolt against rationalism and reason. Contemporary man is approaching the state where his inventions and machines are speeding ahead of him and getting out of control. The realization is setting in that he cannot apply reason to the solution of his everyday problems as he can to scientific problems, that living, thinking organisms cannot be guided by regulations and laws of predictability as in science. Even science is fast approaching the realization of human finitude. Heisenberg's principle of indeterminacy states that there is a point to be reached where man will be unable to predict physical states and where he will saturate his ability to know. The mathematician Kurt Gödel has found that mathematics, the most rational of the sciences, is paradoxical and contains problems that cannot be solved and therefore cannot be integrated into one complete system, that all mathematical systems will

FIGURE 24. *The Great Train Robbery* (1903): an important step in the development of the western as folk art.

be incomplete. Thus, there is an end to rationalism and reason with our existentialist western hero. By accepting this hero, we acknowledge that there is a limit to reason, that the only way we can solve our difficulties is by being men of faith, faith in the all-knowing and self-sufficient earthy western hero.

America has never fully developed a folk-type art form. America has produced jazz, abstract painting, and the "private-eye" detective story, but to be other than provincial, the form must be universal enough to cut through all strata of the culture (i.e., capable of expressing a wide range of emotions and feelings about our culture) and finally be performed almost daily. Classical jazz has never been fully appreciated by all or made available at the flick of a dial. Abstract painting has not been accepted by all strata or given ample exposure. The "private eye" has lacked universality and is too contemporaneous. And the story is much the same with each of several other creative forms: no universality and not enough exposure.

However, we have shown that the adult western is the first folk-type art form to have features of universality. Also, it has achieved mass penetration on television, where it can be observed by the masses as part of their everyday life. The adult western, therefore, has come at the right time (it is universal enough to be appreciated by a wide range of people as the answer to their current problems) and the right place (television).

And so, the development of our art form has taken a long time to evolve from its inception in Owen Wister's late-nineteenth-century *The Virginian*, through its movie precursors *The Great Train Robbery* (1903), *Stagecoach* (1939), *High Noon* (1952), and *Shane* (1953), and its radio precursor *Gunsmoke*, to its classical form on television. But the thing that is unique is that we are only now ready for the "adult western." It could not have occurred at a different time.

NOTE

1. Reprinted in this volume, p. 106. [Editors' note.]

CHAPTER 12

PURITANISM REVISITED: AN ANALYSIS OF THE CONTEMPORARY SCREEN-IMAGE WESTERN

PETER HOMANS

ONE OF THE MOST NOTICEABLE characteristics of popular culture is the rapidity with which new forms are initiated and older, more familiar ones revitalized. While narrative forms of popular culture, such as the detective story, the romance, and the soap opera, have generally been less subject to sudden losses or gains in popularity, the western has within the past few years undergone a very abrupt change in this respect. Formerly associated with a dwindling audience of adolescents, who were trading in their hats and six-guns for space helmets and disintegrators, the western has quite suddenly engaged an enormous number of people, very few of whom could be called adolescent.

This new and far-reaching popularity is easily established. Whereas before the western story was told from four to six in the afternoon, on Saturday mornings, in comic books, and in some pulp fiction, now it is to be seen during the choicest television viewing hours, in a steady stream of motion pictures, and in every drugstore pulp rack. At present, on television alone, more than thirty western stories are told weekly, with an estimated budget of sixty million dollars. Four of the five top nighttime shows are westerns, and of the top twenty shows, eleven are westerns. In addition to this, it is estimated that women now compose one-third of the western's heretofore male audience.

Such evidence invariably leads to attempts to explain the phenomenon. Here there has been little restraint in trying to analyze the unique status that the western has gained. Some have suggested that it is the modern

Peter Homans, "Puritanism Revisited: An Analysis of the Contemporary Screen-Image Western," *Studies in Public Communication* 3 (1961): 73–84. Reprinted with the permission of the author's estate.

story version of the Oedipal classic, others find it a parallel of the medieval legends of courtly love and adventure, while those enamored of psychiatric theory see it as a form of wish fulfillment and "escape" from the realities of life into an oversimplified world of good and evil.

Such theories, I suppose, could be described at greater length—but not much. They not only betray a mindless, off-the-top-of-the-head superficiality, but also suffer from a deeper fault characteristic of so many of the opinions handed down today about popular culture—a twofold reductionism that tends to rob the story of its concrete uniqueness.

This twofold reductionism first appears as the failure to attend fully and with care to the historical roots of any form. For example, to say that the western is a retelling of chivalric tales is partly true. There is some similarity between the quest of the knight and the quest of the western hero—they both seek to destroy an evil being by force. However, the tales of chivalry grew out of medieval culture, and any effort to account for them must consider their relationship to their culture. Similarly, the western must be seen in relation to its culture—eastern American life at the turn of the century. To relate the two forms without first considering their historical contexts is what may be called historical reductionism.

The second form of reductionism is the failure of most theories to attend to the unique details of the story that set it apart from prior forms. This can also be seen in the idea of chivalric tales retold. Holders of this theory notice that both heroes are engaged in a quest, the destruction of evil, and that they both earn some kind of special status in the eyes of the communities they have served. But what is not noticed is that the modern tale betrays an intense preoccupation with asceticism and colorlessness, while the medieval one dwells upon color, sensuousness, and luxury, or that the medieval hero exemplifies tact, manners, and elaborate ceremony and custom, while his modern counterpart seeks to avoid these. Again, the western rules out women; the older story would not be a story of chivalry did not women play an important part. The refusal to attend with care to specific and possibly inconsequential details is a form of reductionism that may be called textual reductionism.

Both types of reductionism rob a particular form of possible uniqueness and independence. They force it to be merely a dependent function of some prior form, whatever that form may be. Together, they have become the two main errors that have obscured analysis of many present-day forms of popular culture.

However, these two foci are more than pitfalls to be avoided. The textual and historical aspects of any popular art form are the very points that should be scrutinized most carefully and elaborately. If these points are properly attended, they will yield the greatest insight into the meaning and significance of the story.

TEXTUAL ANALYSIS

Any effort to analyze a particular form of popular culture must begin with the problem of text. Each of us, in thinking and talking about the western, has in mind an overall understanding of it—an ordered vision of character, event, and detail shaped by all the hundreds of different versions that we have seen. Therefore, one must first set forth and defend precisely what it is one thinks the western is, before indicating what it means. Indeed, disagreements as to meaning can often be traced to disagreements as to text.

But we cannot simply lump together everything that has ever happened in every western, fearful of omitting something important. Nor can we refuse to include anything that does not appear in each and every version. There are westerns that omit details that all critics would agree are characteristic of the story, just as there are others that include details that all would agree are of no consequence. The task consists in selecting from the endless number of westerns we have a basic construct of narrative, character, and detail that will set forth clearly the datum for subsequent analysis. This critic's basic construct can be set forth as follows.

BACKGROUND

The western takes place in a stark, desolate, abandoned land. The desert, as a place deprived of vitality and life as we know it, is indispensable. The story would not be credible were it set in an equatorial jungle, a fertile lowland, or an Arctic tundra. As the classical versions have told us again and again, the hero emerges from the desert, bearing its marks, and returns to it. Already we are instructed that our story deals with a form of existence deprived of color and vitality.

This desert effect is contradicted by the presence of a town. Jerry-built, slapped-together buildings, with false fronts lined awkwardly along a road that is forever thick with dust or mud, tell us that the builders themselves did not expect them to endure. And of these few buildings, only three stand out as recognizable and important—the saloon, the bank, and the marshal's office (hero's dwelling). Recent westerns have added stores, courthouses, homes, and even churches. But for the classical versions, such contrived togetherness has never really been necessary.

The saloon is by far the most important building in the western. First of all, it is the only place in the entire story where people can be seen together time after time. It thereby performs the function of a meeting-house, social center, church, and so on. More important, however, is its function as locus for the climax of the story, the gunfight. Even in today's more fashionable westerns, which prefer Main Street at high noon, the gunfight often begins in the saloon and takes place just outside it.

The bank, we note, is a hastily constructed, fragile affair. Poorly guarded (if at all), it is an easy mark, there for the taking. Its only protection consists of a sniveling, timid clerk, with a mustache and a green eyeshade, who is only too glad to hand over the loot. Has there ever been a western in which a robber wondered whether he could pull off his robbery? There is a great deal of apprehension as to whether he will elude the inevitable posse but never as to the simple act of robbery. The bank is surprisingly unprotected.

The marshal's office appears less regularly. Most noticeable here is the absence of any evidence of domesticity. We rarely see a bed, a place for clothes, or any indication that a person actually makes his home here. There is no mirror, an omission that has always intrigued me. The overall atmosphere is that of austerity, to be contrasted sharply with the rich carpeting, impressive desk, curtains, pictures, and liquor supply of the saloon owner or evil gambler. Such asceticism is not due to the hero's lack of funds or low salary; rather, because of his living habits, there is no need for anything else. Indeed, we are led to suspect that such austerity is in some way related to our hero's virtue.

The town as a whole has no business or industry. People have money, but we rarely see them make it. And we are not concerned as to how they got their money unless they stole it. This town and its citizens lead a derivative, dependent existence, serving activities that originate and will continue outside the town. It is expendable and will disappear as soon as the activities it serves no longer exist.

Home life, like economic life, is conspicuous by its absence. There simply are no homes, families, domestic animals, or children. The closest thing to a home is a hotel, and this is rarely separated from the saloon. Recent westerns have included homes, along with cozy vignettes of hearth, wife, kitchen, and the like. Such innovations do little more than indicate how harassed scriptwriters have become, for these scenes do not contribute to the basic action and imagery of the story. Classically, home life in the western simply isn't.

SUPPORTING PEOPLE

As in any good form of popular culture, the number of important people is small. Such people I prefer to call "types." A type is an important figure recurring again and again, whose basic actions and patterns of relationship are relatively enduring from one version of the story to another. The particular vocation, clothing, mannerisms, personal plans, names are all conventions—concessions to plausibility—that seemingly identify as new someone we know we've seen before. Such conventions I would like to call "role." When we refer to a particular person in a story with the preface "the"—e.g., "the" hero or "the" good girl—we have penetrated beyond the role and identified a type.

One of the most interesting types is the "derelict-professional." He is one who was originally trained in one of the traditional eastern professions (law, medicine, letters, ministry), but who has, since his arrival in the West, become corrupted by such activities as drink, gambling, sex, or violence. Most celebrated is Doc Holliday, who trained in the East as a dentist, then came west to practice medicine whenever he was sober enough to do so. The derelict-professional sometimes appears as a judge or lawyer, sometimes as an ex-writer; in other instances he is a gun-toting preacher. The point is the same: the traditional resources of society (healer, teacher, shepherd, counselor) cannot exist in an uncorrupted state under the pressures of western life.[1]

Somewhat similar is the "nonviolent easterner." He often appears as a well-dressed businessman or as a very recent graduate of Harvard, although the roles, as always, vary. Constantly forced to defend himself, he is simply not up to it. Indeed, he is usually thrashed shortly upon his arrival in town. Sometimes this is so humiliating that he tries to become a westerner. It never works. He is either humiliated even more or killed. Another role for this type is the pastor (a recent addition) who, when the chips are down, has only a prayer to offer. The East, we soon note, is incapable of action when action is most needed.

The "good girl" is another supportive type. Pale and without appetites, she too is from the East. Classically represented as the new schoolmarm, she also appears as the daughter of a local rancher, someone en route to a more distant point, or the wife of a cattleman. She has her eye on the hero. While any dealings between them come about as the result of her initiative, she is rarely flirtatious or coy. She does not allow any feminine allure to speak for itself—surely one reason she ends up doing most of the talking. The "good girl" fails to understand why men have to drink, gamble, punch, and shoot each other, and she spends a good deal of time making this point to the hero. Usually, she has some kind of protection—brother, father, fiancé, or relative—which makes it possible for her not to work. She is never independent, out in the world, with no attachments.

The "bad girl" is alone in the world, unattached, and works for her living, usually in the saloon as a waitress or dancer. She too has her eye on the hero, attracting him in a way her counterpart does not. She is often flirtatious and coy, but rarely takes the initiative in their meetings. She doesn't try to make him put away his guns and settle down. She is friendly with other men and, like her counterpart, is unhappily stalemated in her relation to the hero.

The "attendant" is another type. The most enduring and easily recognizable role for this type is the bartender, although the sniveling bank clerk is a close second. The attendant observes the action, provides the instruments of it, but never becomes centrally involved with it. Like a child following adults from room to room, he remains passive, deferring again and again to the principals, performing the important function of appearing unimportant.

One final type, of which there are many—"the boys," those drinking, bearded, grimy people who are always "just there," drinking and gambling in the saloon, without any apparent interest in anyone or anything, except their cards, whiskey, and the occasional songstress. Their function is that of an audience. No hero ever shot it out with his adversary without these people watching. Isolated conflicts between hero and adversary are always postponed—sometimes at considerable inconvenience to both—until "the boys" have had a chance to gather. "The boys" are passive functions of the action, important primarily for their presence.

PRINCIPALS AND ACTION

The action of the screen-image western takes place in three phases: the opening, the action, and the closing phases—or everything before the fight, the fight, and everything after the fight.

The opening phase first of all introduces us to the story's setting, to the supporting types (through their roles) and principals. In doing so, however, it not only supplies us with information, but also provides the very important illusion that we are to see for the first time something that we know, in the back of our heads, we have seen many times before. It is important to believe that we are not idiots, watching the same story night after night.

Second, the opening phase prepares us for the action by delineating the hero. He is, first of all, a transcendent figure, originating beyond the town. Classically, he rides into town from nowhere; even if he is the marshal, his identity is in some way dissociated from the people he must save. We know nothing of any past activities, relationships, future plans, or ambitions. Indeed, the hero is himself often quite ambiguous about these. There are no friends, relatives, family, mistresses—not even a dog or cat—with the exception of the horse, and this too is a strangely formal relationship.

His appearance further supports this image. In the preaction phase the hero sets forth a contrived indolence, barely distinguishable from sloth. Lax to the point of laziness, there appears to be nothing directional or purposeful about him. Take that hat, for instance: it sits exactly where it was placed—no effort has been made to align it. His horse is tied to whatever happens to protrude from the ground—and remains tied, although little more than a lazy nod would free it. Clothes and gun belt also betray the absence of any effort toward arrangement and order. With feet propped up on the hitching rail, frame balanced on a chair or stool tilted back on its two rear legs, hat pushed slightly over the eyes, hands clasped over the buckle of his gun belt, the hero is a study in contrived indolence.

I have used the word *contrived* to indicate another quality—that of discipline and control—that remains latent, being obscured by apparent laxity. His indolence is merely superficial and serves to protect and undergird the deeper elements of control that will appear in the action phase. Now he has time on his hands, but he knows his time is coming, and so do we.

The hero's coupling of laxity and control is seen in those recurrent primary images that are ordinarily referred to simply as "typical scenes." With women there is no desire or attraction. He appears somewhat bored with the whole business, as if it were in the line of duty. He never blushes or betrays any enthusiasm; he never rages or raves over a woman. His monosyllabic stammer and brevity of speech clearly indicate an intended indifference. In the drinking scenes we are likely to see him equipped with the traditional shot glass and bottle. The latter becomes his personal property, and therefore he is never questioned as to how many drinks he has taken. We rarely see him pay for more than one. While drinking, he usually stares gloomily at the floor or at all the other gloomy people who are staring gloomily at each other. He gulps his drink, rarely enjoys it, and is impatient to be off, on his way, hurrying to a place we are never told about. In the gambling scenes his poker face is to cards what his gloomy stare was to drink—a mask serving to veil any feelings, enthusiasm, fear, or apprehension. We note, however, that he always wins or else refuses to play. Similarly, he is utterly unimpressed and indifferent to money, regardless of its quantity or source, although the unguarded bank is always just around the corner.

The action phase opens with the threat of evil and extends up to its destruction at the hands of the hero. Although evil is most often referred to as the "villain" or "bad guy" or "heavy," I prefer the terms *evil one* or *adversary*.

Of the many hundreds of seemingly different versions, each is unshaven, darkly clothed, and from the West. Little is known about him. We are not told of his origins, his relationships, habits, or customs. Like the hero, he is from beyond the town, rather than identified with the interests, problems, and resources that characterize it. All details of his personal life are withheld. We can only be sure that the evil one unhesitatingly involves himself in the following: gambling, drink, the accumulation of money, lust, and violence. They are his vocation; with respect to these he is a professional man. It should be noted, however, that he is inclined to cheat at cards, get drunk, lust after women who do not return the compliment, rob banks, and, finally, shoot people he does not care for, especially heroes.

The impact of this evil one on the town is electric, as though a switch had been thrown, suddenly animating it with vitality, purpose, and direction. Indeed, it is evil, rather than good, that actually gives meaning to the lives of these people—his presence elicits commitment to a cause. The townsfolk now share a new identity: they are "those who are threatened by the evil one." Unified by a common threat, the town loses its desolate, aimless quality. It becomes busy. Some hasten to protect others, some to protect themselves; some run for help; some comment fearfully. Nevertheless, they all know (as do we) that they are of themselves ultimately powerless to meet this evil. What is required is the hero—a transcendent power originating from beyond the town.

Notice what has happened to this power. Gone are the indolence, laxity, and lack of intention. Now he is infused with vitality, direction, and seriousness. Before, the most trivial items might have caught his attention; now, every prior loyalty and concern are thoroughly excluded—he drops everything—in order that he may confront with passion and single-mindedness this ultimate threat. Once this radical shift has been accomplished, the hero (and audience) is ready for the final conflict—the central part of the action phase, the climax of the story.

While the fight can take many forms (fistfight, fight with knives, whips, and so on—even a scowling match in which the hero successfully glares down the evil one), the classical and most popular form is the encounter with six-guns. It is a built-up and drawn-out affair, always allowing enough time for an audience to gather. The two men must adhere to an elaborate and well-defined casuistry as to who draws first, when it is proper to draw, when it is not, and so forth. The climax also reflects much of the craft of gunplay, of which both hero and evil one are the skilled artisans (cross draw versus side draw, fanning versus thumbing, whether two guns are really better than one, and more). While these issues are certainly not the main concern of the action, the prominence given them by the story as a whole tends to prolong the climax.

Although the hero's presence usually makes the fight possible—i.e., he insists on obstructing the evil one in some way—it is the latter who invariably attacks first. Were the hero ever to draw first, the story would no longer be a western. Regardless of the issues involved, or of the moral responsibility for what is to follow, the hero's final victorious shot is always provoked by the evil one. With the destruction of the evil one, the action phase is completed.

In the closing phase the town and its hero return to their preaction ways. The electric quality of alarm and the sense of purpose and direction recede. People come out of hiding to acclaim their hero and enjoy his victory. He too returns to his preaction mode of indolence and laxity. At such a moment he is likely to become immediately absorbed in some unimportant detail (like blowing the smoke from his gun), indicating for all to see that he has survived the crisis and is once again his old self.

One more event must take place, however, before the story can conclude. The hero must renounce any involvement with the town that his victory may have suggested. In some way the town offers him the opportunity to identify with it, to settle down. Traditionally, this means marrying the schoolmarm and settling down. The hero always refuses. He cannot identify himself with the situation he has saved. He forfeits any opportunity to renounce his "beyond the town" origin and destiny. When this forfeiture has been made clear, when both savior and saved realize that it cannot be abrogated, then the story is over.

ANALYSIS

The western is, as most people by this time are willing to acknowledge, a popular myth. And by myth I mean three things. First of all, it is a story whose basic patterns of character, plot, and detail are repeated again and again and can be recognized. Second, the story embodies and sets forth certain meanings about what is good and bad, right and wrong— meanings regarded as important by those who view and participate in the myth. And third, some of these meanings are veiled by the story,[2] so that one can affirm them without overtly acknowledging them. Some part of the story (or all of it, perhaps) serves to conceal something from the participant—i.e., there is an unacknowledged aspect to the story. There is, therefore, an embarrassing question that never occurs to those in the sway of the myth—the posing of which is precisely the critic's most important task.

The meanings that the western sets forth center upon the problem of good and evil. Evil, according to the myth, is the failure to resist temptation. It is loss of control. Goodness lies in the power and willingness to resist temptation. It is the ability to remain in the presence of temptation yet remain in control of one's desire. Five activities make up the well-known content of temptation: drinking, gambling, money, sex, and violence.

Whenever any one of these activities appears, it should be seen as a self-contained temptation episode.[3] Such an episode, first of all, presents an object of temptation that can be indulged, should the hero so choose; second, it sets forth the hero in such a way that he can indulge the temptation in a preliminary way without becoming absorbed in it—i.e., without losing control. And, of course, it sets forth the evil one in precisely the opposite way.

In the drinking scenes the hero possesses not one drink but a whole bottle—i.e., he has at his disposal the opportunity for unlimited indulgence and its consequent loss of self-control. Gambling is a situation over which one has rather limited control—you can lose, but the hero does not lose. He wins, thereby remaining in control (cheating simply signifies the failure to acknowledge loss of control). Wealth is not seized, although it is available to him through the unguarded bank, and both good and bad girl seek out the hero in their various ways, but to no avail—he remains a hero. However, each temptation is presented in its peculiar way in order to set forth hero and evil one in their respective functions.

The temptation to do violence is more problematic, so much more so that the climax is given over to its solution. Furthermore, in the climax we find the key to the meaning of the myth as a whole—i.e., it can tell us why each type appears as he does, why the temptation episodes have their unique shape, and why certain fundamental images recur as they do.

We perceive in the evil one a terrible power, one that cannot be overcome by the ordinary resources of the town. However, he has acquired this power at great price: he has forfeited that very control and resistance that sustain and make the hero what he is. The evil one represents, therefore, not temptation so much as "temptation unhesitatingly given into." He is the embodiment of the failure to resist temptation; he is the failure of denial. This is the real meaning of evil in the myth of the western, and it is this that makes the evil one truly evil. Because of this he threatens the hero's resistance (and that of the townsfolk, as well, although indirectly): each taunt and baiting gesture is a lure to the forfeiture of control. This temptation the hero cannot handle with the usual methods of restraint, control, and the refusal to become absorbed, and it leads to a temptation that the hero cannot afford to resist: the temptation to destroy temptation.

The evil one's dark appearance is related to this threat. It tells us two things. First, that to lose control and forfeit resistance is (according to the story) a kind of living death, for black signifies death. In terms of the moral instruction of the story, and speaking metaphorically, we know that the evil one has "lost his life." But his black appearance also tells us, second, that, speaking quite literally, this man will die—because of what he is, he must and will be executed. We are therefore both instructed and reassured.

The embarrassing question can now be posed: why must the hero wait to be attacked, why must he refrain from drawing first? Why does he not take his opponent from behind, while he is carousing, or while he is asleep? Anyone in the power of the myth would reply that the gunfight takes place the way it does because this is the way westerns are; it's natural; this is the way it's always done—or, in the language of the myth itself, it was self-defense. But if one moves beyond the grasp of the myth, if one is no longer loyal to its rules and values, the gunfight is never inevitable. The circumstances that force the hero into this situation are contrived in order to make the violent destruction of the evil one appear just and virtuous. These circumstances have their origin in the inner veiled need to which the story is addressed. This process, whereby desire is at once indulged and veiled, I call the "inner dynamic." It is the key to the western, explaining not only the climax of the story, but everything else uniquely characteristic of it. What is required is that temptation be indulged while providing the appearance of having been resisted.

Each of the minor temptation episodes—the typical scenes setting forth hero and evil one as each encounters drink, cards, money, and sex— takes its unique shape from this need. Each is a climaxless western in itself, a play within a play in which temptation is faced and defeated, not by violent destruction as in the climax but by inner willed control. Or, reversing the relationship, we may say that in the gunfight, we have writ large something that takes place again and again throughout the story. It is precisely for this reason that no western has or needs to have all these episodes. Therefore, westerns can and do depart radically from the composite picture described earlier. We are so familiar with each kind of temptation, and each so reinforces the others, that extraordinary deletions and variations can occur without our losing touch with the central meanings.

The inner dynamic affects the supporting types as well. The derelict-professional is derelict and the nonviolent easterner is weak, precisely because they have failed to resist temptation in the manner characteristic of the hero. Their moderate, controlled indulgence of the various temptations does not conform to the total resistance of the hero. Consequently, they must be portrayed as derelict, weak, and deficient men, contrasting unfavorably with the hero's virtue. In this sense they have more in common with the evil one.

Because these two types both originate in the East, they have something in common with the good girl. We note that everything eastern in the western is considered weak, emotional, and feminine (family life, intellectual life, domestic life, professional life). Only by becoming westernized can the East be redeemed. The western, therefore, is more a myth about the East than it is about the West: it is a secret and bitter parody of eastern ways. This is all the more interesting since it was originally written in the East, by easterners for East reading. It really has little to do with the West.

Woman is split in the western to correspond to the splitting of man into hero and evil one. Primarily, however, the double feminine image permits the hero some gratification of desire while making a stalemate ultimately necessary. To get the good girl, the story instructs us, our hero would have to become like those despicable easterners; to get the bad girl, he would have to emulate the evil one. In such a dilemma a ride into the sunset is not such a bad solution after all.

The attendant sets forth the inner dynamic by being infinitely close to the action (temptations) while never becoming at all involved in it. It is his task to provide the instruments of temptation (drink, money, cards, guns) while never indulging in them himself. He is at once closer to temptation than any other type, yet more removed than any other type.

The boys function to facilitate the action without becoming involved in it. Without them hero and adversary might find other ways to settle their differences. The boys serve to remind them of their obligations to each other and the story as a whole, thereby structuring the myth more firmly. While they are around, nothing less than the traditional gunfight will do. On the other hand, because they never participate in the action but only coerce and reinforce it, they are thoroughly resistant to this temptation as well.

In summary, then: the western is a myth in which evil appears as a series of temptations to be resisted by the hero—most of which he succeeds in avoiding through inner control. When faced with the embodiment of these temptations, his mode of control changes, and he destroys the threat. But the story is so structured that the responsibility for this act falls upon the adversary, permitting the hero to destroy while appearing to save. Types and details, as well as narrative, take their shape from this inner dynamic, which must therefore be understood as the basic organizing and interpretive principle for the myth as a whole.

CULTURAL IMPLICATIONS

The western, I believe, bears a significant relationship—both dynamic and historical—to a cultural force that, for lack of better word, I would call "puritanism." Here I simply refer to a particular normative image of man's inner life in which it is the proper task of the will to rule, control, and contain the spontaneous, vital aspects of life. For the puritan there is little interpenetration between will and feeling, will and imagination. The will dominates rather than participates in the feelings and imagination.

Whenever vitality becomes too pressing, and the dominion of the will becomes threatened, the self must find some other mode of control. In such a situation the puritan will seek, usually unknowingly, any situation that will permit him to express vitality while at the same time appearing to control and resist it. The western provides just this opportunity, for, as we have seen, the entire myth is shaped by the inner dynamic of apparent control and veiled expression. Indeed, in the gunfight (and to a lesser extent in the minor temptation episodes) the hero's heightened gravity and dedicated exclusion of all other loyalties present a study in puritan virtue, while the evil one presents nothing more nor less than the old New England Protestant devil—strangely costumed, to be sure—the traditional tempter whose horrid lures never allow the good puritan a moment's peace. In the gunfight there are deliverance and redemption. Here is the real meaning of the western: a puritan moral tale in which the savior-hero redeems the community from the temptations of the devil.

The western is also related to puritanism through its strong self-critical element—i.e., it attacks, usually through parody, many aspects of traditional civilized life. Self-criticism, however, does not come easily to the puritan. Like vitality, it functions through imagination, and it too is in the service of the will. Therefore, if such criticism is to appear at all, it too must be veiled. The western assists in this difficult problem, for the story is well removed from the puritan's own locale, both geographically and psychically. Because it is always a story taking place "out there" and "a long time ago," self-criticism can appear without being directly recognized as such.

It is tempting to inquire how far certain historical forms of puritanism, such as mass religious revivals, may have actually produced the western. Was it only a coincidence that the same period of 1905–1920, which saw the early emergence of the western myth, also witnessed the nationwide popularity of a Billy Sunday and an Aimee Semple McPherson? Their gospel was a radical triumph of will over feeling and vitality, through which the believer could rely wholly upon his increasingly omnipotent will for the requisite controls. And here too was the familiar inventory of vices, with its characteristic emphasis upon gambling and drinking.

Recently, there has been an even more remarkable religious revival. Beginning in the early 1950s, it reached its point of greatest intensity in 1955. Here the gentle willfulness of the Graham gospel, and the more subtle (but equally hortatory) "save yourself" of the Peale contingent, permitted many respectable people to go to church and become interested in religion, without actually knowing why. However, like its earlier counterpart, this was not so much a religious movement as it was a renewed attack of the will upon the life of feeling and vitality.

That a reappearance of the western should take place precisely at this point is certainly suggestive. The upsurge in its popularity did occur just five years ago, beginning in the same year that the religious revival reached its height. Perhaps the present western revival has been more extensive and pervasive because the recent religious revival was equally so.

Presently, however, the religious revival has subsided, but the western remains almost as popular as ever. This could mean one of two things. On the one hand, the many changes that the western is presently undergoing—in its narrative, its types, and its recurrent primary images—could indicate that the religious recession has permitted the myth to be altered radically, such that it is on the way to becoming something entirely different. On the other hand, should such changes remain responsible to and be contained by the classical version, it could be that our puritanism is simply being expressed through nonreligious sources, most notably through the social sciences (indeed, in the sociologist's and psychologist's denunciation of the violence, historical inaccuracies, and so forth in the western, do we not hear echoes of the puritan hero himself?).

NOTES

1. Such TV versions as *Frontier Doctor* (1958, medicine), *Jefferson Drum* (1958, letters), and *Black Saddle* (1959, law) do not contradict this thesis, although they set forth professional men from the East who are hardly derelict. Close attention, however, reveals a "past" of questionable nature that these men are trying to conceal, but which is always being threatened by exposure. Such figures might best be called "covert" derelict-professionals.

2. This point is drawn from Denis de Rougemont's analysis of the myth of Tristan and Isolde. See de Rougemont, *Love in the Western World* (New York: Pantheon, 1956).

3. I am not suggesting that every western has all of these temptations, or that they appear in any given order. The subject of analysis is the representative version—not any particular version or set of versions. Thus, any particular western might deal with any one or a number of such temptations.

PART III

THE FANTASTIC

Part 3 focuses on the various fantastic genres: horror, fantasy, science fiction. Forrest J. Ackerman's influential fanzine *Famous Monsters of Filmland* began publication in 1958, helping to develop a fan base for these genres that was both popular and scholarly, but before then horror was largely ignored as lowbrow and sensational, fantasy had yet to emerge as a distinct genre, and science fiction film was frequently dismissed for its banalities and scientific inaccuracies, usually by "purists" who preferred science fiction literature. Unlike slapstick comedy or the western, neither horror nor science fiction dominated the generic or critical landscape until after the work of the writers represented here and the rise of grand theory. Once directors such as George A. Romero, John Carpenter, David Cronenberg, and Brian De Palma began reworking horror during the period of intense genre revisionism in the 1970s, a good deal of scholarly work, much of it inspired by the writings of Robin Wood,[1] began to focus on the genre, and it soon replaced the western as the foremost genre of critical interest.

An author, poet, and film critic, Parker Tyler was one of the first to write extensively about experimental cinema as well as Hollywood film. His nine books of film criticism reveal Tyler's distinctive interest in psychoanalysis, in dreams both individual and communal, and in cultural history. All of these interests come together in his essay "Supernaturalism in the Movies," from *Theatre Arts* in 1945, in which he wryly argues that cinema itself is a ghostly presence in contrast to Hollywood's vision of the hereafter, which is entirely earthbound in conception.

Next, in a 1958 *Partisan Review* essay entitled "Reflections on Horror Films," Robert Brustein, author, playwright, producer, and founder of the Yale Repertory Theatre, considers the cycle of teenage-oriented horror movies made during the 1950s. A longtime theater critic for the *New Republic* and author of many books on theater and society, including *The Theatre of Revolt* (1964), in which he invokes Northrop Frye to map a schema of modern drama's treat-ment of spiritual disintegration, Brustein here offers a typology for what he sees as the major types of horror film, categories that subsequently were re-peated with variations by a number of critics to follow. Brustein discusses the horror film's depiction of science as a "black magic" that has replaced super-stition in the genre and the moral and thematic implications of this view in the current cycle of teenage horror films—a significant component of what Thomas Doherty would later call the "juvenilization" of Hollywood at the time.[2]

Next, in his 1959 essay from *Film Quarterly*, "A Brief, Tragical History of the Science Fiction Film," Richard Hodgens offers one of the first sustained critical attacks on the science fiction film as a debasement of the genre in comparison to its literary counterpart. This was a frequent complaint among science fic-tion fans prior to the blockbusters of the late 1970s—Steven Spielberg's *Close Encounters of the Third Kind* (1977), George Lucas's *Star Wars* (1977), *Superman* (1978), and *Star Trek: The Motion Picture* (1979)—the wide successes of which moved the genre from marginal to the mainstream. At the time a graduate student in the English Department at New York University, Hodgens defines the genre in the orthodox manner established by influential writer and editor John W. Campbell as being based on scientific knowledge and method. Echo-ing Brustein, Hodgens sees the science in science fiction films depicted as a form of "black magic," knowledge potentially dangerous that is best left undis-turbed. The major culprit of Hollywood's rejection of science in the genre is *The Thing from Another World* (1951), which violated the scientific detective source story "Who Goes There?" by Campbell and set the tone for the monstrous rep-resentation of the alien Other in the numerous movies of the period, dubbed "Springtime for Caliban" by John Baxter.[3]

Rather more appreciative of film's ability to show scenes of monstrous action and mass destruction is Susan Sontag, whose well-known essay "The Imagination of Disaster" follows. Sontag was a novelist, filmmaker, and cul-tural critic who achieved both critical and popular recognition in the 1960s for such essays as "On Camp" and "Against Interpretation" (both 1964) in which she deftly articulated aspects of the period's countercultural and avant-garde sensibility. Although she wrote mostly on art cinema directors such as Berg-man and Bresson, she also wrote about forms of popular culture—perhaps most controversially on pornography. In her essay on monster movies, origi-nally published in *Commentary* in 1965, Sontag readily admits their unscientific nature and instead seeks to discuss the conventional qualities of the genre in terms of the cinematic medium, as Vivian Sobchack would do several years later,[4] and so celebrates rather than condemns their kinetic sensationalism.

In the brief essay "Extrapolative Cinema" from *Arts in Society* in 1969 that follows, Ivor A. Rogers takes issue with Sontag, arguing that the monster movies she discusses are not true science fiction, which by definition employs extrapolation of the known. Rogers was a professor of theater at the University of Wisconsin in Green Bay and at Drake University in Des Moines, Iowa, where he also ran a science fiction bookshop, and was one of the founding members of the Science Fiction Research Association, the first scholarly organization devoted to the study of science fiction and fantasy film and literature.

The section concludes with R. H. W. Dillard's ode to Universal's horror films of the 1930s from his essay "Even a Man Who Is Pure at Heart: Poetry and Danger in the Horror Film." In this abridged version of a longer essay originally published in W. R. Robinson's 1967 anthology *Man and the Movies*, Dillard, a poet and professor of film studies and creative writing at Hollins College in Virginia, understands the horror film as providing visually poetic means for viewers to negotiate the realities of evil and death.

NOTES

1. Robin Wood, "Introduction to the American Horror Film," in *Planks of Reason: Essays on the Horror Film*, edited by Barry Keith Grant and Christopher Sharrett, rev. ed. (Lanham, MD: Scarecrow Press, 2004), 107–142.

2. Thomas Doherty, *Teenagers & Teenpics: The Juvenilization of American Movies in the 1950s* (Boston: Unwin Hyman, 1988).

3. John W. Campbell's "Who Goes There?" first appeared in *Astounding Science Fiction* in August 1933 and has been widely reprinted since; John Baxter, *Science Fiction in the Cinema* (New York: Paperback Library, 1970), 100.

4. Vivian Sobchack, *The Limits of Infinity: The American Science Fiction Film* (South Brunswick, NJ: Barnes, 1980), revised as *Screening Space: The American Science Fiction Film* (New York: Ungar, 1987).

CHAPTER 13

SUPERNATURALISM IN THE MOVIES

PARKER TYLER

WHAT IS THE SUPERNATURAL? All religions have their answers in the-
ology; poets and saints have had their peculiar answer in visions; medicine and psychology attempt to throw light on the subject in their respective idioms. During the Middle Ages, magic claimed to evoke the Devil
and other wonders and produced legends, such as that of the Golem, that
persisted in literature and finally arrived from the vats of Hollywood as
Frankenstein—the synthetic man. While in horror and ghost thrillers the
movies utilize all manner of supernaturalist conceptions and their de-
graded vestiges, the movie camera itself is the source of an illusion of "the
supernatural."

Movie-camera trickery is of a magic-carpet kind—but here this expression not only is a figure of speech but denotes an actual vision, albeit
only an image recorded by one mechanism and thrown by another onto
a screen, an image as insubstantial as a ghost itself. With this power to
render the human substance into mere symbolic ectoplasm, the movie
camera possesses a perambulation parallel to the movements supposedly
initiated in actual Ghost Land. Thus, the ancient superstition of savages
that inanimate objects could be the source of spirits—Aladdin's lamp is a
relatively civilized example—has been effected by an object that can sci-
entifically project anything from the visible Hedy Lamarr to the Invisible
Man.

When the movie camera first appeared as a bioscope, it was a kind of
magician's toy. The fact that photographs could move was itself an aston-

Parker Tyler, "Supernaturalism in the Movies," *Theatre Arts* 29, no. 6 (1945): 362–
369. Reprinted by permission of Collier Associates, PO Box 20149, West Palm
Beach, FL 33416.

ishment that held adult persons as enthralled as a snake holds a rabbit. The first imaginative step of the cinematographer exploited the capacity of the bioscope for magic illusion—such as that of appearing and disappearing persons. As to theatrical illusion, the movie camera could perform all the feats the stage could, and much more simply in terms of physical operation. Fantasies of several kinds, including *A Trip to the Moon* (1902), which was vaguely like a Ziegfeld Follies spectacle, were soon being unveiled to patrons of the new "art." Today, of course, certain naturalistic illusions, such as those of "prop" cities and ocean scenes (often fabricated miniatures), take a good deal of time and trouble, but in the end are simpler than using actual urban or oceanic backgrounds for the elaborate realism now achieved. Amusing it is to reflect that the pioneer production of *Intolerance* (1916) by D. W. Griffith, in the early days of American film, made use of actually constructed sets and tremendous architectural backgrounds, such as those of Babylon, whereas nowadays Babylon (and Nineveh and Tyre) would, in the scenic en masse, be at least four-fifths beaverboard and paint and possibly no higher than your shoulder.

Super is not only an adjective but a real quality that was early corralled by Hollywood, so it seems only in the logical course of events to add to it ... *natural*. I need hardly add that no suspicion is implied that the invisible spiritual universe has anything to do with producing the supernatural within the towering outer escarpments of the Movie City. Yet considering the facility with which the technical magic of the movies can produce visions of the supernatural (about which poets, saints, and philosophers have only *talked*), who is there not to agree that, with the inception of the movies in this century, the supernatural came in for some entirely unsuspected, if equally unorthodox, propaganda?

The overpowering incense offered by Hollywood to the supernatural is certainly not grounded in theological considerations. Rather, it is embedded in the highly tangible objective of entertaining the naive and susceptible; its motive is the opposite of the ethereal. Yet in willy-nilly thrusting supernaturalism on its payroll, Hollywood may have grasped something as slippery as the "ghost girl" who keeps eluding Gildersleeve in the recent film *Gildersleeve's Ghost* (1944). Those who have escorted their unquiet risibilities through this opus recall that a luscious moll, with blonde locks as copious as storm clouds, keeps luring Gildersleeve into frantic clutches, spine-tingling kisses, and other devices suggestive of feminine avoirdupois, only to fade without notice into pure atmosphere. I thought it an especially telling device that, when the young lady's well-curved chassis made its due impression against a comfy chair cushion, the dent was visible but she was not. No one had ever seen a lady's—or, for that matter, a gentleman's—"dent" before. This apparition also had a hint of poetical fantasy. Certainly, if Poe had thought of that tantalizing dent, he would have introduced it into a poem or story.

In Freud's investigations of human vagary, amid what Poe termed "the ghoul-haunted woodland of Weir,"[1] the Vienna maestro identified Poe's woodlands as the dream world and showed very convincingly that things are to be known by something besides dictionary labels—for instance, that attraction and repulsion may be harbored by a human being for the same object. Taking a relatively primer view of this as of all truths, Hollywood has had recourse to such painfully obvious fables as *Dr. Jekyll and Mr. Hyde* (1931), in which the attraction is "Jekyll" and the repulsion is "Hyde," and *Frankenstein* (1931), in which the attraction is "soul" and the repulsion "body." Stevenson's rather casual little fantasy is a symbolic drama of brute beast versus civilized beast in the human personality and remains a somewhat Grimm treatment of the split-personality neurosis. But this much is to be observed of the Stevenson thriller: in the tooth-by-tooth, hair-by-hair transformation of Dr. Jekyll into Mr. Hyde, the camera has invented a more valid means of illustrating *what is supposed to have taken place* than the means Stevenson himself invented. During this sequence (in which Fredric March was the Lon Chaney), I could not help recalling the accelerated growth of a flower illusorily produced by the movie camera. Camera science, in setting forth the internal dynamics of nature, adds eloquent testimony to the logical possibility of the use of such dynamics outside the so-called bounds of nature. What is sauce for the goose may also be the elementary means of sustenance for the ghost!

In general, when a fable is stripped of its original literary form and prepared for its cinematic fitting, it has a better chance of becoming palatable to both taste and reason. Certainly, this is truest of ghost stories. One writer, Thorne Smith, whose libidinal brews seem inflected exclusively toward the literary taste of the readers of *Esquire*, has risen clear out of his literary class with three cinematizations—all charades of the supernatural: *Topper* (1937), *I Married a Witch* (née *The Passionate Witch* [1942]), and *Turnabout* (1940). The first indulges in invisible chicanery, the second is a variation on the Devil-welcoming witch theme, and the third is a notably ingenious confection based on the exchange of sexuality between husband and wife. In *I Married a Witch*, as the result of a tribal curse that started in *Scarlet Letter* days, a young woman (Veronica Lake by name) and her father (Charles Winninger) find themselves imprisoned in bottles and thus, in a double significant sense, are spirits. They emerge from and go

FIGURE 25. Veronica Lake and Fredric March in *I Married a Witch* (1942).

back into their ex-alcoholic homes as vapors, but materialize in human shape at will. It is the girl's mission to avenge herself on the young male scion of the family responsible for their imprisonment, but lo! she falls in love with him, and from then on, deciding to keep her human shape permanently, joins him in getting rid of her still wrathful and conspicuously bibulous parent. The two young lovers succeed in permanently corking up poor pater in his own sizzling juices (keeping the bottle at home in a special niche as an heirloom and, no doubt, as a moral precept for their growing children). At the same time, what an opportunity there was here for a Society for the Prevention of Cruelty to Ghosts!

Rightly, the above treatment might be termed "magical" rather than supernatural. But what of the infinite hierarchy of the thoroughly dead, where spirits wander in a literally distinct portion of geography? What is that world like? And, more pertinently, why do spirits aspire to be ghosts, to return to this world in their diaphanous shapes? A purely theological answer to the second question is supplied by the repeat version of *Outward Bound* (1930), now dubbed the more portentous *Between Two Worlds* (1944). We find that the "other world" is a mere replica of this one, the interval of travel between them being occupied by a voyage on a well-

FIGURE 26. *Between Two Worlds* (1944): the other world as mere replica of this one.

appointed but curiously deserted ocean liner. It suited Hollywood's scope to learn from the Sutton Vane play that the modern Styx is to the ancient one as Billy Rose's aquacade to a bathtub. There is plenty of time for the most substantial dead humans to get acquainted with the idea that they're both healthy and dead: a completely novel combination. A zany-minded newspaperman proves this fact with a revolver shot, said shot, with the customary innocuousness of those fired on stage and screen every day of the week, failing to make a hole in the recipient. Thus, it is a stage illusion in reverse: the bullet is real, but the man is a blank. However, I must say that Mr. Vane's play always seemed to me the most discouraging alleged news about the hereafter that I ever heard of.

The parental ghost, appearing as counsellor against evil as well as general nuisance, has been given front-stage space rather frequently on the screen. I call to mind *Our Town* (1940) and the fairly recent *The Uninvited* (1944). In the former, the spirits have sentry duty to perform at the head of their own graves, so that they have returned to substantiality only as their own breathing, speaking tombstones. Otherwise, they merely haunt the premises, doing the same chores for their young that they did in life; the young don't benefit except that they thus feel the weight and dignity of family and tribal tradition. A dubiously edifying business, despite good taste in handling and superb photography. Something in the strictly bona fide tradition of "hants" was *The Uninvited*, wherein a benevolent spirit, a young woman robbed of life and the rights of motherhood by a dastardly crime, tries to save her now-grown daughter from the workings of the same malevolent agent that wrought her own undoing. During the proceedings, a rigged-up Ouija board has a significant role in helping the frantic ghost get her message across. At first the ghost suffers all the desperate pangs of a victim of mistaken identity, but it turns out that the evil proceeds from a perfectly identifiable human source in this world, whereas all the most feared adjuncts of ghosts, such as frigid perfume and their ability to wither things, are shown as mere conventions of the postmortem state, and not necessarily signs of evil.

With the casual help of literature, Hollywood progresses toward some sophistication in the realm of the supernatural, as awkward and painful as the process sometimes is, and as far removed from a Dantesque majesty. Even so, in the movies, the underworld phase of the preternatural is more persuasive, generally, than the superworld phase. One of the many confusions of modern life is concerned with this very distinction. Is the "under" always *evil*, the "super" always *good*? Is Frankenstein's inspiration

FIGURE 27. The séance in *The Uninvited* (1944).

to remake mankind really from way down under, where Mr. Hyde's soul also abides in its half-portion state (Dr. Jekyll presumably having gone to heaven)? These are moral questions of importance, and so hardly a legitimate concern of Hollywood's. The basic nature of the movie camera as a magician's toy accounts for Hollywood's supernatural entertainment value. The screen's juggling with the supernatural mechanism affords the purest enjoyment, in the long run, among movie devices.

I call to witness a recent potpourri with a hefty spice of many things spine-nibbling: Olsen and Johnson's *Ghost Catchers* (1944). It intrigues because the jolly charade of its all being the plot of criminals to "scarify" tenants of an old house from a rich liquor haul in its cellar is saucily mingled with the perfectly "real" ghost who haunts his former haunt (after a mortal fall from his own window) because he did not finish the party he was throwing. There are some moments of melting pathos with Elmer, the ghost, who at last materializes in seraphically white evening clothes to aid the tenants walled up below stairs by the villains. Not the least of these moments is the one when Elmer is routed from the premises by a ballet of jitterbugs accompanied by a symphony of swing. After all, Elmer thrived in the soft-shoe era, and when his transcendental eyes observe some aerial jiving over the most august bedstead in the house, he raises the white flag of his Klan and evacuates conspicuously by the front door. I can think of Hollywood revelations of spirit whimsy far less worth the money, and of corridor stalkings far less profound in implication.

NOTE

1. Edgar Allan Poe, "Ulalume: A Ballad," in *Selected Prose, Poetry, and Eureka*, edited by W. H. Auden (San Francisco: Rinehart Press, 1950), 474.

CHAPTER 14

REFLECTIONS ON HORROR MOVIES

ROBERT BRUSTEIN

ALTHOUGH HORROR MOVIES HAVE recently been enjoying a vogue, they have always been perennial supporting features among grade B and C fare. The popularity of the form is no doubt partly explained by its ability to engage the spectator's feelings without making any serious demand on his mind. In addition, however, horror movies covertly embody certain underground assumptions about science that reflect popular opinions.

The horror movies I am mainly concerned with I have divided into three major categories: Mad Doctor, Atomic Beast, and Interplanetary Monster. They do not exhaust all the types, but they each contain two essential characters, the Scientist and the Monster, toward whom the attitudes of the movies are in a revealing state of change.

The Mad Doctor series is by far the most long-lived of the three. It suffered a temporary decline in the 1940s when Frankenstein, Dracula, and the Wolfman (along with their countless offspring) were first loaned out as straight men to Abbott and Costello and then set out to graze in the parched pastures of the cheap all-night movie houses, but it has recently demonstrated its durability in a group of English remakes and a Teenage Monster craze. These films find their roots in certain European folk myths. Dracula was inspired by an ancient Balkan superstition about vampires, the werewolf is a Middle European folk myth recorded, among other places, in the Breton *lais* of Marie de France, and even Frankenstein, though out of Mary Shelley by the Gothic tradition, has a medieval prototype in the Golem, a monster the Jews fashioned from clay and earth to free them from oppression. The spirit of these films is still medieval,

Robert Brustein, "Reflections on Horror Movies," *Partisan Review* 25, no. 2 (1958): 288–296. Copyright © by Robert Brustein. Reprinted by permission of the author.

FIGURE 28. Colin Clive (*far right*) as the mad doctor in *Frankenstein* (1931).

combining a vulgar religiosity with folk superstitions. Superstition now, however, has been crudely transferred from magic and alchemy to creative science, itself a form of magic to the untutored mind. The devil of the vampire and werewolf myths, who turned human beings into baser animals, today has become a scientist, and the metamorphosis is given a technical name—it is a "regression" into an earlier state of evolution. The alchemist and devil-conjuring scholar Dr. Faustus gives way to Dr. Frankenstein, the research physician, while the magic circle, the tetragrammaton, and the full moon are replaced by test tubes, complicated electrical apparatus, and Bunsen burners.

Frankenstein, like Faustus, defies God by exploring areas where humans are not meant to trespass. In Mary Shelley's book (it is subtitled "A Modern Prometheus"), Frankenstein is a latter-day Faustus, a superhuman creature whose aspiration embodies the expansiveness of his age. In the movies, however, Frankenstein loses his heroic quality and becomes a lunatic monomaniac, so obsessed with the value of his work that he no longer cares whether his discovery proves a boon or a curse to mankind. When the mad doctor, his eyes wild and inflamed, bends over his intricate equipment, pouring in a little of this and a little of that, the spectator is confronted with an immoral being whose mental superiority is only a measure of his madness. Like the popular image of the theoretical scientist engaged in basic research ("Basic research," says Charles Wilson, "is science's attempt to prove that grass is green"),[1] he succeeds only in creating something badly that nature has already made well. The Frankenstein monster is a parody of man. Ghastly in appearance, clumsy in movement, criminal in behavior, imbecilic of mind, it is superior only in physical strength and resistance to destruction. The scientist has fashioned it in the face of divine disapproval (the heavens disgorge at its birth), not to mention the disapproval of friends and frightened townspeople — and it can lead only to trouble.

For Dr. Frankenstein, however, the monster symbolizes the triumph of his intellect over the blind morality of his enemies, and it confirms him in the ultimate soundness of his thought ("They thought I was mad, but this proves who is the superior being"). When it becomes clear that Dr. Frankenstein's countrymen are unimpressed by his achievement and regard him as a menace to society, the monster becomes the agent of his revenge. As it ravages the countryside and terrorizes the inhabitants, it embodies and expresses the scientist's own lust and violence. It is an extension of his own mad soul, come to life not in a weak and ineffectual body but in a body of formidable physical power. (In a movie like *Dr. Jekyll and Mr. Hyde* [1920, 1931, 1941], the identity of monster and doctor is even clearer; Mr. Hyde, the monster, is the aggressive and libidinous element in the benevolent Dr. Jekyll's personality.) The rampage of the monster is the rampage of mad, unrestrained science, which inevitably turns on the scientist, destroying him too. As the lava bubbles over the sinking head of the monster, the crude moral of the film frees itself from the horror and is asserted. Experimental science (and, by extension, knowledge itself) is superfluous, dangerous, and unlawful, for in exploring the unknown, it leads man to usurp God's creative power. Each of these films is a victory for obscurantism, flattering the spectator into believing that his intellectual inferiority is a sign that he is loved by God.

The Teenage Monster films, a very recent phenomenon, amend the assumptions of these horror movies in a startling manner. Their titles — *I Was a Teenage Werewolf* (1957), *I Was a Teenage Frankenstein* (1957), *Blood of Dracula* (*Blood of the Demon* [1957]), and *Teenage Monster* (1958) (some wit awaits one called "I Had a Teenage Monkey on My Back") — suggest a Hollywood prank, but they are deadly serious, mixing the conventions of early horror movies with the ingredients of adolescent culture. The doctor, significantly enough, is no longer a fringe character whose madness can be inferred from the rings around his eyes and his wild hair but

FIGURE 29. Michael Landon as the adolescent lycanthrope in *I Was a Teenage Werewolf* (1957).

a respected member of society, a high school chemistry teacher (*Blood of Dracula*) or a psychoanalyst (*I Was a Teenage Werewolf*) or a visiting lecturer from Britain (*I Was a Teenage Frankenstein*). Although he gives the appearance of benevolence—he pretends to help teenagers with their problems—behind this facade he hides evil experimental designs. The monster, on the other hand, takes on a more fully developed personality. He is a victim who begins inauspiciously as an average, though emotionally troubled, adolescent and ends, through the influence of the doctor, as a voracious animal. The monster as teenager becomes the central character in the film, and the teenage audience is expected to identify and sympathize with him.

In *I Was a Teenage Werewolf*, the hero is characterized as brilliant but erratic in his studies and something of a delinquent. At the suggestion of his principal, he agrees to accept therapy from an analyst helping maladjusted students. The analyst gets the boy under his control and, after injecting him with a secret drug, turns him into a werewolf. Against his will he murders a number of his contemporaries. When the doctor refuses to free him from this curse, he kills him and is himself killed by the police. In death, his features relax into the harmless countenance of an adolescent.

The crimes of the adolescent are invariably committed against other youths (the doctor has it in for teenagers) and are always connected with those staples of juvenile culture, sex and violence. The advertising displays show the male monsters, dressed in leather jackets and blue jeans, bending ambiguously over the diaphanously draped body of a luscious young girl, while the female teenage vampire of *Blood of Dracula*, her nails long and her fangs dripping, is herself half-dressed and lying on top of a struggling male (whether to rape or murder him is not clear). The identification of sex and violence is further underlined by the promotional blurbs: "In her eyes DESIRE! In her veins—the blood of a MONSTER!" (*Blood of Dracula*); "A Teenage Titan on a Lustful Binge That Paralyzed a Town with Fear" (*Teenage Monster*). It is probable that these crimes are performed less reluctantly than is suggested and that the adolescent spectator is more thrilled than appalled by this "lustful binge" that captures the attention of the adult community. The acquisition of power and prestige through delinquent sexual and aggressive activity is a familiar juvenile fantasy (the same distributors exploit it more openly in films like *Reform School Girl* [1957] and *Drag Strip Girl* [1957]), one that we can see frequently acted out by delinquents in our city schools. In the Teenage Monster films, however, the hero is absolved of his aggressive and libidinous impulses. Although he both feels and acts on them, he can attribute the responsibility to the mad scientist who controls his behavior. What these films seem to be saying, in their underground manner, is that behind the harmless face of the high school chemistry teacher and the intellectual countenance of the psychoanalyst lies the warped authority responsible for teenage violence. The adolescent feels victimized by society—turned into a monster by society—and if he behaves in a delinquent manner, society and not he is to blame. Thus, we can see one direction in which the hostility for experimental research, explicit in the Mad Doctor films, can go—it can be transmuted into hatred of adult authority itself.

Or it can go underground, as in the Atomic Beast movies. The Mad Doctor movies, in exploiting the supernatural, usually locate their action in Europe (often a remote Bavarian village), where wild fens, spectral castles, and ominous graveyards provide the proper eerie background. The Atomic Beast movies depend for their effect on the contemporary and familiar, and there is a corresponding change in locale. The monster (or "thing," as it is more often called) appears now in a busy American city— usually Los Angeles to save the producer money—where average men walk about in business suits. The thing terrorizes not only the hero, the heroine, and a few anonymous (and expendable) characters in Tyrolean costumes, but the entire world. Furthermore, it has lost all resemblance to anything human. It appears as a giant ant (*Them!* [1954]), a prehistoric animal (*The Beast from 20,000 Fathoms* [1953]), an outsized grasshopper (*Beginning of the End* [1957]), or a monstrous spider (*Tarantula* [1955]). Although these films, in their deference to science fiction, seem to smile more benignly on scientific endeavor, they are unconsciously closer to the antitheoretical biases of the Mad Doctor series than would first appear.

All these films are similarly plotted, so the plot of *Beginning of the End* will serve as an example of the whole genre. The scene opens on a pair of adolescents necking in their car off a desert road. Their attention is caught by a weird clicking sound, the boy looks up in horror, the girl screams, the music stings, and the scene fades. In the next scene, we learn that the car has been completely demolished, and its occupants have disappeared. The police, totally baffled, are conducting fruitless investigations when word comes that a small town nearby has been destroyed in the same mysterious way. Enter the young scientist hero. Examining the wreckage of the town, he discovers a strange fluid that when analyzed proves to have been manufactured by a giant grasshopper. The police ridicule his conclusions and are instantly attacked by a fleet of these grasshoppers, each fifteen feet high, which wipe out the entire local force and a few state troopers. Interrupting a perfunctory romance with the heroine, the scientist flies to Washington to alert the nation. He describes the potential danger to a group of bored politicians and yawning big brass, but they remain skeptical until word comes that the things have reached Chicago and are crushing buildings and eating the occupants. The scientist is then put in charge of the army and air force. Although the military men want to evacuate the city and drop an atomic bomb on it, the scientist devises a safer method of

FIGURE 30. Science and the military respond to the threat of giant grasshoppers in *Beginning of the End* (1957).

destroying the creatures and proceeds to do so through exemplary physical courage and superior knowledge of their behavior. The movie ends on a note of foreboding: have the things been completely exterminated?

Externally, there seem to be very significant changes indeed, especially in the character of the scientist. No longer fang-toothed, long-haired, and subject to delirious ravings (Bela Lugosi, John Carradine, Basil Rathbone), the doctor is now a highly admired member of society, muscular, handsome, and heroic (John Agar). He is invariably wiser, more reasonable, and more humane than the boneheaded bureaucrats and trigger-happy brass that compose the members of his "team," and he even has sexual appeal, a quality that Hollywood's eggheads have never enjoyed before. The scientist-hero, however, is not a very convincing intellectual. Although he may use technical, polysyllabic language when discussing his findings, he always yields gracefully to the admonition to "tell us in our own words, Doc" and proves that he can speak as simply as you or I; in the crisis, in fact, he is almost monosyllabic. When the chips are down, he loses his glasses (a symbol of his intellectualism) and begins to look like everyone else. The hero's intellect is part of his costume and makeup, easily shed when heroic action is demanded. That he is always called upon not only to outwit the thing but to wrestle with it as well (in order to save the heroine) indicates that he is in constant danger of tripping over the thin boundary between specialist and average Joe.

The fact remains that there is a new separation between the scientist and the monster. Rather than being an extension of the doctor's evil will, the monster functions completely on its own, creating havoc through its predatory nature. We learn through charts, biological film, and the scientist's patient explanations that ants and grasshoppers are not the harmless little beasties they appear but actually voracious insects that need only the excuse of size to prey upon humanity. The doctor, rather than allying himself with the monster in its rampage against our cities, is in strong opposition to it and reverses the pattern of the Mad Doctor films by destroying it.

Yet if the individual scientist is absolved of all responsibility for the "thing," science somehow is not. These films suggest an uneasiness about science that, though subtle and unpremeditated, reflect unconscious American attitudes. These attitudes are sharpened when we examine the genesis of the thing, for, though it seems to rise out of nowhere, it is invariably caused by a scientific blunder. The giant ants of *Them!*, for example, result from a nuclear explosion that causes a mutation in the species; another fission test has awakened, in *The Beast from 20,000 Fathoms*, a dinosaur encrusted in polar ice caps; the spider of *Tarantula* grows in size after having been injected with radioactive isotopes and escapes during a fight in the lab between two scientists; the grasshoppers of *Beginning of the End* enlarge after crawling into some radioactive dust carelessly left about by a researcher. We are left with a puzzling statement: science destroys the thing, but scientific experimentation has created it.

I think we can explain this equivocal attitude when we acknowledge that the thing "which is too horrible to name," which owes its birth to an atomic or nuclear explosion, which begins in a desert or frozen waste and moves from there to cities, and which promises ultimately to destroy the world, is probably a crude symbol for the bomb itself. The scientists we see represented in these films are unlike the Mad Doctors in another more fundamental respect: they are never engaged in basic research. The scientist uses his knowledge in a purely defensive manner, like a specialist working on rocket interception or a physician trying to cure a disease. The isolated theoretician who tinkers curiously in his lab (and who invented the atomic bomb) is never shown, only the practical working scientist who labors to undo the harm. The thing's destructive rampage

FIGURE 31. The nest of giant ants in *Them!* (1954).

against cities, the rampage of the Frankenstein monster, is the result of too much cleverness, and the consequences for all the world are only too apparent.

These consequences are driven home more powerfully in movies like *The Incredible Shrinking Man* (1957) and *The Amazing Colossal Man* (1957), where the audience gets the opportunity to identify closely with the victims of science's reckless experimentation. The hero of the first movie is an average man who, through contact with fallout while on his honeymoon, begins to shrink away to nothing. As he proceeds to grow smaller, he finds himself in much the same dilemma as the other heroes of the Atomic Beast series: he must do battle with (now) gigantic insects in order to survive. Scientists can do nothing to save him—after a while they can't even find him—so as he dwindles into an atomic particle he finally turns to God, for whom "there is no zero." The inevitable sequel, *The Amazing Colossal Man*, reverses the dilemma. The hero grows to enormous size through the premature explosion of a plutonium bomb. Size carries with it the luxury of power, but the hero cannot enjoy his new stature. He feels like a freak, and his body is proceeding to outgrow his brain and heart. Although the scientists labor to help him and even succeed in reducing an elephant to the size of a cat, it is too late; the hero has gone mad, demolished Las Vegas, and fallen over Boulder Dam. The victimization of man by theoretical science has become, in these two movies, less of a suggestion and more of a fact.

In the Interplanetary Monster movies, Hollywood handles the public's ambivalence toward science in a more obvious way, by splitting the scientist in two. Most of these movies feature both a practical scientist who wishes to destroy the invader and a theoretical scientist who wants to communicate with it. In *The Thing from Another World* (1951), for example, we find billeted among a group of moral altruistic average-Joe colleagues with crew cuts an academic long-haired scientist of the Dr. Frankenstein type. When the evil thing (a highly evolved vegetable that, by multiplying itself, threatens to take over the world) descends in a flying saucer, this scientist tries to perpetuate its life in order "to find out what it knows." He is violently opposed in this by the others, who take the occasion to tell him that such amoral investigation produced the atomic bomb. But he cannot be reasoned with and almost wrecks the entire party. After both he and the thing are destroyed, the others congratulate themselves on remaining safe, though in the dark. In *Forbidden Planet* (1956), a sophisticated thriller inspired in part by Shakespeare's *The Tempest*, the good and evil elements in science are represented, as in *Dr. Jekyll and Mr. Hyde*, by the split personality of the scientist. He is urbane and benevolent (Walter Pidgeon plays the role) and is trying to realize an ideal community on the far-off planet he has discovered. Although he has invented a robot (Ariel) who cheerfully performs man's baser tasks, we learn that he is also responsible, though unwittingly, for a terrible invisible force (Caliban) overwhelming in its destructiveness. While he sleeps, the aggressive forces in his libido activate a dynamo he has been tinkering with that gives them enormous power to kill those the doctor unconsciously resents. Thus, Freudian psychology is evoked to endow the scientist with guilt. In the end, he accepts his guilt and sacrifices his life in order to combat the being he has created.

The Interplanetary Monster series sometimes reverses the central situation of most horror films. We often find the monster controlling the scientist and forcing him to do its evil will. In *It Conquered the World* (1956), the first film to capitalize on *Sputnik* and *Explorer*, the projection of a space satellite proves to be a mistake, for it results in the invasion of America by a monster from Venus. The monster takes control of the scientist who, embittered by the indifference of the masses toward his ideas, mistakenly thinks the monster will free men from stupidity. This

FIGURE 32. The Venusian creature of *It Conquered the World* (1956).

muddled egghead finally discovers the true intentions of the monster and destroys it, dying himself in the process. In *The Brain from Planet Arous* (1957), a hideous brain inhabits the mind of a nuclear physicist with the intention of controlling the universe. As the physical incarnation of the monster, the scientist is at the mercy of its will until he can free himself of its influence. The monster's intellect, like the intellect of the Mad Doctor, is invariably superior, signified graphically by its large head and small body (in the last film named it is nothing but Brain). Like the Mad Doctor, its superior intelligence is always accompanied by moral depravity and an unconscionable lust for power. If the monster is to be destroyed at all, this will be done not by matching wits with it but by finding some chink in its armor. The chink quite often is a physical imperfection: in *The War of the Worlds* (1953), the invading Martians are stopped, at the height of their victory, by their vulnerability to the disease germs of Earth. Before this Achilles' heel is discovered, however, the scientist is controlled to do evil, and with the monster and the doctor in collaboration again, even in this qualified sense, the wheel has come full circle.

The terror of most of these films, then, stems from the matching of knowledge with power, always a source of fear for Americans—when

Nietzsche's Superman enters comic book culture, he loses his intellectual and spiritual qualities and becomes a muscle man. The muscle man, even with X-ray vision, poses no threat to the will, but muscle in collaboration with mind is generally thought to have a profound effect on individual destinies. The tendency to attribute everything that happens in the heavens, from flying saucers to Florida's cold wave, to science and the bomb ("Why don't they stop?" said an old lady on the bus behind me the other day. "They don't know what they're doing") accounts for the extreme ways in which the scientist is regarded in our culture: either as a protective savior or as a destructive blunderer. It is little wonder that America exalts the physician (and the football player) and ignores the physicist. These issues, the issues of the great debate over scientific education and basic research, assert themselves crudely through the unwieldy monster and the Mad Doctor. The films suggest that the academic scientist, in exploring new areas, has laid the human race open to devastation either by human or by interplanetary enemies—the doctor's madness, then, is merely a suitable way of expressing a conviction that the scientist's idle curiosity has shaken itself loose from prudence or principle. There is obviously a more sensitive problem involved here, one that needs more articulate treatment than the covert and superstitious way it is handled in horror movies. That the problem is touched there at all is evidence of how profoundly it has stirred the American psyche.

NOTE

1. See John W. Finney, "Defense Scientists Fear Research Cut," *New York Times*, September 22, 1957, sec. 1, p. 1.

CHAPTER 15

A BRIEF, TRAGICAL HISTORY OF
THE SCIENCE FICTION FILM

RICHARD HODGENS

Cut is the branch that might have grown full straight,
And burned is Apollo's laurel-bough,
That sometime grew within this learned man.
Faustus is gone: regard his hellish fall,
Whose fiendful fortune may exhort the wise,
Only to wonder at unlawful things,
Whose deepness doth entice such forward wits
To practise more than heavenly power permits.
—*DOCTOR FAUSTUS*, EPILOGUE

SOME OF THE MOST ORIGINAL and thoughtful contemporary fiction has been science fiction (SF), and this field may well prove to be of much greater literary importance than is generally admitted. In motion pictures, however, "science fiction" has so far been unoriginal and limited, and both the tone and the implications of these films suggest a strange throwback of taste to something moldier and more "Gothic" than the Gothic novel. But the genre is an interesting and potentially very fruitful one.

Science fiction publishing expanded spectacularly in the late 1940s and dwindled again in the early '50s. Science fiction filming as we know it today began in 1950 with *Destination Moon* and has continued to the present, hideously transformed, as a minor category of production. Earlier examples—like Fritz Lang's *Metropolis* (1927) and *Frau im Mond* (1929); H. G. Wells's powerful essay on future history, *Things to Come* (1936); and

Richard Hodgens, "A Brief, Tragical History of the Science Fiction Film," *Film Quarterly* 13, no. 2 (1959): 30–39. Copyright © 1959 by the Regents of the University of California. Reprinted with permission of the Regents of the University of California.

such nonsupernatural horror films as *The Invisible Ray* (1936)—have not been considered "science fiction," although they were. One of the many painful aspects of most of the recent films involving space travel, alien visitors, or earthly monsters that have followed *Destination Moon* is that they are considered "science fiction," although most of them are something peculiarly different from the literature of the same label.

Motion picture adaptations have ruined any number of good works of literature without casting a pall, in the public mind, over literature in general. The science fiction films, however, seem to have come close to ruining the reputation of the category of fiction from which they have malignantly sprouted. To the film audience, "science fiction" means "horror," distinguished from ordinary horror only by a relative lack of plausibility.

Science fiction involves extrapolated or fictitious science, or fictitious use of scientific possibilities, or it may be simply fiction that takes place in the future or introduces some radical assumption about the present or the past. For those who insist upon nothing but direct treatment of contemporary life, science fiction has little or nothing to offer, of course. But there are issues that cannot be dealt with realistically in terms of the present, or even the past, and to confront such issues in fiction it is better to invent a future-tense society than to distort the present or the past. And in a broader sense there are few subjects that cannot be considered in science fiction, few styles in which it cannot be written, and few moods that it cannot convey. It is, to my mind, the only kind of writing today that offers much surprise—not merely the surprise of shock effects, but the surprise of new or unusual material handled rationally. And conscientious science fiction, more than any other type, offers the reader that shift of focus essential to the appeal of any literature. Often too it presents a puzzle analogous to that of the detective story, but with its central assumptions considerably less restricted.

Science fiction, as most science fiction readers define it and as most science fiction writers attempt to practice it, calls for a plausible or at least possible premise, logically developed. The most damning criticism one can make of a work of science fiction is that it is flatly impossible in the first place and inconsistent in the second. To say the least, many things are possible, and readers may accept a premise that they believe impossible anyway, so long as they do not consider it "supernatural." Often, the distinction between science fiction and fantasy is simply one of attitude, but an impossible premise must at least not contradict itself, and it should be developed consistently in the story.

Science fiction films, with few exceptions, follow different conventions.

The premise is always flatly impossible. Any explanations offered are either false analogy or entirely meaningless. The character who protests "But that's incredible, Doctor!" is always right. The impossible, and often self-contradictory, premise is irrationally developed, if it is developed at all. There is less narrative logic than in the average western. Although antiscientific printed science fiction exists, most science fiction reflects at least an awareness and appreciation of science. Some science fiction, it is true, displays an uncomprehending faith in science and implies that it will solve all problems magically. But in the science fiction films there is rarely any sane middle ground. Now and then, science is white magic. But far more often, it is black, and if these films have any general implications about science, they are that science and scientists are dangerous, raising problems and provoking widespread disaster for the innocent, ignorant good folks, and that curiosity is a deadly sin.

The few exceptions to this bleak picture are the first three SF films produced by George Pal: *Destination Moon*, *When Worlds Collide* (1951), and *The War of the Worlds* (1953). Perhaps there are one or two others. *Destination Moon* may be considered a good semidocumentary, educational film, although today its optimism is rather depressing. Despite its accuracy and consistency, and the extent to which the stereotyped characters were forced to go to explain it, most criticism indicated that the critics did not understand it. The special effects were the film's main attraction and, except for a few shots of the apparent size of the ship in space and the appearance of the stars, were exact and superb. In a fascinating article about the technical problems of this film, Robert Heinlein credits its director, Irving Pichel, with saving it from an arbitrary addition of musical comedy and "pseudoscientific gimmicks which would have puzzled even Flash Gordon."[1]

Those who hoped that the financial success of *Destination Moon* would lead to equally convincing but more sophisticated science fiction films were bitterly disappointed, for nearly everything since has been unconvincing and naive. There was a flood of "science fiction" on the screen, but it followed in the footsteps of *The Thing from Another World* (1951), and it was unbelievably and progressively inane.

Pal's next two productions were satisfactory, however, and although they are not impressive when compared with a film like *Things to Come*, in comparison with their contemporary science fiction competition they seemed masterpieces. In the 1930s Paramount had considered *When Worlds Collide*, a novel by Edwin Balmer and Philip Wylie, for DeMille, and *The War of the Worlds*, by H. G. Wells, for Eisenstein. Pal's films modernized the sources but respected them. Unlike *Destination Moon*, however, both have themes of menace and catastrophe—the end of the world and interplanetary invasion. It appeared that even Pal had decided that science fiction films must be, somehow, horrible.

In *When Worlds Collide*, models were used extensively, and while many of them were not completely convincing, the only major disappointment to most people was the last shot of the lush, green new world, after the single escaping spaceship had landed in impressively rugged territory. H. G. Wells's *War of the Worlds* is a good novel and difficult to ruin. If *War of the Worlds* had been filmed as a period piece, as Disney later treated Jules Verne's *20,000 Leagues under the Sea* (1954), it would still have been effective. The story was carefully modernized, however, as Howard Koch had modernized it in 1938 for Orson Welles's *Mercury Theater on the Air*. One unnecessary modern addition, though, was an irrelevant boy-and-girl theme because, Pal apologized, "Audiences want it."[2]

The theme of Wells's memorable "assault on human self-satisfaction" is still valid, if less startling. No one today expects to be visited by intelligent Martians, but granting this premise the film was quite convincing. The Martians' fantastic weapons were acceptable as products of a superior technology; the Martians themselves, though more terrestrial in appearance than Wells's original conception, were probably the most convincing Things to come from Hollywood, and they were used with surprising restraint and effectiveness—one brief glimpse and, at the end, a lingering shot of the hand of the dying creature. About half the film was painstaking special effects, and the models were nearly perfect.

These three films were spectacular productions, and if the scripts contained moments rather similar to more traditional spectacles, they still contained powerful images that had never been seen before: after take-off, virtually every shot in *Destination Moon*; the red dwarf star nearing the doomed Earth; and the deadly Martian machines, like copper mantas and hooded cobras, gliding down empty streets.

I do not mean to imply that everyone was pleased by these films. Those who like plots with villains were bored by *Destination Moon*, and people who knew nothing about space travel, and did not care, were baffled. *When Worlds Collide* drew harsh words for its concluding shot and its models, and some people seem to have been irritated by the undemocratic survival of the interplanetary Ark. And of *The War of the Worlds* I heard someone say, "That Orson Welles always was crazy, anyway."

George Pal's last science fiction production, *Conquest of Space* (1955), was disappointing. Again there were some visually impressive shots, but

FIGURE 33. The space walk in *Conquest of Space* (1955).

unfortunately that was all. The script attempted to "enliven" a subject that called for serious treatment; the result was an inaccurate, misleading film ending with a miracle that, unlike the "miraculous" end of *The War of the Worlds*, was impossible and pointless. It was an expensive production that could have contributed to the salvation of science fiction in motion pictures. But the monsters had taken the field, and the facile *Conquest of Space* merely seemed to prove that monsters are always necessary.

What the movies were likely to do with science fiction was already evident when *Rocketship X-M* was released in 1950 to compete with *Destination Moon*. An expedition sets out for the moon. The ship's course is altered by the close passage of some noisy meteors, however, and the explorers land on Mars, where they learn that atomic warfare has destroyed Martian civilization. The Martians appear to be entirely human—at least, if memory serves, one savage female was beautifully human—but radiation has bestialized them. The girl scientist and the boy scientist escape from Mars, but, lacking fuel to land on the frantically spinning Earth, they endure a stoic martyrdom. Though *Rocketship X-M* seemed ludicrous, it was levelheaded and superb compared with what followed.

The great villain was *The Thing from Another World*, which appeared in

FIGURE 34. The Americans at the Arctic base in *The Thing from Another World* (1951).

1951. *The Thing* was based on a short novel by John W. Campbell Jr., the editor of *Astounding Science Fiction*, where it appeared in 1938 with the title "Who Goes There?" The story is regarded as one of the most original and effective science fiction stories, subspecies "horror." Its premise is convincing, its development logical, its characterization intelligent, and its suspense considerable. Of these qualities the film retained one or two minutes of suspense. The story and the film are poles apart. Probably for timely interest, the Thing crashed in a flying saucer and was quick-frozen in the Arctic. In Campbell's story "it had lain in the ice for twenty million years" in the Antarctic. In film as in source, when the creature thaws out it is alive and dangerous. In "Who Goes There?," when it gets up and walks away, and later when it is torn to pieces by the dogs and still lives, the nature of the beast makes its invulnerability acceptable. But there is little plausibility about the Hollywood Thing's nine lives. Since this film, presumably dead creatures have been coming back to life with more and more alacrity and with less and less excuse. Instead of the nearly insoluble problem created in Campbell's story, this Thing is another monster entirely. He is a vegetable. He looks like Frankenstein's monster. He roars. He is radioactive. And he drinks blood.[3]

Probably Campbell's protean menace was reduced to this strange combination of familiar elements in the belief that the original idea—the idea that made the story make sense—was too complex. This was probably incorrect, because monsters since that Thing have imitated the special ability of Campbell's Alien, although with far less credibility (*It Came from Outer Space* [1953], *Invasion of the Body Snatchers* [1956]), and there is no indication that anyone found them difficult to understand.

Incidentally, the most stupid character in the film is the most important scientist. The script did its best to imply that his tolerant attitude toward the Thing was his worst idea. And the film ended with a warning to all mankind: "Watch the skies" for these abominably dangerous flying saucers.

The Thing is a most radical betrayal of its source, but since the source was generally unfamiliar, and since the idea of a monster from outer space seemed so original (though the monster itself had blood brothers in Transylvania), the film earned both critical approval and a great deal of money.[4] In addition, it fixed the pattern for the majority of science fiction films that followed, for it proved that some money could be made by "science fiction" that preyed on current fears symbolized crudely by any preposterous monster, and the only special expense involved would be for one monster suit.

Not all science fiction films since *The Thing* have been about monsters, but the majority have. *The Day the Earth Stood Still*, also released in 1951, was almost, but not quite, a monster film. It was a story not of catastrophe, as the title suggests, but of alien visitors. The screenplay deprived another popular science fiction story from *Astounding*, Harry Bates's "Farewell to the Master," of its good ideas, its conviction, and its point. *The Day* substituted a message: Earthlings, behave yourselves. Again, probably because like *The Thing* the story was novel but could be understood without much effort, *The Day* earned good reviews and good money. Whatever reservations one may have about the film, in comparison with *The Thing* and its spawn, *The Day* has a comparatively civilized air, at least.

It Came from Outer Space was another rare exception that appeared rather early in the cycle. One of the virtues of *It Came from Outer Space* is that It is here by accident and wants to go home.

Following the precedent that *The Thing* set, *The Beast from 20,000 Fathoms* (1953) and *Them!* (1954) established major variations of the monster theme. The Beast, a foolish fancy of Ray Bradbury's to begin with, was an amphibious dinosaur. I cannot remember whether nuclear physics was responsible for its resuscitation or its final destruction, but probably it was both. The Beast, like the Thing, thaws to life, but it was a menace of terrestrial origin. This simplifies the filmmakers' problems. The Beast has been followed by several monsters, revived, we are told, from the distant past, and all of them instinctively attack populous cities. (King Kong, un-like these "atom beasts," had some sort of motivation.) The monsters in *Them!* were giant ants, also dangerous, in the sewers of Los Angeles. Im-possibly large insects with a taste for human flesh have appeared in *The Deadly Mantis* (1957), *The Spider* (*Earth vs. the Spider* [1958]), and others. The milder monster of *Creature from the Black Lagoon* (1954) proved so popular that he himself returned in *Revenge* (1955),[5] but of all the earthly monsters, only that of *The Magnetic Monster* (1953), with a script by Curt Siodmak, displayed much originality and consistency.

The Incredible Shrinking Man (1954) created its bloated-insect horror by shrinking the hero until an ordinary spider became typically perilous. The unfortunate young man of the title passes through a strange cloud while sunbathing on his cabin cruiser and begins to shrink—evenly, all over. The screenplay, by Richard Matheson from his own novel, is a pro-tracted and occasionally amusing agony. Soon the incredible shrinking man is too small to live an ordinary life. He finds brief happiness with a beautiful midget, but he breaks off their relationship when he discovers that he has become too short for her. He is plagued by reporters. When his wife walks downstairs, the dollhouse in which he lives shakes with unbearable violence. The cat chases him. He gets lost in the cellar. Then the spider chases him. Although the premise of the story is impossible, the end improves upon it, for the incredible shrinking man does not die because "in the mind of God there is no zero." Even God, in the science fiction films, is a poor mathematician. *The Incredible Shrinking Man* began its own minor series of increasingly poor films about people who are too small or too big.

In a persuasive review of Matheson's novel and Frank M. Robinson's *The Power*, Damon Knight argues that these works are popular successes precisely because they are irrational and antiscientific—considering, for instance, the inconsistent diminution of Matheson's hero, one of the novel's faults that is not repeated in the film, where one wouldn't notice it much. Knight goes too far, however, when he remarks, "Spiders don't scream, as even Matheson might know; but gutted scientists do."[6] *The Incredible Shrinking Man* is certainly unscientific, but this sinister implication Knight suggests in the impalement of the screaming "symbolic" spider does not follow. In many of the science fiction films, though, such sinister implications are conventional.

Invasions from space did not cease. *The Blob* (1958) came in color, and Martian Blood Rust sprouted in black and white in *Space Master X-7* (1958). When Japan is invaded by aliens in *The Mysterians* (1957), the aggressors' one insupportable demand is intermarriage with human females "because there is so much strontium-90 in our bones." If one can safely judge by title and advertising, *I Married a Monster from Outer Space* (1958) involves a similar unlikely prospect and takes the same attitude toward it. This is like expecting the Thing to pollinate Godzilla, but monstrous union is in line with this sort of film, and, considering the attitude they display toward almost every Thing in them, an intolerant view of mixed marriage is to be expected. The Mysterians, incidentally, look very much like human beings, except that they melt. Space travel is rare in science fiction films now, but we have discovered human beings native to Mars, Venus, and various nonexistent planets. Sometimes space travel and monsters are ingeniously combined, as when the *First Man into Space* (1959) returns a monster. *Forbidden Planet* (1956) and *This Island Earth* (1955) were expensive color productions that involved space travel and managed to have their monsters too. In *Forbidden Planet* it had something to do with the Id, but it might as well have been Grendel. *This Island Earth*, an unbelievable adaptation of a somewhat less unbelievable novel by Raymond F. Jones, included a horrendous Thing called, of all things, a Mutant.

The most recent big science fiction is *The Fly* (1958), in CinemaScope and Horror-color, and popular enough to call for *Return of the Fly* (1959). *The Fly* is not from the short story of that title by Arthur Porges, originally in the *Magazine of Fantasy and Science Fiction*, but from another story of the same title by George Langelaan, originally in *Playboy.*[7] Porges's story presents an interesting situation that could not be filmed without expansion and, inevitably, ruination, and it would be called "Invasion of the Atom-Fly from Another World." Since Langelaan's story is impossible to begin with, is inconsistent anyway, and is a horror story as horrifying as the most horrible science fiction films, one might expect that it could endure motion picture adaptation. The film, however, managed to be more impossible and less consistent, to add clichés and bright blood, and to contrive a happier ending with some morally repugnant implications.

Even if one accepts, for the sake of entertainment, the initial premise that Andre Delambre has built, in his basement, a working matter transmitter, nothing else follows. The machine behaves differently each time it makes a mistake. The molecular structure of a dish is reversed. A cat with a pitiable wail disappears entirely. Finally, Andre himself is somehow mixed up with a fly. The result is a handsome young scientist with "the head of a fly" (and an arm, too) and "the fly with the head of a man!"[8] Of course, there is a certain ingenuity about the accident: it creates two "monsters" instead of one. But why is Andre with the head of the fly still Andre, and why does his fly leg have (evidently) a fly's volition? Why was the part of the fly grafted to Andre enlarged to fit him so well? How does he eat? Breathe? Why does he gradually begin to think a bit like a fly, and why is he then tempted to maul his poor wife, Helene? Why destroy the lab? The series of physical impossibilities in the script is not helped by the psychology. After squashing the man with the head of the fly in a hydraulic press, Helene neither commits suicide nor is she confined, as in the story. Helene is saved from grief and inconvenience by Commissaire Charas, who, at the last minute, notes the fly with the head of a man and squashes it with a rock. What else, indeed, could be done with it? Although it is clear that Andre's death (i.e., Andre in the press) was suicide in which Helene cooperated, the script chooses to ignore the moral problem presented by the suicide, or the mercy killing, or whatever it was. Instead, the issue is that Helene killed a mere Thing. After all, it is not improper to kill a Thing, and one may safely kill a man if he is no longer entirely human. This follows repetitious dialogue about the Sacredness of Life, but apparently they meant natural, original life forms only, and the cat is more sacred than Andre in either combination. In the last scene of the film, Andre's surviving brother delivers a little proscience speech to Andre's son while Helene listens, smiling sweetly. Father, the boy's uncle tells him, was like Columbus. What will be remembered, of course, is that Father was like a fly.

The Fly, like most science fiction films, has a rather strange, very old moral. A search for knowledge or any worldly improvements may go too far, it may be blasphemous, and one may be punished with an unnatural end.[9] The premises of science fiction films are all antique and carelessly handled. Twenty years ago, the matter transmitter in the present-day cellar might have been almost convincing, but now one would expect it in a more credible context and expect it to function with some consistency. Most science fiction films, however, do not take place in the future, where such an invention might be acceptable. The film *1984* (1956) is a rare recent exception, but if Orwell's novel had not forced the date, it would have been 1960.

It is true that magazine science fiction developed and exploited the stereotyped mad scientist and the evil bug-eyed monster. But that, again, was about twenty years ago. Giant insects, shrinking men, and dinosaurs can be found in science fiction of the same period. It is true that some science fiction stories are as unoriginal, illogical, and monstrous as science fiction films, but you have to know where to look in order to find many of them.

Apart from such incidental lessons as the immorality of attempting to prolong life and the advisability of forgetting anything new that one happens to learn, there are two vague ideas that appear in science fiction films with some regularity. Sometimes, the menace or the Thing does not merely kill its victims but deprives them of their identity, their free will, or their individual rights and obligations as members of a free society. In *Attack of the Puppet People* (1958), for instance, the combination doll maker and mad superscientist who shrinks the people he likes is a sort of pathetic, benevolent dictator. Many science fiction films derive whatever emotional effect they have from their halfhearted allegorization of the conflict between individuality and conformity. Usually, the conflict remains undeveloped, and although the characters tend to resist such menaces, their reasons may often be that the menace is a slimy, repulsive Thing or that they would resist any change, even one for the better. The movie *1984* is the only science fiction film that took this conflict as its subject, although it is common in science fiction novels.

The other vague idea is that atomic power is dangerous. The point has been made again and again, ever since the Geiger counter reacted to the presence of the first Thing. The point is indisputable, but these films rarely show any awareness of the ways in which the atom is dangerous. The danger of atomic war is explicit in Arch Oboler's *Five* (1951), the recent *The World, the Flesh, and the Devil* (1959), and the forthcoming *On the Beach* (1959). These films are not only exceptional; they are not generally considered to be science fiction. In the ordinary science fiction film, atomic bombs raise dragons and shrink people. Even *The Fly*, which had nothing to do with the effects of radiation, real or imagined, was advertised as if its poor monsters were the realistic, possible outcome of fallout on flesh. It may be argued that all the atomic monsters of science fiction films are symbols, and I suppose that they are, but they are inapt, inept, or both.

If the creators of monster films had intended any comment on the problems raised by the atomic bomb, or even on feelings about it, as some kindly critics have assumed, they would not have made their monster films at all. The most obvious advantage of science fiction, and the three

FIGURE 35. The diminutive detainees of the mad doctor in *Attack of the Puppet People* (1958).

films mentioned above, is that one can deal with such problems and feelings by extending the situation into the future and showing a possible effect or resolution. There is no need for indirect discussion or for a plot with a "symbol" as its mainspring. A twelve-ton woman-eating cockroach does not say anything about the bomb simply because it, too, is radioactive, or crawls out of a test site, and the filmmakers have simply attempted to make their monster more frightening by associating it with something serious.

One should realize that, like them or not, the invaders in Wells's *War of the Worlds*, the stranded Alien in Campbell's "Who Goes There?," or the parasites in Heinlein's *The Puppet Masters* (clumsily parodied by *The Brain Eaters* [1958], the monsters of which are complex parasitic animals that evolved when there were no hosts for them) are a different sort of monster from those of most SF films. They may be symbols too, but first they are beings. Campbell may invent a creature that evokes a complex of ancient fears—fear of the ancient itself, the fear that death may not be final, that evil is indestructible, and fear rising from the imitation motif, fear of possession, of loss of identity, all the fears that gave rise to tales of demons, ghosts, witches, vampires, shape-shifters. But in "Who Goes There?" it is a realistically conceived being that evokes these fears and creates the suspense, not an impossible symbol; the story is not hysterical, but a study of man under stress.

The science fiction films abuse their borrowed props and offer nothing but hysteria. The films resemble unpleasant dreams, but rarely resemble them well. One cannot condemn an attempt to make a film suggesting nightmare illogic, of course. But surrealism is not what the makers of these films have in mind.

Fantasy and science fiction are not convincing if they are not consistent. Convincing the audience to accept the initial premise of the story may be difficult enough without violating that premise in each scene. Expensive and careful treatment of a careless script cannot overcome the script's bad logic in science fiction or anything else. And while careful science fiction scripts are rare, careful treatment is even more rare. Most of the special effects in science fiction films, for instance, would not deceive a myopic child in the back of the theater—not even all the third-degree burns and running sores that have become so popular. The films convey the impression that everyone involved is aware that he is working on something that is not only beneath his talent but beneath the audience as well. It seems that even the makeup department, called upon by the pointless turns of a morbid plot to disintegrate a bored actor, has neither the time nor the heart to waste any effort and produces something that looks like the unraveling of an old vacuum-cleaner bag. Perhaps this is a good thing. But it is strange that if you hire a group of talented people and ask for another science fiction–horror, you will get a film that is not merely abominable in conception and perverse in implication but halfhearted in execution.

Reginald Bretnor's symposium *Modern Science Fiction* contains an interesting article by Don Fabun, "Science Fiction in Motion Pictures, Radio, and Television," a detailed examination that concludes with this hope: "In time we may see the modern literary form called science fiction legitimately married to novel and exciting techniques of presentation, a combination which should bring us fresh and exciting entertainment superior to what we see and hear today."[10] That was in 1953. Today, there seems little cause for hope from the present level where "science fiction" is indistinguishable from "horror" and "horror" from sadism. An audience for good science fiction films probably exists, but it is unlikely that producers will take that chance now. During the period when it seemed reasonable to expect some good science fiction films, the only chances that producers were willing to take with unfamiliar material were with material from contemporary life—"unfamiliar material" only in their previous films. With science fiction, everyone has followed the easy examples of a few successful horror films, in cheaper and cheaper productions that plagiarized their poverty of ideas and their antiscientific tone. Perhaps the problem of producing good SF films is more difficult than that of producing simply good films. Complex, individual, and intelligent films are rare, and films of this quality with unfamiliar, fantastic subjects are few indeed. *Things to Come, The Cabinet of Dr. Caligari* (1920), *Orphée* (*Orpheus* [1950]), and *The Seventh Seal* (1957) are uncommon individual achievements; probably, good science fiction films will appear only in the form of such unusual achievements.[11] For the rest, if SF films continue to be produced, they will take the easy way of the scream instead of the statement and continue to tell their increasingly irrational and vicious stories of impossible monsters, evil professors, and helpless victims. ("See a stripteaser completely stripped—of flesh!" invites the latest poster.)

A possible explanation for the impossible, self-contradictory creatures and plots of these films is that their creators do not think it could matter to anyone: the monsters are unnatural—or unnaturalness—anyway, and the calculated response is "Quick! Kill it, before it reproduces!" (Poor Andre, poor Thing.) The assumption may be partially correct, and if many people like this sort of entertainment, the clear impossibility of creatures and plots may help ease the conscience. If the monsters are anything, they are evil conveniently objectified. But the "evils" that they represent, while sometimes pain and death, are just as often man's power, knowledge, and intelligence. Their part used to be played by the Devil or his demons. The destruction of the Things and of the mad scientists, and the senseless martyrdoms of the more rare "good" (if not "sane") scientists, resembles nothing so much as exorcism and the burning of witches and heretics.

Unfortunately, science fiction films have associated science, the future, the different, and the unknown with nothing but irrational fear. There are enough dangers; in these films the dangers are not natural, but impossible and monstrous—of the same character as those that one was believed to risk when, in another time, one forsook the True Faith for the Black Arts. What the equivalent of the Black Arts is imagined to be is often all too clear in each film. But the True Faith is never plainly shown, perhaps because if it is anything at all, it is simply an absence of any thinking.

NOTES

1. Robert Heinlein, "Shooting *Destination Moon*," *Astounding Science Fiction* 45, no. 5 (1950): 18. Reprinted in *The Science Fiction Film*, edited by William Johnson (Englewood Cliffs, NJ: Prentice Hall, 1972), 52–64.

2. George Pal, "Filming *War of the Worlds*," *Astounding Science Fiction* 52, no. 2 (1953): 100–111.

3. It may be pointed out that Wells's Martians shared this improbable habit, but they were not vegetable bipeds, and that was about fifty years before.

4. Vague approval of this film is found even today, when its "novelty" is no excuse. For instance, Frank Hauser, although aware of the fiction of Bradbury and Heinlein, makes this wild understatement: "The film, unfortunately, is not a complete success." "Science Fiction Films," in *International Film Annual*, no. 2, edited by William Whitebait (New York: Doubleday, 1958), 88.

5. *The Creature Walks among Us*, the third film in the series, was released in 1956. [Editors' note.]

6. Damon Knight, *In Search of Wonder: Essays on Modern Science Fiction* (Chicago: Advent, 1956), 283.

7. George Langelaan, "The Fly," *Playboy*, June 1957, 17–18, 22, 36, 38, 46, 64–68. Reprinted in *The Ghouls*, edited by Peter Haining (New York: Pocket Books, 1972), 251–284.

8. In the story, Andre attempts to rectify this error and merely mixes himself with the vanished cat as well as the housefly; this explains why the author did away with the cat, if not how. No doubt the makers of the film considered this too complicated, but retained the cat's disappearance for the unique poignancy of the scene.

9. In *The Return of the Fly*, the same thing happens, and the moral is the same.

10. Don Fabun, "Science Fiction in Motion Pictures, Radio, and Television," in *Modern Science Fiction: Its Meaning and Its Future*, edited by Reginald Bretnor, 43–70 (New York: Coward-McCann, 1953), 70.

11. Despite his success with *La belle et le bête* (*Beauty and the Beast* [1946]), Cocteau had trouble obtaining backing for *Orpheus*.

CHAPTER 16

THE IMAGINATION OF DISASTER

SUSAN SONTAG

THE TYPICAL SCIENCE FICTION film has a form as predictable as a western and is made up of elements that, to a practiced eye, are as classic as the saloon brawl, the blonde schoolteacher from the East, and the gun duel on the deserted main street.

One model scenario proceeds through five phases.

(1) The arrival of the thing (emergence of the monsters, landing of the alien spaceship, etc.). This is usually witnessed or suspected by just one person, a young scientist on a field trip. Nobody, neither his neighbors nor his colleagues, will believe him for some time. The hero is not married, but has a sympathetic though also incredulous girlfriend.

(2) Confirmation of the hero's report by a host of witnesses to a great act of destruction (if the invaders are beings from another planet, a fruitless attempt to parley with them and get them to leave peacefully). The local police are summoned to deal with the situation and massacred.

(3) In the capital of the country, conferences between scientists and the military take place, with the hero lecturing before a chart, map, or blackboard. A national emergency is declared. Reports of further destruction. Authorities from other countries arrive in black limousines. All international tensions are suspended in view of the planetary emergency. This stage often includes a rapid montage of news broadcasts in various languages, a meeting at the UN, and more

Susan Sontag, "The Imagination of Disaster," *Commentary* (October 1965): 42–48.

conferences between the military and the scientists. Plans are made for destroying the enemy.

(4) Further atrocities. At some point the hero's girlfriend is in grave danger. Massive counterattacks by international forces, with brilliant displays of rocketry, rays, and other advanced weapons, are all unsuccessful. Enormous military casualties, usually by incineration. Cities are destroyed and/or evacuated. There is an obligatory scene here of panicked crowds stampeding along a highway or a big bridge, being waved on by numerous policemen who, if the film is Japanese, are immaculately white-gloved, preternaturally calm, and call out in dubbed English, "Keep moving. There is no need to be alarmed."

(5) More conferences, whose motif is: "They must be vulnerable to something." Throughout the hero has been working in his lab to this end. The final strategy, upon which all hopes depend, is drawn up; the ultimate weapon—often a superpowerful, as yet untested, nuclear device—is mounted. Countdown. Final repulse of the monster or invaders. Mutual congratulations, while the hero and girlfriend embrace cheek to cheek and scan the skies sturdily. "But have we seen the last of them?"

The film I have just described should be in color and on a wide screen. Another typical scenario, which follows, is simpler and suited to black-and-white films with a lower budget. It has four phases.

(1) The hero (usually, but not always, a scientist) and his girlfriend, or his wife and two children, are disporting themselves in some innocent, ultranormal middle-class surroundings—their house in a small town or on vacation (camping, boating). Suddenly, someone starts behaving strangely, or some innocent form of vegetation becomes monstrously enlarged and ambulatory. If a character is pictured driving an automobile, something gruesome looms up in the middle of the road. If it is night, strange lights hurtle across the sky.

(2) After following the thing's tracks, or determining that It is radioactive, or poking around a huge crater—in short, conducting some sort of crude investigation—the hero tries to warn the local authorities, without effect; nobody believes anything is amiss. The hero knows better. If the thing is tangible, the house is elaborately barricaded. If the invading alien is an invisible parasite, a doctor or friend is called in, who is himself rather quickly killed or "taken possession of" by the thing.

(3) The advice of whoever further is consulted proves useless. Meanwhile, It continues to claim other victims in the town, which remains implausibly isolated from the rest of the world. General helplessness.

(4) One of two possibilities: either the hero prepares to do battle alone, accidentally discovers the thing's one vulnerable point, and destroys it, or he somehow manages to get out of town and succeeds in laying his case before competent authorities. They, along the lines of the first script but abridged, deploy a complex technology that (after initial setbacks) finally prevails against the invaders.

Another version of the second script opens with the scientist-hero in his laboratory, which is located in the basement or on the grounds of his tasteful, prosperous house. Through his experiments, he unwittingly causes a frightful metamorphosis in some class of plants or animals that turn carnivorous and go on a rampage. Or else his experiments have caused him to be injured (sometimes irrevocably) or "invaded" himself. Perhaps he has been experimenting with radiation or has built a machine to communicate with beings from other planets or transport him to other places or times.

Another version of the first script involves the discovery of some fundamental alteration in the conditions of existence of our planet, brought about by nuclear testing, which will lead to the extinction in a few months of all human life. For example, the temperature of the Earth is becoming too high or too low to support life, or the Earth is cracking in two, or it is gradually being blanketed by lethal fallout.

A third script, somewhat but not altogether different from the first two, concerns a journey through space—to the moon or some other planet. What the space voyagers discover commonly is that the alien terrain is in a state of dire emergency, itself threatened by extraplanetary invaders or nearing extinction through the practice of nuclear warfare. The terminal dramas of the first and second scripts are played out there, to which is added the problem of getting away from the doomed or hostile planet and back to Earth.

I AM AWARE, OF COURSE, that there are thousands of science fiction novels (their heyday was the late 1940s), not to mention the transcriptions of science fiction themes that, more and more, provide the principal subject matter of comic books. But I propose to discuss science fiction films (the present period began in 1950 and continues, considerably abated, to this day) as an independent subgenre, without reference to other media—

FIGURE 36. *The Beast from 20,000 Fathoms* (1953) displays the conventional plot of monster movies.

and, most particularly, without reference to the novels from which, in many cases, they were adapted. While novel and film may share the same plot, the fundamental difference between the resources of the novel and the film makes them quite dissimilar.

Certainly, compared with the science fiction novels, their film counterparts have unique strengths, one of which is the immediate representation of the extraordinary: physical deformity and mutation, missile and rocket combat, toppling skyscrapers. The movies are, naturally, weak just where the science fiction novels (some of them) are strong—on science. But in place of an intellectual workout, they can supply something the novels can never provide—sensuous elaboration. In the films it is by means of images and sounds, not words that have to be translated by the imagination, that one can participate in the fantasy of living through one's own death and more, the death of cities, the destruction of humanity itself.

Science fiction films are not about science. They are about disaster, which is one of the oldest subjects of art. In science fiction films disaster is rarely viewed intensively; it is always extensive. It is a matter of quantity and ingenuity. If you will, it is a question of scale. But the scale, particu-

larly in the wide-screen color films (of which the ones by Japanese director Inoshiro Honda and American director George Pal are technically the
most convincing and visually the most exciting), does raise the matter to
another level.

Thus, the science fiction film (like that of a very different contemporary
genre, the Happening) is concerned with the aesthetics of destruction,
with the peculiar beauties to be found in wreaking havoc, making a mess.
And it is in the imagery of destruction that the core of a good science fiction film lies. Hence, the disadvantage of the cheap film—in which the
monster appears or the rocket lands in a small dull-looking town. (Hollywood budgetary needs usually dictate that the town be in the Arizona or
California desert. In *The Thing from Another World* [1951] the rather sleazy
and confined set is supposed to be an encampment near the North Pole.)

Still, good black-and-white science fiction films have been made. But
a bigger budget, which usually means color, allows a much greater play
back and forth among several model environments. There is the populous
city. There is the lavish but ascetic interior of the spaceship—either the
invaders' or ours—replete with streamlined chromium fixtures and dials
and machines whose complexity is indicated by the number of colored
lights they flash and strange noises they emit. There is the laboratory
crowded with formidable boxes and scientific apparatuses. There is a comparatively old-fashioned-looking conference room, where the scientists
unfurl charts to explain the desperate state of things to the military. And
each of these standard locales or backgrounds is subject to two modali-
ties—intact and destroyed. We may, if we are lucky, be treated to a panorama of melting tanks, flying bodies, crashing walls, awesome craters and
fissures in the earth, plummeting spacecraft, colorful deadly rays, and to a
symphony of screams, weird electronic signals, the noisiest military hardware going, and the leaden tones of the laconic denizens of alien planets
and their subjugated earthlings.

Certain of the primitive gratifications of science fiction films—for instance, the depiction of urban disaster on a colossally magnified scale—
are shared with other types of films. Visually, there is little difference between mass havoc as represented in the old horror and monster films and
what we find in science fiction films, except (again) scale. In the old monster films, the monster always headed for the great city, where he had to do
a fair bit of rampaging, hurling buses off bridges, crumpling trains in his
bare hands, toppling buildings, and so forth. The archetype is King Kong,
in Schoedsack and Cooper's great film of 1933, running amok, first in the
native village (trampling babies, a bit of footage excised from most prints),

then in New York. This is really no different in spirit from the scene in Inoshiro Honda's *Rodan* (1957) in which two giant reptiles—with a wingspan of five hundred feet and supersonic speeds—by flapping their wings whip up a cyclone that blows most of Tokyo to smithereens. Or the destruction of half of Japan by the gigantic robot with the great incinerating ray that shoots forth from his eyes, at the beginning of Honda's *The Mysterians* (1959). Or the devastation by the rays from a fleet of flying saucers of New York, Paris, and Tokyo in *Battle in Outer Space* (1960). Or the inundation of New York in *When Worlds Collide* (1951). Or the end of London in 1966 depicted in George Pal's *The Time Machine* (1960). Neither do these sequences differ in aesthetic intention from the destruction scenes in the big sword, sandal, and orgy color spectaculars set in biblical and Roman times—the end of Sodom in Aldrich's *Sodom and Gomorrah* (1962), of Gaza in DeMille's *Samson and Delilah* (1949), of Rhodes in *The Colossus of Rhodes* (1961), and of Rome in a dozen Nero movies. Griffith began it with the Babylon sequence in *Intolerance* (1916), and to this day there is nothing like the thrill of watching all those expensive sets come tumbling down.

In other respects as well, the science fiction films of the 1950s take up familiar themes. The famous 1930s movie serials and comics of the adventures of Flash Gordon and Buck Rogers, as well as the more recent spate of comic book superheroes with extraterrestrial origins (the most famous is Superman, a foundling from the planet Krypton, currently described as having been exploded by a nuclear blast), share motifs with more recent science fiction movies. But there is an important difference. The old science fiction films, and most of the comics, still have an essentially innocent relation to disaster. Mainly, they offer new versions of the oldest romance of all—of the strong, invulnerable hero with a mysterious lineage come to do battle on behalf of good and against evil. Recent science fiction films have a decided grimness, bolstered by their much greater degree of visual credibility, which contrasts strongly with the older films. Modern historical reality has greatly enlarged the imagination of disaster, and the protagonists—perhaps by the very nature of what is visited upon them— no longer seem wholly innocent.

The lure of such generalized disaster as a fantasy is that it releases one from normal obligations. The trump card of the end-of-the-world movies—like *The Day the Earth Caught Fire* (1962)—is that great scene with New York or London or Tokyo discovered empty, its entire population annihilated. Or, as in *The World, the Flesh, and the Devil* (1959), the whole movie can be devoted to the fantasy of occupying the deserted metropolis and starting all over again, a world Robinson Crusoe.

FIGURE 37. The fantasy of the deserted metropolis in *The World, the Flesh, and the Devil* (1959).

Another kind of satisfaction these films supply is extreme moral sim-plification—that is to say, a morally acceptable fantasy where one can give outlet to cruel or at least amoral feelings. In this respect, science fiction films partly overlap with horror films. This is the undeniable pleasure we derive from looking at freaks, beings excluded from the category of the human. The sense of superiority over the freak conjoined in varying proportions with the titillation of fear and aversion makes it possible for moral scruples to be lifted, for cruelty to be enjoyed. The same thing hap-pens in science fiction films. In the figure of the monster from outer space, the freakish, the ugly, and the predatory all converge—and provide a fantasy target for righteous bellicosity to discharge itself and for the aes-thetic enjoyment of suffering and disaster. Science fiction films are one of the purest forms of spectacle; that is, we are rarely inside anyone's feel-ings. (An exception is Jack Arnold's *The Incredible Shrinking Man* [1957].) We are merely spectators; we watch.

But in science fiction films, unlike horror films, there is not much hor-ror. Suspense, shocks, surprises are mostly abjured in favor of a steady, inexorable plot. Science fiction films invite a dispassionate, aesthetic view of destruction and violence—a technological view. Things, objects, machinery play a major role in these films. A greater range of ethical values is embodied in the decor of these films than in the people. Things, rather than the helpless humans, are the locus of values because we experience them, rather than people, as the sources of power. According to science fiction films, man is naked without his artifacts. They stand for different values, they are potent, they are what get destroyed, and they are the indispensable tools for the repulse of the alien invaders or the repair of the damaged environment.

THE SCIENCE FICTION FILMS are strongly moralistic. The standard message is the one about the proper, or humane, use of science versus the mad, obsessional use of science. This message the science fiction films share in common with the classic horror films of the 1930s, like *Frankenstein* (1931), *The Mummy* (1932), *Island of Lost Souls* (1932), and *Dr. Jekyll and Mr. Hyde* (1931). (George Franju's brilliant *Les yeux sans visage* [*Eyes without a Face / The Horror Chamber of Doctor Faustus* (1960)] is a more recent example.) In the horror films, we have the mad or obsessed or misguided scientist who pursues his experiments against good advice to the contrary, creates a monster or monsters, and is himself destroyed—often recognizing his folly himself and dying in the successful effort to destroy his own creation. One science fiction equivalent of this is the scientist, usually a member of a team, who defects to the planetary invaders because "their" science is more advanced than "ours."

This is the case in *The Mysterians*, and, true to form, the renegade sees his error in the end, and from within the Mysterian spaceship destroys it and himself. In *This Island Earth* (1955), the inhabitants of the beleaguered planet Metaluna propose to conquer Earth, but their project is foiled by a Metalunan scientist named Exeter who, having lived on Earth a while and learned to love Mozart, cannot abide such viciousness. Exeter plunges his spaceship into the ocean after returning a glamorous pair (male and female) of American physicists to Earth. Metaluna dies. In *The Fly* (1958), the hero, engrossed in his basement-laboratory experiments on a matter-transmitting machine, uses himself as a subject, exchanges head and one arm with a housefly that had accidentally gotten into the machine, becomes a monster, and with his last shred of human will destroys his laboratory and orders his wife to kill him. His discovery, for the good of mankind, is lost.

Being a clearly labeled species of intellectual, scientists in science fiction films are always liable to crack up or go off the deep end. In *Conquest of Space* (1955), the scientist-commander of an international expedition to Mars suddenly acquires scruples about the blasphemy involved in the undertaking and begins reading the Bible midjourney instead of attending to his duties. The commander's son, who is his junior officer and always addresses his father as "General," is forced to kill the old man when he tries to prevent the ship from landing on Mars. In this film, both sides of the ambivalence toward scientists are given voice. Generally, for a scientific enterprise to be treated entirely sympathetically in these films, it needs the certificate of utility. Science, viewed without ambivalence, means an efficacious response to danger. Disinterested intellectual curiosity rarely appears in any form other than caricature, as a maniacal dementia that cuts one off from normal human relations. But this suspicion is usually directed at the scientist rather than his work. The creative scientist may become a martyr to his own discovery, through an accident or by pushing things too far. But the implication remains that other men, less imaginative—in short, technicians—could have administered the same discovery better and more safely. The most ingrained contemporary mistrust of the intellect is visited, in these movies, upon the scientist-as-intellectual.

The message that the scientist is one who releases forces that, if not controlled for good, could destroy man himself seems innocuous enough. One of the oldest images of the scientist is Shakespeare's Prospero, the overdetached scholar forcibly retired from society to a desert island, only partly in control of the magic forces in which he dabbles. Equally classic is the figure of the scientist as satanist (Doctor Faustus and stories of Poe and Hawthorne). Science is magic, and man has always known that there is black magic as well as white. But it is not enough to remark that contemporary attitudes—as reflected in science fiction films—remain ambivalent, that the scientist is treated as both satanist and savior. The proportions have changed, because of the new context in which the old admiration and fear of the scientist are located. His sphere of influence is no longer local, himself or his immediate community. It is planetary, cosmic.

ONE GETS THE FEELING, particularly in the Japanese films but not only there, that a mass trauma exists over the use of nuclear weapons and the possibility of future nuclear wars. Most of the science fiction films bear witness to this trauma and, in a way, attempt to exorcise it.

The accidental awakening of the superdestructive monster who has slept in the earth since prehistory is, often, an obvious metaphor for the Bomb. But there are many explicit references as well. In *The Mysterians*, a probe ship from the planet Mysteroid has landed on Earth, near Tokyo.

FIGURE 38. The aliens attack in *The Mysterians* (1957).

Nuclear warfare having been practiced on Mysteroid for centuries (their civilization is "more advanced than ours"), 90 percent of those now born on the planet have to be destroyed at birth because of defects caused by the huge amounts of strontium-90 in their diet. The Mysterians have come to Earth to marry Earth women and possibly to take over our relatively un-contaminated planet. . . . In *The Incredible Shrinking Man*, the John Doe hero is the victim of a gust of radiation that blows over the water while he is out boating with his wife; the radiation causes him to grow smaller and smaller, until at the end of the movie he steps through the fine mesh of a window screen to become "the infinitely small." . . . In *Rodan*, a horde of monstrous carnivorous prehistoric insects, and finally a pair of giant flying reptiles (the prehistoric Archeopteryx), are hatched from dormant eggs in the depths of a mine shaft by the impact of nuclear test explosions and go on to destroy a good part of the world before they are felled by the molten lava of a volcanic eruption. . . . In the English film *The Day the Earth Caught Fire*, two simultaneous hydrogen bomb tests by the United States and Russia change by eleven degrees the tilt of the earth on its axis and alter the earth's orbit so that it begins to approach the sun.

Radiation casualties—ultimately, the conception of the whole world as a casualty of nuclear testing and nuclear warfare—is the most ominous of all the notions with which science fiction films deal. Universes become ex-pendable. Worlds become contaminated, burned-out, exhausted, obsolete.

In *Rocketship X-M* (1950) explorers from Earth land on Mars, where they learn that atomic warfare has destroyed Martian civilization. In George Pal's *The War of the Worlds* (1953), reddish spindly alligator-skinned creatures from Mars invade Earth because their planet is becoming too cold to be inhabitable. In *This Island Earth*, also American, the planet Metaluna, whose population has long ago been driven underground by warfare, is dying under the missile attacks of an enemy planet. Stocks of uranium, which power the force field shielding Metaluna, have been used up, and an unsuccessful expedition is sent to Earth to enlist earth scientists to devise new sources for nuclear power. In Joseph Losey's *The Damned* (*These Are the Damned* [1961]), nine icy-cold radioactive children are being reared by a fanatical scientist in a dark cave on the English coast to be the only survivors of the inevitable nuclear Armageddon.

THERE IS A VAST AMOUNT OF wishful thinking in science fiction films, some of it touching, some of it depressing. Again and again, one detects the hunger for a "good war," which poses no moral problems, admits of no moral qualifications. The imagery of science fiction films will satisfy the most bellicose addict of war films, for a lot of the satisfactions of war films pass, untransformed, into science fiction films. Examples: the dogfights between earth "fighter rockets" and alien spacecraft in the *Battle in Outer Space*; the escalating firepower in the successive assaults upon the invaders in *The Mysterians*, which Dan Talbot correctly described as a nonstop holocaust; and the spectacular bombardment of the underground fortress of Metaluna in *This Island Earth*.

Yet at the same time, the bellicosity of science fiction films is neatly channeled into the yearning for peace, or for at least peaceful coexistence. Some scientist generally takes sententious note of the fact that it took the planetary invasion to make the warring nations of the earth come to their senses and suspend their own conflicts. One of the main themes of many science fiction films—the color ones usually, because they have the budget and resources to develop the military spectacle—is this UN fantasy, a fantasy of united warfare. (The same wishful UN theme cropped up in a recent spectacular that is not science fiction, *55 Days in Peking* [1963]. There, topically enough, the Chinese, the Boxers, play the role of Martian invaders who unite the earthmen, in this case the United States, England, Russia, France, Germany, Italy, and Japan.) A great-enough disaster cancels all enmities and calls upon the utmost concentration of Earth resources.

Science—technology—is conceived of as the great unifier. Thus, the science fiction films also project a Utopian fantasy. In the classic models of Utopian thinking—Plato's Republic, Campanella's City of the Sun, More's Utopia, Swift's Land of the Houyhnhnms, Voltaire's Eldorado—society had worked out a perfect consensus. In these societies reasonableness had achieved an unbreakable supremacy over the emotions. Since no disagreement or social conflict was intellectually plausible, none was possible. As in Melville's *Typee*, "they all think the same." The universal rule of reason meant universal agreement. It is interesting, too, that societies in which reason was pictured as totally ascendant were also traditionally pictured as having an ascetic or materially frugal and economically simple mode of life. But in the Utopian world community projected by science fiction films, totally pacified and ruled by scientific consensus, the demand for simplicity of material existence would be absurd.

YET ALONGSIDE THE HOPEFUL fantasy of moral simplification and international unity embodied in the science fiction films lurk the deepest anxieties about contemporary existence. I don't mean only the very real trauma of the Bomb—that it has been used, that there are enough now to kill everyone on earth many times over, that those new bombs may very well be used. Besides these new anxieties about physical disaster, the prospect of universal mutilation and even annihilation, the science fiction films reflect powerful anxieties about the condition of the individual psyche.

Science fiction films may also be described as a popular mythology for the contemporary negative imagination about the impersonal. The otherworld creatures that seek to take "us" over are an "it," not a "they." The planetary invaders are usually zombielike. Their movements are either cool, mechanical, or lumbering, blobby. But it amounts to the same thing. If they are nonhuman in form, they proceed with an absolutely regular, unalterable movement (unalterable save by destruction). If they are human in form—dressed in space suits, and so forth—then they obey the most rigid military discipline and display no personal characteristics whatsoever. And it is this regime of emotionlessness, of impersonality, of regimentation, which they will impose on Earth if they are successful. "No more love, no more beauty, no more pain," boasts a converted earthling in the *Invasion of the Body Snatchers* (1956). The half-earthling, half-alien children in *Children of the Damned* (1964) are absolutely emotionless, move as a group and understand each other's thoughts, and are all prodigious intellects. They are the wave of the future, man in his next stage of development.

These alien invaders practice a crime that is worse than murder. They do not simply kill the person. They obliterate him. In *The War of the Worlds*, the ray that issues from the rocket ship disintegrates all persons and objects in its path, leaving no trace of them but a light ash. In Honda's *The H-Man* (1959), the creeping blob melts all flesh with which it comes in contact. If the blob, which looks like a huge hunk of red Jello and can crawl across floors and up and down walls, so much as touches your bare foot, all that is left of you is a heap of clothes on the floor. (A more articulated, size-multiplying blob is the villain in the English film *The Creeping Unknown* [1956].) In another version of this fantasy, the body is preserved, but the person is entirely reconstituted as the automatized servant or agent of the alien powers. This is, of course, the vampire fantasy in new dress. The person is really dead, but he doesn't know it. He is "undead"; he has become an "unperson." It happens to a whole California town in *Invasion of the Body Snatchers*, to several earth scientists in *This Island Earth*, and to assorted innocents in *It Came from Outer Space* (1953), *Attack of the Puppet People* (1958), and *The Brain Eaters* (1958). As the victim always backs away from the vampire's horrifying embrace, so in science fiction films the person always fights being "taken over"; he wants to retain his humanity. But once the deed has been done, the victim is eminently satisfied with his condition. He has not been converted from human amiability to monstrous "animal" bloodlust (a metaphoric exaggeration of sexual desire), as in the old vampire fantasy. No, he has simply become far more efficient—the very model of technocratic man, purged of emotions, volitionless, tranquil, obedient to all orders. (The dark secret behind human nature used to be the upsurge of the animal—as in *King Kong*. The threat to man, his availability to dehumanization, lay in his own animality. Now the danger is understood as residing in man's ability to be turned into a machine.)

The rule, of course, is that this horrible and irremediable form of murder can strike anyone in the film except the hero. The hero and his family, while greatly threatened, always escape this fate, and by the end of the film the invaders have been repulsed or destroyed. I know of only one exception, *The Day Mars Invaded Earth* (1963), in which after all the standard struggles, the scientist-hero, his wife, and their two children are "taken over" by the alien invaders—and that's that. (The last minutes of the film show them being incinerated by the Martians' rays and their ash silhouettes flushed down their empty swimming pool, while their simulacra drive off in the family car.) Another variant but upbeat switch on the rule occurs in *The Creation of the Humanoids* (1962), where the hero discovers at the end of the film that he, too, has been turned into a metal robot, complete with highly efficient and virtually indestructible mechanical insides, although he didn't know it and detected no difference in himself. He learns, however, that he will shortly be upgraded into a "humanoid," having all the properties of a real man.

Of all the standard motifs of science fiction films, this theme of dehumanization is perhaps the most fascinating. As I have indicated, it is scarcely a black-and-white situation, as in the old vampire films. The attitude of the science fiction films toward depersonalization is mixed. On the one hand, they deplore it as the ultimate horror. On the other hand, certain characteristics of the dehumanized invaders, modulated and disguised—such as the ascendancy of reason over feelings, the idealization of teamwork and the consensus-creating activities of science, a marked degree of moral simplification—are precisely traits of the savior-scientist. It is interesting that when the scientist in these films is treated negatively, it is usually done through the portrayal of an individual scientist who holes up in his laboratory and neglects his fiancée or his loving wife and children, obsessed by his daring and dangerous experiments. The scientist as a loyal member of a team, and therefore considerably less individualized, is treated quite respectfully.

There is absolutely no social criticism, of even the most implicit kind, in science fiction films. No criticism, for example, of the conditions of our society that create the impersonality and dehumanization that science fiction fantasies displace onto the influence of an alien It. Also, the notion of science as a social activity, interlocking with social and political interests, is unacknowledged. Science is simply either adventure (for good or evil) or a technical response to danger. And, typically, when the fear of science is paramount—when science is conceived of as black magic rather than white—the evil has no attribution beyond that of the perverse will of an individual scientist. In science fiction films the antithesis of black magic and white is drawn as a split between technology, which is beneficent, and the errant individual will of a lone intellectual.

Thus, science fiction films can be looked at as thematically central allegory, replete with standard modern attitudes. The theme of depersonalization (being "taken over") that I have been talking about is a new allegory reflecting the age-old awareness of man that, sane, he is always perilously close to insanity and unreason. But there is something more here than just a recent popular image that expresses man's perennial, but largely unconscious, anxiety about his sanity. The image derives most of its power from a supplementary and historical anxiety, also not experienced consciously by most people, about the depersonalizing conditions of modern urban life. Similarly, it is not enough to note that science fiction allegories are one of the new myths about—that is, one of the ways of accommodating to and negating—the perennial human anxiety about death. (Myths of heaven and hell, and of ghosts, had the same function.) Again, there is a historically specifiable twist that intensifies the anxiety. I mean the trauma suffered by everyone in the middle of the twentieth century when it became clear that, from now on to the end of human history, every person would spend his individual life under the threat not only of individual death, which is certain, but of something almost insupportable psychologically—collective incineration and extinction that could come at any time, virtually without warning.

From a psychological point of view, the imagination of disaster does not greatly differ from one period in history to another. But from a political and moral point of view, it does. The expectation of the apocalypse may be the occasion for a radical disaffiliation from society, as when thousands of eastern European Jews in the seventeenth century, hearing that Sabbatai Zevi had been proclaimed the Messiah and that the end of the world was imminent, gave up their homes and businesses and began the trek to Palestine. But people take the news of their doom in diverse ways. It is reported that in 1945 the populace of Berlin received without great agitation the news that Hitler had decided to kill them all, before the Allies arrived, because they had not been worthy enough to win the war. We are, alas, more in the position of the Berliners of 1945 than of the Jews of seventeenth-century eastern Europe, and our response is closer to theirs, too. What I am suggesting is that the imagery of disaster in science fiction is above all the emblem of an inadequate response. I don't mean to bear down on the films for this. They themselves are only a sampling, stripped of sophistication, of the inadequacy of most people's response to the unassimilable terrors that infect their consciousness. The interest of the films, aside from their considerable amount of cinematic charm, consists in this intersection between a naive and largely debased commercial art product and the most profound dilemmas of the contemporary situation.

OURS IS INDEED AN age of extremity. For we live under continual threat of two equally fearful, but seemingly opposed, destinies: unremitting banality and inconceivable terror. It is fantasy, served out in large rations by the popular arts, that allows most people to cope with these twin specters. One job that fantasy can do is to lift us out of the unbearably humdrum and to distract us from terrors—real or anticipated—by an escape into exotic, dangerous situations that have last-minute happy endings. But another of the things that fantasy can do is to normalize what is psychologically unbearable, thereby inuring us to it. In one case, fantasy beautifies the world. In the other, it neutralizes it.

The fantasy in science fiction films does both jobs. The films reflect worldwide anxieties, and they serve to allay them. They inculcate a strange apathy concerning the processes of radiation, contamination, and destruction that I for one find haunting and depressing. The naive level of the films neatly tempers the sense of otherness, of alienness, with the grossly familiar. In particular, the dialogue of most science fiction films, which is of a monumental but often touching banality, makes them wonderfully, unintentionally funny. Lines like "Come quickly. There's a monster in my bathtub," "We must do something about this," "Wait, Professor. There's someone on the telephone," "But that's incredible," and the old American standby, "I hope it works!" are hilarious in the context of picturesque and deafening holocaust. Yet the films also contain something that is painful and in deadly earnest.

There is a sense in which all these movies are in complicity with the abhorrent. They neutralize it, as I have said. It is no more, perhaps, than the way all art draws its audience into a circle of complicity with the thing represented. But in these films we have to do with things that are (quite literally) unthinkable. Here, "thinking about the unthinkable"—not in the way of Herman Kahn, as a subject for calculation, but as a subject for fantasy—becomes, however inadvertently, itself a somewhat questionable act from a moral point of view. The films perpetuate clichés about identity, volition, power, knowledge, happiness, social consensus, guilt, and responsibility that are, to say the least, not serviceable in our present extremity. But collective nightmares cannot be banished by demonstrating that they are, intellectually and morally, fallacious. This nightmare—the one reflected, in various registers, in the science fiction films—is too close to our reality.

CHAPTER 17

EXTRAPOLATIVE CINEMA

IVOR A. ROGERS

THE SCIENCE FICTION FILM has been the "closet case" of the serious film critic. If the film is any good, it is seldom labeled SF, but every film that violates science, art, truth, and beauty is invariably mislabeled science fiction. This situation probably originated with a producer who, knowing nothing of science except that he "didn't understand it," constructed a potbellied syllogism (undistributed middle) of "Everything I don't understand is Science." This mutated to the point that every film that violated the canons of belief was labeled science fiction. The situation has not been helped by those film critics who seem to understand Krafft-Ebing better than the second law of thermodynamics. Indeed, there even seems to be a vogue in film criticism, which for want of a better term might be labeled the Buck Rogers Syndrome, that considers any film containing a space vehicle as fit fare for "children of all ages."

It is far past time to claim respectability for the science fiction or extrapolative film. As Susan Sontag pointed out in her rather uninformed but stimulating article "The Imagination of Disaster," it is relatively easy to represent visual catastrophe but quite difficult to provide an intellectual workout, which is the real mission and challenge of science fiction.[1]

Miss Sontag has clearly seen the failings and inadequacies of the films detailing the radioactive and hyperthyroid monsters that have been spawned in countless special effects laboratories. There is some question as to whether these films should even be considered as true science fiction, but Miss Sontag has failed to consider the best of the extrapolative films in her article.

Ivor A. Rogers, "Extrapolative Cinema," *Arts in Society* 6 (Summer–Fall 1969): 287–291. Reprinted by permission of University of Wisconsin–Extension.

As Carlos Clarens, a far more perceptive critic of the science fiction film, has observed, many recent films have turned away from the glorification of disaster and the placid recounting of technological marvels to a more mature introspection of man and his deeds.[2] This is partly due to the fact that important directors have begun to work in the genre. (A western directed by John Ford, while still in the western genre, has more depth and psychological significance than the average B western produced by Monogram or Republic.) With the advent of directors like Kubrick, Truffaut, Hitchcock, and Godard into the field, we are assured, if not better science fiction films, at least a higher level of craftsmanship. This influence has even been felt in television, where we are finally permitted to see "aliens from outer space" who are not foam-rubber abominations (*The Invaders* [1967–1968]) and a TV series (*Star Trek* [1966–1969]) that is willing to discuss serious themes in a nonhysterical fashion. *Star Trek* has on occasion even managed to produce a plausible love story—a feat hitherto achieved by only a few science fiction writers and French science fiction filmmakers.

To completely appreciate the extrapolative science fiction film, it is necessary to define the genre carefully so that we do not lump the latest crawler from the radioactive lagoon with such classics as *Metropolis* (1927), *Destination Moon* (1950), *Dr. Strangelove* (1964), and *2001: A Space Odyssey* (1968).

Even after eliminating the horror, vampire, and werewolf films as being alien to science fiction, there is still a large corpus of science fiction works that might be described as monster or "thing" films. Although there is often a scientist (mad) or two associated with these efforts, the net result is usually antiscientific in tone if not invariably in content. Science fiction writer Charles Beaumont once said of this type of film that it is easier to believe in a monster ape with a human brain than a monster producer with a human brain. There are a few films that attempt to work within the science fiction framework but are so carelessly researched and shoddily produced that they can scarcely be called *science* fiction. (It must be pointed out that even the best science fiction films often run into technical problems, not only because the proper speculation of today may be the scientific implausibility of tomorrow, but because most interplanetary epics are not yet able to shoot on location.) Eliminating the grosser examples of non–science fiction, there still remains a respectable core that may be considered science fiction extrapolative films. These may not all be outstanding works of art, but, freed from the onus of being associated with the mass of junk that has masqueraded under the science fiction label, they may be able to stand on their own as a genre worthy of critical notice.

Perhaps the most neglected subgenre of the science fiction film is the film of political extrapolation. Ranging from such borderline examples as *The Manchurian Candidate* (1962), *Advise & Consent* (1962), and *Seven Days in May* (1964) to obvious examples such as *Dr. Strangelove* and *On the Beach* (1959), these films attempt to explore the impacts of a hypothesized political event (a political assassination, the sudden death of the president during crucial international negotiations, a military coup, and the consequences of our military control over atomic weapons). While a few critics have asserted the political importance of some of these films, there has been no adequate study of them to compare, for example, with Susan Sontag's examination of the psychology of the "destruction" science fiction film.

Closely allied to the political extrapolation subgenre is the film of social extrapolation. This has been even less considered than the political films. One explanation is obvious: there are relatively few good films made in this genre—the best examples being the British film *The Man in the White Suit* (1951) and the recently released *Charly* (1968). This state of affairs is surprising since the science fiction story investigating the social consequences of a new invention or discovery is staple fare in fiction writing. We are living in an age where scientific and technological developments literally transformed both man and his environment, and one would expect some indication of this upheaval echoed in the mass media. Instead we get *Prudence and the Pill* (1968), which does no sociological investigating at all. *The Man in the White Suit* demonstrated that social exploration could be funny. *Seconds* (1966) indicated that Rock Hudson could even act a bit, and Joseph Losey's *The Damned* (*These Are the Damned* [1963]) proved that there was drama in the genre. It would appear that there is a vital need for cinematic exploration of many themes concerning the relationship of man to the scientific and technological changes in his environment. I can think of no film that adequately explores the impact of automation and computerization upon the individual, much less upon society as a whole. I strongly suspect that we have not yet seen the ultimate in the creation of the Cardpunchman, and it would certainly seem to be a most fertile subject for a filmmaker. Perhaps social extrapolation might be best approached by a fusion of the techniques of the documentary and the fictive film, but such a development awaits much more effort in the area and more recognition by critics of the importance of the genre.

Several critics have commented that the rash of monster destruction

FIGURE 39. *The Man in the White Suit* (1951): an example of humorous social comment in the science fiction film.

movies of the 1950s was a direct result of the anxiety created by living in an atomically armed society in which instant nuclear devastation was a constant threat. There is another pervasive anxiety in our scientific-technological civilization: the anxiety that results from the speed at which our society changes. Literary critics have noted that the development of the concept of the imaginary voyages to the moon and the planets was largely an outgrowth of the astronomical discoveries of the seventeenth century. In a real sense these fictive works enabled readers to allay growing fears of the future by presenting them in an imaginative form. By depicting what the future *may* bring, the reader/viewer can perhaps face the future and its uncertainties with a degree of equanimity.

J. M. (apparently Joseph Morgenstern) in the *Newsweek* review of *Charly* made the following rather astounding statement: "It is science fiction, or the art of the impossible, with all of its coarse ineptitude supposedly exonerated by the possibility that today's fiction will be tomorrow's science."[3] Whether J. M. means that science fiction is inept or the film is inept, he is still missing the point in implying that the only value of science fiction is predictive. Science fiction is also enjoyed because it can provide a good

FIGURE 40. *Destination Moon* (1950): the sense of wonder in science fiction.

adventure story (*Forbidden Planet* [1956]), because it can suggest a new sexual fillip (*Barbarella* [1968]), or because it can create a sense of wonder (*Destination Moon*). The history of extrapolative fiction would indicate that an author usually writes a wholly predictive tale (from *The Battle of Dorking* to *1984*) in order to help thwart the actual occurrence of the events he describes. If we frankly accept the idea that rocket ships and the other paraphernalia of the space epic are standard genre devices, as the butler and the locked room are genre devices of the mystery story, and if we recognize the sociological implications of science fiction upon an audience, we will be better able to evaluate science fiction films on a rational basis. To claim that a film is worthless because it is science fiction is an ad hominem argument at best; to downgrade a film because it allegedly does poorly what it never claimed to do is senseless.

Perhaps the most exciting type of extrapolative film may not even be true science fiction at all. It does not utilize the devices and speculations of technology but has its point of origin in the philosophy of science, mathematical speculation, and basic (as opposed to practical) science. The concept of time has since Einstein been a favorite subject of the mathematician and scientific philosopher, and some creative artists have found dramatic elements in this very abstract field of study. J. B. Priestley utilized the theories of the twentieth-century mathematician J. W. Dunne in a series of plays that proved to be immensely popular successes. It is just as well that the majority of these plays were never filmed, since they would have created chaos in the world of the film critic. It is a peculiarity of the mathematician that he may create a mathematical universe that has no congruence to the real world yet, because his construct has internal validity, be highly esteemed by his colleagues. (If you can understand minus numbers, this is apparent to you; if you were unable to grasp this concept, you probably had bad grades in high school algebra.) Most film critics, with both feet mired in the bog of reality, can turn quite hostile in their reviews when confronted with a filmic universe that is non-Euclidean or based on any order of imaginative reality. This may explain the mixed reaction given to Chris Marker's film *La jetée* (1962). If the film is to be faulted, it is because of oversimplification. It is a minor *recherche du temps perdu* with the added elements of catastrophic atomic disaster, a form of time travel, and a future civilization (attempting to avert the final destruction of mankind). It is also a love story of the bitter-ending-in-futility school with a wry ironic twist at the end. It has a fair amount of honesty in treatment and, at its best, reminds one of the early novels of Judith Merril.

While Marker's *La jetée* was a trivial exploration into the philosophy of time, *Last Year at Marienbad* (1961) was a full-scale effort. If understood as a true science fiction film, Marker's Bergsonesque study of time and remembrance opens the way for consideration of *Marienbad* as a film that is an authentic extrapolative exploration of time. It is no secret that both the writer-collaborator, Alain Robbe-Grillet, and the director, Alain Resnais, are interested in exploring the concepts of time and reality as the basis for artistic insight. I think that it was wrong for critics of this film to assert that the elimination of linear development and the stress on a sense of timelessness were techniques used to assert an artistic style: in fact, these creators are concerned with an investigation of the phenomenon more of time itself. This becomes apparent if one reads the novels of Robbe-Grillet, and some perceptive critics have noted Resnais's persistent preoccupation with time from *Nuit et brouillard* (*Night and Fog* [1955]) to *Muriel, ou, Le temps d'un retour* (1963). *Marienbad*, *Muriel*, and Antonioni's study of reality *Blow-Up* (1966) are creative works of genius in their own right, but if they are also considered as investigations into time-space, they achieve another dimension of significant sensibility.

There is one other genre I would like to discuss, and that is the group of films that attempt to make a philosophical comment on the nature of man and utilize the science fiction framework to isolate the characters from the realistic world. The science fiction premise of such films, while not integral to the structure of the story, still serves a vital artistic function. Just as the phrase "once upon a time" plays a very valid role in a narrative, so, too, the casting of a film into the science fiction mold can serve as a most useful plotting device.

The sense of isolation developed in the novel (and in the film version by Peter Brook) of *Lord of the Flies* (1963) is due largely to the science fictional atomic war framework of the story. It is possible that a group of boys could have been shipwrecked on a remote island in a realistic version of the story without damaging the suspension of disbelief, but the impact of the pessimistic ending would have been considerably weakened. The bestiality and conflict of the young boys echo their elders' fatal involvement in an atomic war, and the only intrusions into their primitive world are reminders of this tragic occurrence (the dead pilot and the rescuers from a warship). William Golding is able to utilize similar techniques of isolation from reality in *Pincher Martin* and *Free Fall*, and an isolation in time in *The Inheritors*, but the only successful dramatization of his work (if we except his comedy *The Brass Butterfly*) is in the science fiction framework of the film version of *Lord of the Flies*.

Stanley Kubrick has twice used the science fiction framework for his films: once for the bitterly satirical, politically oriented *Dr. Strangelove* and most recently for the incomparably superior *2001: A Space Odyssey*. Perhaps the only fantastic element of *2001* is the reception given the film by the critics. Bitterly attacked by most of the critics in the science fiction press and fan publications and greeted by the majority of film critics with massive incomprehension, the film is not a zap-zap action-suspense story as evidently expected by science fiction fans or a comment on God (as most film critics—confronted by a non-Freudian universe—seem to have expected on the basis of their own subconscious urgings).

It is simply a story of Man, epic in its simplicity, and breathtakingly cinematic in its recounting. We have in the reaction of both specialized groups a feast-and-famine problem. The science fiction fans, long accustomed to brilliantly orchestrated set pieces of scientific extrapolation by such authors as Hal Clement and Robert Heinlein (whose fictive universes are so minutely detailed that a cosmic engineer would have little trouble in constructing a world to their specifications), were taken aback by seeing a film in which the speculation was philosophical rather than technological. The film critics, with Pavlovian responses reinforced by

FIGURE 41. *2001: A Space Odyssey* (1968): an epic story of Man.

countless monster and radioactive destruction films, turned to rend another "spaceship picture."

The film is not an unqualified success: at times it moves with the ponderous tread of a brontosaurus, certain portions of the first episode may be most charitably described as unfortunate, and the internal logic of the film is not always what one would expect of either Clarke or Kubrick. As always, there is the cry that "you should have seen it before it was cut by the commercializers," and there may be a certain justification in the claim this time, but all errors and flaws included, it is still the most successfully ambitious film since the introduction of sound.

What Kubrick has apparently attempted is to utilize the trappings of science and technology as a framework for his comment upon the nature of man. The basic premise—that preman was helped in his development from the ape to man the toolmaker by some "alien" race or entity, and, now that he has almost reached the peak of his powers as *Homo faber*, is about to be given a further boost into what can best be called *Homo superior*—was originally conceived by Kubrick's collaborator, Arthur C. Clarke. Film critics not familiar with the writing of Clarke should be as wary as those science fiction critics who are not familiar with the films of Kubrick. The indications are that this was a true collaboration and that each man provided an artistic stimulus for the other—a true blending of art and science-technology. The final version of the film goes far beyond the bald statement of plot that would have been very satisfying to the reader of printed science fiction and totally bewildering to the average filmgoer, because the film attempts to make a comment on the plot: it says simply that the construction of bigger and better tools is not the sole purpose of human existence. The film is not antiscientific; it is antitech-nological. The berserk computer is not a stab at science, but a reminder that tools are not gods. The film is not about man and God; it is about man and his friends in the universe. God and his strictures are not mentioned in the film, but one is left with an optimistic wish-fantasy that there are hope and reason in the universe and an admonition that the machine can be a useful companion but should not be deified.

Sir Charles Snow commented on the division of the world of intelli-gence into two cultures that are unable to communicate or aid each other in their struggle to comprehend the universe.[4] Science fiction has been conceived as a bridge between these two cultures, and it is deplorable that in practice the science fiction film has been responsible for the erec-tion of more walls than bridges. Partly it is the fault of the commercial filmmakers who find it more rewarding to build another rubber monster than to use their imaginations; partly it is the fault of the audiences who will pay money to see another abomination from outer space; partly it is the fault of those film critics who apparently can see artistic quality only in sin, sex, and sadism; and partly it may be the fault of our materialis-tic society that considers imagination and the imaginative as fit only for children.

NOTES

1. Susan Sontag, "The Imagination of Disaster," reprinted in this volume. [Editors' note.]

2. Carlos Clarens, *An Illustrated History of the Horror Film* (New York: Capricorn, 1967), 162.

3. Joseph Morgenstern, "Maverick Enzyme," *Newsweek*, September 30, 1968, 96–97.

4. See C. P. Snow, *The Two Cultures and a Second Look* (Cambridge: Cambridge University Press, 1962).

CHAPTER 18

EVEN A MAN WHO IS PURE AT HEART: POETRY AND DANGER IN THE HORROR FILM

R. H. W. DILLARD

WE ARE SITTING, you and I, in the plush (if somewhat worn) seats of a darkened movie house—featureless, all of us seated in rows, hearing the first dark chords of a somber score, waiting for the hard grin of death's skull to chill us all to the bone that will outlast our flesh and set on end our hair that legend says will grow long after we are dead.

And on the screen, dark figures move among the mists and tilting stones of a central European graveyard—a hunchbacked dwarf, a tall young man. There is the clank of shovels under a full moon. High, scudding clouds. The action is unclear. A body is raised from its rest, and heavy clods thump on the empty coffin lid. And somehow, a stone tower, the fury of a storm, the mad harmony of thunder, lightning, and the buzzing of machines that spit and crackle life into the shrouded figure on the table. It moves, first a hand, an arm; it rises and lurches unsteadily on sewn and cumbrous limbs. And its face is the face of death, the pain and incomprehensibility of death, the death that waits for us all.

For those of you who remember, who have seen the same films and dreamed the same dreams, I offer you here a voyage of shared memories, ones like that of Poe's traveler in "The Domain of Arnheim"—one that twists and winds loosely from recollection to idea, a voyage of discovery into a dark world where, maybe, with luck, we too can find a land "glittering in the red sunlight with a hundred oriels, minarets, and pinnacles;

and seeming the handiwork, conjointly, of the Sylphs, of the Fairies, of the Genii, and of the Gnomes."[1]

WHEN I WAS NINE YEARS OLD, my father took me to see my first horror film, a double feature, *Frankenstein* and *Dracula* (both 1931)—nurses in attendance at all performances and an ambulance parked and ready at the theater door. My grandmother had already frightened me with tales of the monster and his blind and destructive fury, but I was totally unprepared for what I saw: the open graves, the dead that walked, the dark as I had never pictured dark before. And heard: Count Dracula's poised and foreign voice, his mad victim crying out for spiders and dreaming of "acres and acres of rats." But, most of all, the monster, the poignancy of his reaching for the light, the horror of his wounded bellow, and the slowly dying embers of his flaming tomb.

I have shared that monster's fate more than once in my sleep, have feared him and been him in the same dream, and I suspect that perhaps even you have lived through a similar night. Or was it in the Carpathians as Count Dracula welcomed you to his webbed castle where you were to feel the light touch of teeth on your throat and were to rise at night yourself, undead and hot with a thirst for living blood? Or did you seek freedom from the wolf's curse that drove you, all shaggy hair and sharp fangs, through moonlit streets, hungry for death and life? Or did you linger, scarred and mad, in the catacombs of the Paris Opera or stalk the night protecting the mummified remains of a princess you loved thirty-seven hundred years ago? These dreams are as much a part of us now as the doubts of Hamlet or the frenzy of Lear. They come to us from a variety of sources—perhaps even, as Robert Eisler suggested in *Man into Wolf*, from "the subhuman animal strata of the 'collective unconscious.'"[2] But certainly they have come most clearly to us today from the films of our youth, the horror movies we sat through eagerly showing after showing and dreamed of during those hectic nights that found us shivering under covers even in a hot and sultry summer.

There is a Shamanist myth that tells of a boy, innocent of women yet ready for manhood, coming to his uncle, the Bwili of Lol-narong. In a ritual rich in symbolic significance, the uncle severs the boy's limbs from his body as they both laugh. Even the boy's head, cut from his body, continues to laugh, and with the affirmation of the boy's trust and of their laughter together the uncle restores the boy whole and a man. This primitive tale contains within it the essence of sacrificial awakening, for in it the youth learns to live in a world of suffering and darkness and still be

FIGURE 42. *Frankenstein* (1931): a poetic initiation into the mysteries of life and death.

able to see the light by an act of personal faith and sacrifice and with the ministering wisdom of an older guide. The myth is magical and certainly unrealistic, but it is true to the essence of cruel experience if not to its daily details. It is a work of imaginative art, concerned with intuitive and emotional truth more than with surface fact. It satisfied those Shamanist believers simply because, in its mystery and magic, it rang true to life—it explained a phenomenon everyone knew but could not understand.

    Frankenstein and *Dracula*, that double bill of terror, operated for me in much the same way as the ritual of the Bwili of Lol-narong terrified and satisfied that young boy and the other members of his society. I am not claiming that I understood the initiation at the time, nor is what I am saying absolutely true. Certainly, those horror films were not my sole initiation into the realities of adult life—that initiation is a continuing one that runs from birth to death itself—but they were a part of that initiation, that fall into life that we all must experience time and again, and they were an important part, for they helped shape my imagination to life and free my dreams to art.

    James Agee, a film critic as well as a poet and novelist, seldom wrote of horror films, but on the few occasions that he did, he sensed the quality that makes the good ones real works of art. He wrote of Val Lewton's *The Body Snatcher* (1945) that it was a better film than *Isle of the Dead* (1945), the ending of which made it "as brutally frightening and gratifying a horror movie as I can remember" because "it explodes into an even finer, and a far more poetic, horror-climax." He enjoyed being frightened, but he preferred being frightened in a "poetic" manner. And again, when he reviewed Lewton's earlier *Curse of the Cat People* (1944) (a film that is presently high in the favor of devotees of art cinema), he spoke of it as "decent and human" in its concern with "the poetry and danger of childhood."[3] What exactly Agee meant by poetic would be difficult to say, but his use of the words *human* and *poetic* in conjunction with *horror* and *danger* is the key to what I believe to be the nature and function of the horror film as an art form.

To define "poetic" at all is a futile task, but the horror film is a part of the great imaginative tradition of art as opposed to the realistic tradition, and as such it shares an aesthetic approach to life with works of literature as varied as Spenser and Kafka, Poe and Lewis Carroll. This imaginative tradition is not of an essentially mimetic art, but rather of a re-creative art, one that fashions new worlds from the familiar pieces of the old, which gives us a world made new while still as ancient as before. As Poe, that most articulate of imaginative and Gothic aesthetic theorists, puts it: "Inspired by an ecstatic prescience of the glories beyond the grave, we struggle, by multiform combinations among the things and thoughts of Time, to attain a portion of that Loveliness whose very elements, perhaps, appertain to eternity alone."[4] The poetic may not have to appertain to eternity in quite Poe's way to be of this tradition, but it does have to concern itself with the nature of being beyond the simple facts of life, with the human spirit, and with what Poe called "Beauty" and Agee called "poetry and danger."

I suppose that all significant Western art, at least since the medieval period, has been directly concerned with the original Fall of man and the consequent introduction of sin and death into the world. Certainly, sin (or, if you prefer, human evil) and death must be the central concerns of any artist seriously involved with life; poetry can never be totally divorced from danger and still be of the highest order. The horror film is, at its best, as thoroughly and richly involved with the dark truths of sin and death as any art form has ever been, but its approach is that of parable and metaphor—an approach that enables it on occasion to achieve a metaphysical grandeur, but that also may explain why its failures are so very awful and indefensible.

Like a medieval morality play, the horror film deals with the central issue of Christian life—the struggle between the spirits of good and evil for the possession of man's immortal soul. In the morality play personified abstractions (Friendship, Knowledge, Evil Deeds, Good Deeds, Riches, Good Angel, Evil Angel, Death) argue for Vice and Virtue, and their actions free the soul to heaven or cast it down to hell. The plays were totally unrealistic and as completely serious, for they were attempts to image in the flesh on a stage the dreadful battle within the spirit between the divided forces of man's own nature—the love of God and other men versus the corrupt love of self and evil. To a medieval Catholic those plays were as true as art could ever be. The horror film is quite as unrealistic and, I believe, quite as concerned with the truth available to art.

If the morality play personified the elements of the human soul and set them forth for all to see in an instructive pageant, the horror film personifies those very elements in a dark and beautiful dream that, for all its vagueness and artificiality, is quite as instructive. The horror film is a pageant of death, the death that breeds in all things—entropy, mutability, and corruption. The morality play taught the method of salvation to which a Christian should adhere in order to pass through the temptations and sufferings of life to the peace and joy of union with God; Death was the dangerous and unexpected bailiff who cast man before the final bar of justice, and Death was, then, also the liberator to the new and true life of the spirit freed of the crippling results of the Fall. The horror film teaches an acceptance of the natural order of things and an affirmation of man's ability to cope with and even prevail over the evil of life that he can never hope to understand; death is the unknown and unknowable end to life, but it is also the natural and peaceful end to the turmoil and terror of life in a fallen world. To die in irredeemable sin is the primary danger in the morality play; to be unable to die and find peace and the possibility of heaven for the suffering spirit is the great danger in the horror film.

I have certainly set the horror film a mighty task—to make us accept death as the natural ending of life, an ending to be desired. But that task is really no more possible or impossible than any of the tasks art ever attempts. The bold method of the horror film is as old as Aristotle and older; it sets out to purge us of our fear of death by exposing us to death as we have never seen it before, by distorting the fact of death into all possible contortions to help us see its simple and natural reality. The mirror the horror film holds up to death is the distorting mirror of a deserted funhouse that frightens us out of fear and frees our fancy to find the truth more surely.

Death in the horror film is most often grotesque; innocent and guilty alike are slaughtered horribly—drained of their blood by vampires, strangled or flung aside casually by a mummy's hand or the sewn hand of a monster made from dead flesh and bone, mangled by a werewolf's teeth and claws, strangled by the severed hands of a dead man, given to savage and unnatural beasts by mad and sadistic scientists, burked by a body snatcher desperate for a fresh corpse, and on and hideously on. But what is more horrible, even death and the repose of the grave are impermanent; the dead rise or are disturbed in a variety of ways: they rise as vampires thirsting for blood, their mummified remains return after nearly four thousand years to seek revenge for the desecration of a princess's tomb, they are eaten by ghouls and snatched by body snatchers, their bodies are dissected and sewn together anew as a monster, they are enslaved as zombies, and, if nothing worse, they are dug up for inspection by those left fighting whatever evil killed them.

The central figure of the film, the monster or evil whatever his particular form, suffers perhaps worst of all from the failure of death, and his grotesque death not only saves the world he inhabits from his evil, but also frees him to a natural and permanent death from the painful striving of his unnatural life. The vampire is peaceful and his features calm and even beautiful once the stake is driven through his heart, his head severed, and his mouth stuffed with garlic; the Frankenstein monster's blundering search for understanding and love in a society that is horrified by him is at the only end it could possibly have; the mummy's centuries of living death are resolved by a true death; the madman is freed of his distorting insanity; the invisible man, whose invisibility imprisoned his mind as it freed his flesh, rests quietly and visibly. This peace, the peace of death, is the object and end of the horror film; it is not merely the peace that follows the destruction of an antagonist, for it benefits the villainous opponent as well as his heroic slayers.

The werewolf story is perhaps the clearest example of this important ambiguity of death in the horror film. The werewolf, whether we consider *Werewolf of London* (1935) or *The Wolf Man* (1941) or any of their long line of imitators, is the hero as well as the villain of the film. He is an innocent man who has been bitten by a werewolf and has, because of the supernatural properties of the bite, become a werewolf himself, doomed to change under the full moon into a wolf who must kill to stay alive. Through no action of his own, the evil and madness inherent in every fallen man are released in him, or, as the gypsy's poem in *The Wolf Man* has it:

FIGURE 43. *The Wolf Man* (1941) is at once monster, hero, and victim.

Even a man who is pure at heart
And says his prayers by night
May become a wolf when the wolfbane blooms
And the moon is full and bright.

He destroys life and hurts the one he loves, but he cannot stop himself.
As a wolf, he is a creature of blind animal evil; as a man, he suffers the
tortures of the damned, for he knows the evil he does and can do nothing
about it. Walking through a normal environment in a business suit, he
is separated only by the anguish of his face from the ordinary pattern of
natural life, a life made intensely beautiful in its mundanity by his separation from it and by the alienation of his darker self from all of its standards, its humanity, its simple decencies. He can die, as the best version
of the story has it, only by a wound from a silver weapon (a knife, a bullet,
the head of a cane) wielded by one who loves him dearly.

This situation makes great demands of the observer, the theatergoer
in his or her plush seat, for he or she must wish for the hero's victory, his

release from the curse, by desiring that he die, that he be killed by someone who loves him. Death itself, our final villain, must be made the instrument of the hero's salvation. This is a paradox worthy of the highest
art, for here the spiritual struggle of one man bursts out into the visible
world in hair, claws, and fangs, and the cruelty of man's love for his fel-
lows is painfully enacted in the murder of love, the sacrifice for the last
victory of the soul. When Lawrence Talbot lies in the arms of his father,
his evil pelt gone in death, he is no Oedipus or poisoned Hamlet, but his
story is akin to theirs—he is the victim of the nature of a fallen world, and
his death restores what order there is possible to that world. The act of
love that killed him was one of overwhelming sacrifice, and its victory is
paradoxical and incomprehensible to the reason of our normal world. The
werewolf film is a work of fantasy, and thus, to eyes and minds trained by
realistic standards, it seems a fragile and finally insignificant entertainment. But, whatever the merits of its performance, its form and lines are
sound. Its revelation of the dark and its affirmation of redeeming love
are valid; its metaphysics and its moral structure, whatever their variance
from theological standards, are true to the Christian understanding and
perhaps even, for those of you who demand it, to a modern existential
understanding of the quality of our lives, of the way things really are.

The other central figures in the best horror films, the ones that have
become a part of all our memories, are also victims as well as villains:
vampires who are undead by no choice of their own, monsters who are
placed in a world that doesn't want them and hates them, mummies who
are driven by a curse put on them by long-dead priests of a religion that
is also dead. All of these creatures find the victory of peace in the defeat
of death. And we are, then, doubly relieved at their deaths and perhaps
saddened, too. In this ambiguity the beauty lies, the poetry inextricably a
part of the danger.

But what of the living, those who survive the horrors and live on at the
end of the film? I said that the horror film (as, I suspect, all great art must)
affirms man's ability to cope with evil beyond his ken and even to prevail
over it. The elements of that enduring ability are two, a working combination of reason and faith, of practical understanding and belief. Neither is
properly efficacious without the other. Belief alone may save one's soul,
but it will give him only the direction for any temporal and practical victory. The priest and the superstitious gypsy are allied in belief, for they
both know that there are things in this world beyond the scope of reason
and of scientific thought. Their knowledge is ineffectual, however, because
it is too often fatalistic; they hold the devil in too high regard to strive to

foil him; they will pray for the dead, but they can offer little beyond spiritual solace to the living. Reason, too, is ineffectual, because it denies the existence of any evil that does not fit the immutable laws of a logical and orderly universe. The myriad doctors, scientists, and believers in a rational world are baffled by occurrences that can fit in no possible way into their system; they examine the happenings of the night by daylight and cannot understand the mysteries of the dark. Theirs is a more foolish innocence than that of the superstitious peasant, for their scientific optimism often leads them to deny evil as an active force in human affairs altogether.

Evil must be known to be combated, and the knowing must lead to respect for its power but never to fearful surrender to it. He who can fuse reason and belief into an imaginative and active force is the hero of the horror film, but he is neither the tragic hero nor the comic hero. He is not even the central figure of the story, for although he restores order by his action, he does not control the movement of events at all (no Hamlet is he, nor powerful Prospero). Rather, he copes with events beyond human control. He is the older and wiser guide who reveals the mystery to the votary. The usual pattern is that a young, intelligent person is suddenly faced with an evil beyond his grasp, an evil that does not usually shatter his will to resist but that a former teacher, a professor interested in the occult, a scientist, even on occasion a priest, arrives and teaches the young man to respect all truth no matter what its sources and to fight with what weapons are needed, whether they be the practical weapons of violent force or the incantations and rituals of primitive belief.

Edward Van Sloan is the actor who always seemed to be this heroic guide, perhaps because as Professor Abraham Van Helsing in *Dracula* he surely rendered most fully the strength of this figure—brave, intelligent, aware of the limitations of his humanity, but never faltering in his quest for securing the safety of those menaced by evil, for restoring order. He is a fully educated and practical man with an understanding of modern science and philosophy, but he never rejects the wisdom and beliefs of older orders and systems, whether they be the Transylvanian lore of vampires and werewolves, the curses of the ancient Egyptians (Van Sloan as Dr. Muller in *The Mummy* [1932]), or the old belief that there are directions in which man must not inquire and search too far without breaking the bounds set for him by God (again Van Sloan as Dr. Waldman in *Frankenstein*). He prevails over the personifications of evil, not because he is superior to it in power and appeal, but rather because he is human, weak, and fallen but continually striving to better himself and his world, to earn some of the love that is his by God's grace.

FIGURE 44. *Dracula* (1931): Dr. Van Helsing (Edward Van Sloan) confronts Count Dracula (Bela Lugosi).

The heroic man and the young people whom he guides fight for human values and the natural order of things, the right to live freely without submitting to evil and the right to die peacefully and forever. The evil they do battle with, for all its supernatural trappings, is also human—the vampires and werewolves, monsters and mummies are all human at source and are all personifications of that potentiality for evil and sin that is so much a part of us all. Hero and villain are much the same—both human, both flawed unto death—and the complexity of their struggle and the dark nature of the order recovered by that struggle give the horror film its moral and metaphysical weight. It is a morality play for our times, approaching the very paradox of human life in its fantastic simplicity. It is religious and as mysterious as all art finally proves to be; it transmutes danger into poetry and affirms humanity in the very face of horror. . . .

THERE IS ONE APPARENT contradiction in all this, one fact upon which all my pleadings stand or fall. The horror film is a meaningful and viable art form, concerned with the eternal verities, making them new. And the horror film, I have said, is almost a dead form, a genre of lifeless imitation after its one period of full blossom some twenty and more years ago.

The answer to that contradiction is simply that it is but another example of the unending paradox of art, that the very acts of making new must themselves continually be made new. The thirties and early forties were a time of social crisis and a dominance of artistic social realism. The horror film in America, much like the fiction of Kafka, Nabokov, and many of the surrealists, carried the burden of the imaginative tradition, the tradition of parable. The world war, its horrors, and the horrors of the years following it did not end the need for this kind of art; they did change its terms and forced, as the passage of time always does, another metamorphosis in the surfaces of the same familiar truths, the ones that never change, however much we may try.

Oddly enough, then, one reason that the pure horror film died is that its mode of truth making was so valid that it had to change. Another reason is that the use of the elements of fantasy and dream as a primary artistic technique has become so widespread today in all Western literature and art. Louis MacNeice noted, in his *Varieties of Parable*, that "parable writing is today the concern of only a minority. It is a growing minority and, I think, a very important one."[5] Beckett and Golding are his examples; others are easy to find: Gunter Grass and Tommaso Landolfi, J. R. R. Tolkien, John Hawkes, and Thomas Pynchon and, in film, Ingmar Bergman, whom Federico Fellini has called "a conjurer—half witch and half showman," and Fellini himself.[6] They have all explored in their art those ancient truths available to imagination beneath the surfaces of fact. These are the real descendants of James Whale and Tod Browning, Karloff and Lugosi, not the later horror films or even their science fiction offspring, good as some of them have been.

And perhaps in another way that line of aesthetic descent has been responsible for our failure to accord the horror films of the thirties and early forties the appreciation they truly earned and deserve. The later horror films (with the exception of several of the first Hammer films and an occasional film like Mario Bava's *Black Sunday* [1961]), with the unique talents of Barbara Steele, have been so very cheap and tawdry, so thoroughly meaningless and formless, that we have forgotten the quality of their forebears. Their illegitimate but obvious line of descent obscured the honorable but subtle true line, that line running from the rituals of primitive initiation and sacrifice perhaps to the mass itself and on to the morality play, the medieval and Renaissance allegory, the visions of the romantics, the dreams of Eden of the Victorians, and on to Kafka and the moderns, in America from Poe, Hawthorne, and Melville to Mark Twain, and on to the horror film, one of our major contributions to the literature of the fallen human spirit laid bare.

The horror film does, I am sure, deserve its historical position in that long and continuing tradition, and, I feel, those few superb films are still able to make truth new to those who can come to them fresh, who can see them without the accumulated refuse of their bastard offspring. Because they were made with care and sensitivity, they maintain their imaginative force, their danger, and their poetry.

And, too, there is something about us, even in an age of continually imminent nuclear destruction, that requires the particular dangers of the night and strange beasts that have prowled it in the lore of superstition and simple belief. Those dangers, supernatural as they may be, are always human and always reflect that human evil in us all, that failure of spirit and love that is the source of all evil. The drama of nuclear disaster shifts the focus away from man to his devices and is finally unsatisfactory in its attempt to exorcise the mortal terror of the human spirit. That is art's limitation and its value; it is and must always be human, of and about the truths of the human heart.

NOTES

1. Edgar Allan Poe, "The Domain of Arnheim," in *Complete Stories and Poems of Edgar Allan Poe* (Garden City, NY: Doubleday, 1966), 582.

2. Robert Eisler, *Man into Wolf: An Anthropological Interpretation of Sadism, Masochism and Lycanthropy* (London: Routledge and Kegan Paul, 1951), 44.

3. James Agee, *Agee on Film: Reviews and Comments* (New York: Beacon Press, 1964), 175, 86.

4. Edgar Allan Poe, "The Poetic Principle," in *Selected Prose, Poetry, and Eureka*, edited by W. H. Auden (San Francisco: Rinehart Press, 1950), 418.

5. Louis MacNeice, *Varieties of Parable* (Cambridge: Cambridge University Press, 1965), 25.

6. Federico Fellini, *Fellini on Fellini*, edited by Anna Keel and Christian Strich, translated by Isabel Quigley (New York: Delta, 1977), 99.

PART IV

CRIME AND PUNISHMENT

The history of crime films extends back to the period of early silent cinema, while gangster films, although having antecedents and influences, didn't establish clear conventions until after the coming of sound, when, as with slapstick comedy before, the genre experienced in the 1930s what many have regarded as its classic or "golden age," beginning with the release of *Little Caesar* (1931), *The Public Enemy* (1931), and *Scarface* (1932). While the sense of nostalgia in these essays is not nearly as pronounced as with the writing on silent comedy, there is an implicit notion of classical perfection, and John Baxter does conclude by proclaiming the death of the great gangster movies.

Part 4 begins with Robert Warshow's famous essay "The Gangster as Tragic Hero." Warshow was one of the first critics to write seriously about various forms of popular culture, including comic books and, of course, movies. In this essay, first published in *Partisan Review* in 1948, Warshow considers the gangster film as embodying the ideological tensions of American capitalist democracy, the figure of the gangster representing the drive for success while at the same time suffering the fate of the individual who rises above the crowd. Further, says Warshow, the conventional rise-and-fall narrative of the genre allows spectators to indulge their individualist impulses while at the same time satisfying their need for accepting social responsibility—a double satisfaction that is essential to the experience of several other genres as well.

Next, Claude Chabrol begins his essay "Evolution of the Thriller" (*policier*) by dismissing the formulaic gangster and mystery films of the period that ultimately merged to form the hard-boiled thriller that has attracted numerous talented directors. Chabrol was a major figure of the French nouvelle vague, and more than any of the other filmmakers associated with this group he worked within one particular genre, the crime film, in works such as *Le beau serge* (1958), inspired by Hitchcock's *Shadow of a Doubt* (1943); *Les biches* (1968); *La femme infidèle* (1969); and *Le boucher* (1970). Like Godard, François Truffaut,

Eric Rohmer, and Jacques Rivette, Chabrol wrote as a film critic for *Cahiers du Cinéma* before becoming a director, and, with Rohmer, he cowrote the first book of auteur criticism, *Hitchcock: The First Forty-Four Films* (1957), a thematic and stylistic analysis of the films made by Hitchcock up to *The Wrong Man* (1956). Among his most well-known pieces for *Cahiers* was the later article "Little Themes" ("Les petites sujets" [1959]), which may be, as James Monaco claims, "the shortest and most succinct defense of genre films ever published" in the pages of *Cahiers*, but it is also the magazine's most excessive defense of auteurism.[1] Thus, it is no surprise that in his essay here, from *Cahiers du Cinéma* in 1955, Chabrol, while aware of the genre's changing formulas, steadfastly ascribes responsibility for the most important thrillers to the personal vision of the directors who inflected them.

According to James Naremore, "In an important sense, the French invented the American film noir."[2] No work was responsible for this cultural influence more than *Panorama du film noir américain, 1941–1953* by two cineastes from the southern city of Toulouse, Raymond Borde and Etienne Chaumeton. First published in France in 1955, it was the first book on the genre, and, although not the first critical work to use the term *film noir*,[3] it persuasively argued for noir as a distinctive type of American film even before the concept was recognized as such by either American filmmakers or American audiences. In chapter 2 of their book, "Toward a Definition of Film Noir," reprinted here, Borde and Chaumeton argue for film noir as a series rather than a genre, a group of films bounded as much by time as by space—that is, rooted in a particular localized cultural moment—and the question of whether film noir is in fact a genre or mode, cycle or series, or attitude and tone that cut across genres has been debated ever since. While Borde and Chaumeton are especially interested in the portrayal of violence in film noir and go on to relate it to the postwar American context, their discussion anticipates the more recent and growing critical attention being given to the idea of series and cycles.[4]

Next, British film critic Raymond Durgnat provides a characteristically encyclopedic discussion of film noir, including its cultural antecedents, international variations, and taxonomy of cycles and themes. Less well known than Paul Schrader's somewhat similar piece on the various cultural influences that came together to form noir, published two years later, Durgnat's sometimes quirky comments in "Paint It Black: The Family Tree of the Film Noir," published in *Cinema* in 1970, often reveal surprising affinities between films that show the dynamics of the studio and genre systems at work. Durgnat worked apart from the developing schools of British film and cultural criticism, but his observations demonstrate a keen awareness of ideology nonetheless.

Part 4 and the book conclude with John Baxter's short introduction to his book *The Gangster Film*, which, like Durgnat's essay, was published in 1970, the year that, as we explain in our introduction to this volume, genre criticism entered a period of new productivity and theorization. While Baxter's aesthetic judgments about specific gangster films and the genre more generally remain largely implicit and mark him as less open to ongoing and possible developments than Durgnat, both writers, by seeking to circumscribe the genres they are writing about, begin from a position that assumes the existence and important place of film genres in the cinema and in film studies. Thus, their writing, like all the work included in this volume, contributed substantially to the theoretical and critical work in film genre to follow.

NOTES

1. James Monaco, *The New Wave: Truffaut, Godard, Chabrol, Rohmer, Rivette* (New York: Oxford University Press, 1976), 256. Chabrol's "Little Themes" is translated into English in *The New Wave*, edited by Peter Graham (Garden City, NY: Doubleday, 1968), 73–79.

2. James Naremore, "A Season in Hell; or, The Snows of Yesteryear?," introduction to *A Panorama of American Film Noir, 1941–1953*, by Raymond Borde and Etienne Chaumeton, translated by Paul Hammond (San Francisco: City Lights Books, 2002), ix.

3. The term's origin is generally credited to Nino Frank, in the essay "Un nouveau genre 'policier': L'aventure criminelle," *L'Ecran Français*, no. 61 (1946): 8–9, 14.

4. See, for example, Amanda Ann Klein, *American Film Cycles: Reframing Genres, Screening Social Problems, and Defining Subcultures* (Austin: University of Texas Press, 2011); Leger Grindon, "Cycles and Clusters: The Shape of Film Genre History," in *Film Genre Reader IV*, edited by Barry Keith Grant (Austin: University of Texas Press, 2012), 42–59; and Amanda Ann Klein and R. Barton Palmer, eds., *Cycles, Sequels, Spin-Offs, Remakes, and Reboots* (Austin: University of Texas Press, 2016).

CHAPTER 19

THE GANGSTER AS TRAGIC HERO

ROBERT WARSHOW

AMERICA, AS A SOCIAL AND political organization, is committed to a cheerful view of life. It could not be otherwise. The sense of tragedy is a luxury of aristocratic societies, where the face of the individual is not conceived of as having a direct and legitimate political importance, being determined by a fixed and suprapolitical—that is, noncontroversial—moral order or fate. Modern egalitarian societies, however, whether democratic or authoritarian in their political forms, always base themselves on the claim that they are making life happier; the avowed function of the modern state, at least in its ultimate terms, is not only to regulate social relations, but also to determine the quality and the possibilities of human life in general. Happiness thus becomes the chief political issue—in a sense, the only political issue—and for that reason it can never be treated as an issue at all. If an American or a Russian is unhappy, it implies a certain reprobation of his society, and therefore, by a logic of which we can all recognize the necessity, it becomes an obligation of citizenship to be cheerful; if the authorities find it necessary, the citizen may even be compelled to make a public display of his cheerfulness on important occasions, just as he may be conscripted into the army in time of war.

Naturally, this civic responsibility rests most strongly upon the organs of mass culture. The individual citizen may still be permitted his private unhappiness so long as it does not take on political significance, the extent of this tolerance being determined by how large an area of private life the society can accommodate. But every production of mass culture is a public act and must conform with accepted notions of the public good.

Robert Warshow, "The Gangster as Tragic Hero," *Partisan Review* 15, no. 2 (1948): 240–248. Reprinted by permission of Collier Associates, West Palm Beach, FL.

Nobody seriously questions the principle that it is the function of mass culture to maintain public morale, and certainly nobody in the mass audience objects to having his morale maintained.[1] At a time when the normal condition of the citizen is a state of anxiety, euphoria spreads over our culture like the broad smile of an idiot. In terms of attitudes toward life, there is very little difference between a "happy movie" like *Good News* (1947), which ignores death and suffering, and a "sad" movie like *A Tree Grows in Brooklyn* (1945), which uses death and suffering as incidents in the service of higher optimism.

But whatever its effectiveness as a source of consolation and a means of pressure for maintaining "positive" social attitudes, this optimism is fundamentally satisfying to no one, not even to those who would be most disoriented without its support. Even within the area of mass culture, there always exists a current of opposition, seeking to express by whatever means are available to it that sense of desperation and inevitable failure that optimism itself helps to create. Most often, this opposition is confined to rudimentary or semiliterate forms: in mob politics and journalism, for example, or in certain kinds of religious enthusiasm. When it does enter the field of art, it is likely to be disguised or attenuated: in an unspecific form of expression like jazz, in the basically harmless nihilism of the Marx Brothers, in the continually reasserted strain of hopelessness that often seems to be the real meaning of soap opera. The gangster film is remarkable in that it fills the need for disguise (though not sufficiently to avoid arousing uneasiness) without requiring any serious distortion. From its beginning, it has been a consistent and astonishingly complete presentation of the modern sense of tragedy.[2]

In its initial character, the gangster film is simply one example of the movies' constant tendency to create fixed dramatic patterns that can be repeated indefinitely with a reasonable expectation of profit. One gangster film follows another as one musical or one western follows another. But this rigidity is not necessarily opposed to the requirements of art. There have been very successful types of art in the past that developed such specific and detailed conventions as almost to make individual examples of the type interchangeable. This is true, for example, of Elizabethan revenge tragedy and Restoration comedy.

For such a type to be successful means that its conventions have imposed themselves upon the general consciousness and become the accepted vehicles of a particular set of attitudes and a particular aesthetic effect. One goes to any individual example of the type with very definite expectations, and originality is to be welcomed only to the degree that it intensifies the expected experience without fundamentally altering it. Moreover, the relationship between the conventions that go to make up such a type and the real experience of its audience or the real facts of whatever situation it pretends to describe is of only secondary importance and does not determine its aesthetic force. It is only in an ultimate sense that the type appeals to its audience's experience of reality; much more immediately, it appeals to previous experience of the type itself: it creates its own field of reference.

Thus, the importance of the gangster film, and the nature and intensity of its emotional and aesthetic impact, cannot be measured in terms of the place of the gangster himself or the importance of the problem of crime in American life. Those European moviegoers who think there is a gangster on every corner in New York are certainly deceived, but defenders of the "positive" side of American culture are equally deceived if they think it relevant to point out that most Americans have never seen a gangster. What matters is that the experience of the gangster as an experience of art is universal to Americans. There is almost nothing we understand better or react to more readily or with quicker intelligence. The western film, though it seems never to diminish in popularity, is for most of us no more than the folklore of the past, familiar and understandable only because it has been repeated so often. The gangster film comes much closer. In ways that we do not easily or willingly define, the gangster speaks for us, expressing that part of the American psyche that rejects the qualities and the demands of modern life, that rejects "Americanism" itself.

The gangster is the man of the city, with the city's language and knowledge, with its queer and dishonest skills and its terrible daring, carrying his life in his hands like a placard, like a club. For everyone else, there is at least the theoretical possibility of another world—in that happier American culture that the gangster denies, the city does not really exist; it is only a more crowded and more brightly lit country—but for the gangster there is only the city; he must inhabit it in order to personify it: not the real city, but that dangerous and sad city of the imagination that is so much more important, that is the modern world. And the gangster—though there are real gangsters—is also, and primarily, a creature of the imagination. The real city, one might say, produces only criminals; the imaginary city produces the gangster: he is what we want to be and what we are afraid we may become.

Thrown into the crowd without background or advantage, with only those ambiguous skills that the rest of us—the real people of the real city—can only pretend to have, the gangster is required to make his own way, to make his life and impose it on others. Usually, when we come upon him, he has already made his choice or the choice has already been made for him, it doesn't matter which: we are not permitted to ask whether at some point he could have chosen to be something else than what he is.

The gangster's activity is actually a form of rational enterprise, involving fairly definite goals and various techniques for achieving them. But this rationality is usually no more than a vague background: we know, perhaps, that the gangster sells liquor or that he operates a numbers racket; often we are not given even that much information. So his activity becomes a kind of pure criminality: he hurts people. Certainly, our response to the gangster film is most consistently and most universally a response to sadism; we gain the double satisfaction of participating vicariously in the gangster's sadism and then seeing it turned against the gangster himself.

But on another level, the quality of irrational brutality and the quality of rational enterprise become one. Since we do not see the rational and routine aspects of the gangster's behavior, the practice of brutality—the quality of unmixed criminality—becomes the totality of his career. At the same time, we are always conscious that the whole meaning of this career is a drive for success: the typical gangster film presents a steady upward progress followed by a very precipitate fall. Thus, brutality itself becomes at once the means to success and the content of success—a success that is defined in its most general terms, not as accomplishment or specific gain, but simply as the unlimited possibility of aggression. (In the same way, film presentations of businessmen tend to make it appear that they achieve their success by talking on the telephone and holding conferences and that success *is* talking on the telephone and holding conferences.)

From this point of view, the initial contact between film and its audience is an agreed conception of human life: that man is a being with the possibilities of success or failure. This principle, too, belongs to the city; one must emerge from the crowd, or else one is nothing. On that basis the necessity of the action is established, and it progresses by inalterable paths to the point where the gangster lies dead and the principle has been modified: there is really only one possibility—failure. The final meaning of the city is anonymity and death.

In the opening scene of *Scarface* (1932), we are shown a successful man; we know he is successful because he has just given a party of opulent proportions and because he is called Big Louie. Through some monstrous lack of caution, he permits himself to be alone for a few moments. We understand from this immediately that he is about to be killed. No

FIGURE 45. Edward G. Robinson as successful gangster Rico in *Little Caesar* (1931).

convention of the gangster film is more strongly established than this: it is dangerous to be alone. Yet the very conditions of success make it impossible not to be alone, for success is always the establishment of an individual preeminence that must be imposed on others, in whom it automatically arouses hatred; the successful man is an outlaw. The gangster's whole life is an effort to assert himself as an individual, to draw himself out of the crowd, and he always dies because he is an individual; the final bullet thrusts him back, makes him, after all, a failure. "Mother of God," says the dying titular character in *Little Caesar* (1931), "is this the end of Rico?"—speaking of himself thus in the third person because what has been brought low is not the undifferentiated man but the individual with a name, the gangster, the success; even to himself he is a creature of the imagination.[3] (T. S. Eliot has pointed out that a number of Shakespeare's tragic heroes have this trick of looking at themselves dramatically; their true identity, the thing that is destroyed when they die, is something outside themselves—not a man, but a style of life, a kind of meaning.)[4]

At bottom, the gangster is doomed because he is under the obligation to succeed, not because the means he employs are unlawful. In the deeper layers of the modern consciousness, all means are unlawful, every attempt to succeed an act of aggression, leaving one alone and guilty and defenseless among enemies: one is punished for success. This is our intolerable dilemma: that failure is a kind of death and success is evil and dangerous is—ultimately—impossible. The effect of the gangster film is to embody this dilemma in the person of the gangster and resolve it by his death. The dilemma is resolved because it is his death, not ours. We are safe. For the moment, we can acquiesce in our failure; we can choose to fail.

NOTES

1. In her testimony before the House Un-American Activities Committee, Leila Rogers said that the movie *None but the Lonely Heart* (1944) was un-American because it was gloomy. Like so much else that was said during the unhappy investigation of Hollywood, this statement was at once stupid and illuminating. One knew immediately what Rogers was talking about; she had simply been insensitive enough to carry her philistinism to its conclusion.

2. Efforts have been made from time to time to bring the gangster film into line with the prevailing optimism and social constructiveness of our culture; *Kiss of Death* (1947) is a recent example. These efforts are usually unsuccessful; the reasons for their lack of success are interesting in themselves, but I shall not discuss them here.

3. Robinson's actual line in the film is "Mother of mercy, is this the end of Rico?" [Editors' note.]

4. See Eliot's essay "Shakespeare and the Stoicism of Seneca," in *Selected Essays* (New York: Harcourt, Brace & World, 1950), 107–120, esp. 110. [Editors' note.]

CHAPTER 20

EVOLUTION OF THE THRILLER

CLAUDE CHABROL
TRANSLATED BY LIZ HERON

IN MEMORIAM

SUCCESS CREATES THE FASHION, which in turn shapes the genre. What corresponded to the vogue for the detective story between the two wars, in American cinema—with many poor imitations elsewhere—was the creation of a genre that rapidly gave way, predictably, to mediocrity and slovenly formulas. To begin with, it generated some films that were interesting and well made, if less than admirable: adaptations of the best-selling novels of S. S. Van Dine or Earl Derr Biggers, like the famous *The Canary Murder Case* (1929), which is unforgettable, though for reasons not directly connected with those I have mentioned (namely, Louise Brooks). The tremendous success of these films prompted shrewd businessmen to manufacture an infinite number of cheap by-products, usually rehashed by some Tom, Dick, or Harry, with Charlie Chan, Perry Mason, Philo Vance, or Ellery Queen turning up regularly in some new adventure and generally bearing an extraordinary resemblance to one another (in the shape of Warner Oland, Warren William, or any other highly specialized actor), all with the purpose, I suppose, of giving their none-too-demanding audiences the impression that they were reading a regular Sunday comic strip.

An experience similar in every respect was the lot of those gangster films that emerged out of the very complex social, economic, and political conjunctions of the 1930s. Some—the early ones—were masterpieces, based on the exploits of the famous Italian bootleggers of the Prohibition era, and were what is called "topical." But this topicality did not last, and with it departed a fine source of inspiration. From then on, the by-products without such drawbacks as topicality had the lion's share.

Strange to say, despite a downhill course that was all too obvious even in 1935, there was virtually no merging of the two genres before 1939. The attempts at adapting the novels of Dashiell Hammett only succeeded in reducing the hero of *The Thin Man* to the proportions of a series detective who persisted, tireder, sadder, and more monotonous, until around the end of the war. Thus, the state of the thriller genre—of all the thriller genres—was far from brilliant in 1940. The mystery story either visibly stood still or became impossible to transfer to the screen. Prohibition had long since been forgiven by whiskey lovers, and the crime syndicate had not yet reached the public eye. The films were turning into baleful police stories, definitively condemned to tiny budgets and even smaller talents.

It was then that an unexpected rediscovery of Dashiell Hammett, the appearance of the first Chandlers, and a favorable climate suddenly gave the tough-guy genre its aristocratic credentials[1] and opened the doors of the studios to it once and for all. The trend in these films, from Raoul Walsh's *High Sierra* (1941) and John Huston's *The Maltese Falcon* (1941) onward, continued to grow until 1948. The notion of the series underwent important modifications: if it was still a matter of exploiting a lucrative vein according to preestablished recipes, nevertheless each work was distinguishable from the others, in the best cases, by its tone or style. And if the same character appeared in several films, one had to put it down to chance, or locate it in identical literary sources: no idiocy made it obligatory to identify the Marlowe of *Murder, My Sweet* (1944) with the Marlowe of *Lady in the Lake* (1947). Many of these films were of high quality and often exceeded one's expectations of their directors (I have in mind Dmytryk, Hathaway, and Daves). There are two reasons for this: the subjects of these films were the work of talented writers, all of them specialists in the genre, like Chandler, Burnett, Jay Dratler, or Leo Rosten, and the film-makers had settled for a standard mise-en-scène that worked extremely well and was rich in visual effects, perfectly suited to a genre in which refinement seemed inappropriate.

Misfortune willed that the genre in question should carry within it the seeds of its own destruction. Built as it was on the elements of shock and surprise, it could offer even the most imaginative of scriptwriters and the most conscientious of directors only a very limited number of dramatic situations that, by force of repetition, ended up no longer producing either shock or surprise. If the film noir thriller—and with it the novel—managed to last eight years, it was thanks to the precise combina-

FIGURE 46. Sam Spade (Humphrey Bogart) and femme fatale Brigid O'Shaughnessy (Mary Astor) in *The Maltese Falcon* (1941).

tion of two elements that were at first external: suspense[2] and reportage. There, too, the dice were loaded. Suspense, in introducing a new and infinitely dangerous instrument—anticipation—could ring the changes on only a very small number of situations and covered up the problem without resolving it. As for reportage, its multiple possibilities were stifled by the very nature of the genre, which could preserve only its most superficial features and quickly let it become dull and boring. Thus locked in the prison of its own construction, the thriller could only go around in circles, like a trapped bird unable to find a way out of its cage. Robert Montgomery's gratuitous attempts at subjective camera shots in *Lady in the Lake*, the time disorientation in Sam Wood's *Ivy* (1947), Robert Florey's childish and grotesque avant-gardism in his amnesiac's story (*The Beast with Five Fingers* [1946]) all sounded the death knell. One day Ben Hecht gave it the finishing touch, producing, from a tenth-rate novel by Eleazar Lipsky, an admirable script that was a supreme example of all the features of the detective story genre combined. As if to illustrate perfectly both the strength and the weakness of such a conception, it was Henry

Hathaway, a skilled technician without an ounce of personality (author of the highest expression of the genre: the first half of *Dark Corner* [1946]), who made *Kiss of Death* (1947), swan song of a formula, end of a recipe, and the bottom of a gold mine, which at once blew up in the faces of the tycoons who had made their money but were now in trouble.

NOBILISSIMA VISIONE

And so the film thriller is no more, the novel likewise. The source has dried up; renewal is impossible. What is left but to go beyond it? Following in the footsteps of all the other genres that created the past glory of the American cinema, the thriller, now without an existence of its own, remains a wonderful pretext.

Within civilizations—Valery was instructive about their fate—no successes, no fashions, no genres are immortal. What remain are the works, successes or failures, but a *sincere* expression of the preoccupations and ideas of their authors. In this particular case, another historical panorama is now being unveiled, offering to our eyes *One Exciting Night* (1922), *Underworld* (1927), and *Scarface* (1932), followed by a long bleak and empty plain: well, these few films prefigure the thriller of tomorrow.

There's no question in these films of renovating a genre, either by extending its boundaries or by intellectualizing it in some way. In fact, there's no question of renovation at all, simply of expression, through the telling of a not-too-confusing tale. Aren't the best criteria of an authentic work most often its complete lack of self-consciousness and its unquestionable necessity? So there's nothing to restrict a preference for the freshness and intelligence of that almost impenetrable imbroglio *Out of the Past* (1947), directed by Jacques Tourneur and scripted clumsily, and utterly sincerely, by Geoffrey Homes [Daniel Mainwaring], rather than for *Dark Passage* (1947), with its skillful construction, its judicious use of the camera in its first half, and its amusing surreal ending. But what, you may ask, makes the first of the two films more sincere than the other? The very fact of its clumsiness! A film's total assimilation within a genre often means nothing more than its complete submission to it; to make a thriller, the essential and only prerequisite is that it be conceived as such and, by corollary, that it be constituted exclusively of the elements of the thriller. It is the genre that reigns over inspiration, which it holds back and locks into strict rules. Therefore, it clearly takes exceptional talent to remain oneself in such a strange enterprise (that's the miracle of *The Big Sleep* [1946]), or else it takes inspiration, aspirations, and a vision of the world that are naturally in accordance with the laws of the genre (*Laura* [1944] is yet another miracle, and in a certain sense Lang and Hitchcock too).

There is no doubt that the superiority of *The Big Sleep* derives in part from the quite functional perfection achieved by director and scriptwriters; the plot of the film is a model of the thriller equation, with three unknowns (the blackmailer, the murderer, the avenger), so simple and so subtle that at first all is beyond comprehension; in fact, on a *second* viewing there is nothing easier than the unraveling of this film. The only difference between the viewer and the Marlowe-Bogart character is that the latter works it all out and understands the first time around. And so it seems this film only resembles the others insofar as it towers above them, but deep roots and firm connections link it to the body of Hawks's work. It is not just accidental that here the private eye is more intelligent and sharper than we are and more directly than anywhere else confronted with the brutal strength of his adversaries. Beyond the shadow of a doubt, *The Big Sleep* is closer to *Scarface*, *The Thing* (1951), and even *Monkey Business* (1952) than to Robert Montgomery's *Lady in the Lake*. It is no less true that here the function subordinates the creation, surpassed by it of course, but definitively, since the Hawksian treatment of the tough-guy theme cannot be repeated without in its turn creating a dull and sterile cliché.

Things take a rather different shape in Otto Preminger's *Laura*. In this film the pure thriller element is entirely subordinate to a predetermined narrative style that in some way transmutes it. The film's inspiration, a Vera Caspary novel, is a classic detective story, or rather neoclassic—in other words, based on a less stereotyped kind of realism. At any rate, it is a flawless testimony to the inadequacies of a thoroughly worn-out formula. It is at the level of the characters that the displacement operates: the authors (Preminger and Jay Dratler) push them to their inevitable paroxysm, thus creating characters who are intrinsically fascinating, for whom the course they follow becomes *the only possible one*. Everything happens as if the characters had been created before the plot (it usually happens the other way around, of course), as if they themselves were constructing the plot, transposing it on to a level to which it never aspired. To accentuate this impression, Preminger thought up a new narrative technique (which, moreover, gave his film great historical importance): long sequences shot from a crane, following the key characters in each scene in their every move, so that these characters, *immutably* fixed in the frame (usually in close-up or in two-shot), see the world around them evolving and changing in accordance with their actions. Here was the proof that a thriller can also be beautiful and profound, that it is a question of style

FIGURE 47. The troubled screenwriter Dix Steele (Humphrey Bogart, *right*) in *In a Lonely Place* (1950).

and conviction. Vera Caspary had written a detective story. Preminger filmed a story of characters who meant something to him. Nonetheless, *Laura* is still far from exemplary, since its success postulates a preexisting detective story plot that fits in with the filmmaker's purpose, or, more exactly, demands of the filmmaker a vision that can be integrated into a given thriller theme. There again it is the director who takes the initiative and adapts to the genre. And the result, which one cannot deny is admirable, is worth infinitely more than the principle, which is no more than a half-measure.

At the same time, one can easily understand that these films have constituted decisive stages in the peaceful struggle for the liberation of the genre and the shattering of its formulas; where they have not provided examples, they have worked as stimulants. Thus, one could see an ensemble of aggressive works, some of them failures, but often extraordinary, in any case personal and sincere, whose thriller theme was only a pretext or a means but never an end in itself. Some random examples: Welles's *The Lady from Shanghai* (1947), Nick Ray's *On Dangerous Ground* (1951) and *In a Lonely Place* (1950),[3] Joseph Losey's *The Prowler* (1951), Preminger's

Where the Sidewalk Ends (1950) and *Whirlpool* (1949), and a few others that have endowed the thriller theme with its real aristocratic credentials, films that are not subject to absurd conventions and arbitrary classifications. It is difficult at first to see any connection between *The Lady from Shanghai* and *In a Lonely Place*; the quality of this connection lies in the very difference between the two films, in the astonishing honesty, in relation to themselves, of Welles and Nicholas Ray. The wealth is in the prospectors, no longer in the mine.

There is clearly an objection possible here: all the films I've mentioned—and I've made a deliberate selection—are outstanding primarily because they set themselves miles apart from the genre, attached to it only by tenuous links that have nothing to do with their qualities. Isn't it then a little dishonest to see the future of the thriller only in the dilution of the detective story element within the films, since you only have to take things to their paradoxical conclusion to conceive of an ideal future in the suppression of this element altogether?

In reality, what seems like a dilution is in fact nothing less than enrichment. All these auteurs have one thing in common: they no longer regard crime or any other thriller element as simply a dramatic situation that can lend itself to a range of more or less skillful variations, but see it in ontological (as with Ray, Losey, or Dassin) or metaphysical (Welles, Lang, or Hitchcock) terms.

It is really a matter of valorizing just as Proust tried to do with time or Jouhandeau with homosexuality. In the realm of the cinema, this can be done at the level of mise-en-scène, as with Preminger, or at the level of work done on the script with a certain kind of mise-en-scène (Hitchcock or Welles). It can also be done, dare I say it, independently, in the working out of the script. I shall take my example from this last category since its demonstration is easier on paper.

Let's look at Robert Wise's *Born to Kill* (1947), a film that has received less than its fair share of attention. In this film, then, it's the script itself that is admirable and completely new; the weak spot is the mise-en-scène. Technically, it is beyond reproach and in places quite powerful but, alas, dreadfully *ordinary* and typical of the genre, which was precisely what the film aimed to break away from and grind into dust. The script is a faithful adaptation—if, because of the time constraint, a little simplified—of a novel by someone called James Gunn. This young man wrote his book as an "exercise in creative writing." The university gave him the first page, and by the second he had already eliminated all its superfluous elements, cleverly choosing as the framework for his story two well-exhausted

FIGURE 48. Sam (Lawrence Tierney) with the coldhearted Helen (Claire Trevor) in *Born to Kill* (1947).

themes of the dying genre: the woman who is more monstrous than the most monstrous man (*Deadlier than the Male* is the original title) and the old woman who turns detective in order to avenge a murdered friend. He literally explodes these themes before our eyes, through an absolutely extraordinary freedom of development and tone. Pushing each scene to its paroxysm of violence, comedy, or the macabre, he succeeds in giving them all a dimension of the unexpected, the profound, or the poetic and simultaneously justifying the themes chosen, for it is only through them that the characters can be pushed to their limits, that their purification can be brought about, and the style, tone, and ideas justified. Overprudent, Wise could not—or did not know how to—work in tune with this, and *Born to Kill* was by no means the masterpiece and the manifesto that it should have been.

Be that as it may, through the successes and the failures, evolution cannot be denied. Nobody, I think, would lament the passing of films like *After the Thin Man* (1936), or more recent films like *Murder, My Sweet*, on seeing new films like *In a Lonely Place* or *The Prowler*. For those who remain unconvinced of the rigor of my argument, I have kept an ace up my sleeve. Better than pages of analysis, there is one film that can testify to the new truth. Enter the thriller of tomorrow, freed from everything and especially from itself, illuminating with its overpowering sunlights the depths of the unspeakable.[4] It has chosen to create itself out of the worst material to be found, the most deplorable, the most nauseous product of a genre in a state of putrefaction: a Mickey Spillane story. Robert Aldrich and A. I. Bezzerides have taken this threadbare and lackluster fabric and splendidly rewoven it into rich patterns of the most enigmatic arabesques.[5] In *Kiss Me Deadly* (1955) the usual theme of the detective series of old is handled offscreen and taken up again in a whisper only for the sake of the foolish: what it's really about is something more serious—images of Death, Fear, Love, and Terror pass by in succession. Yet nothing is left out: the tough detective whose name we know so well, the diminutive[6] and worthless gangsters, the cops, the pretty girls in bathing suits, the platinum-blonde murderess. Who would recognize them, and without embarrassment, these sinister friends of former times, now unmasked and cut down to size?

A shortage of themes, says the honest man! As if themes were not what auteurs make of them!

NOTES

1. The genre had, however, already been around for some time. It has its acknowledged origins in the magazine *Black Mask*, which was where Chandler, Hammett, Cornell Woolrich, and Raoul Whitfield published their first stories. Moreover, *The Maltese Falcon* and *The Glass Key* had both been the subjects of low-budget adaptations around 1933.

2. It is very difficult to draw a clear line between what constitutes "suspense" and the "thriller." In literature the first is closer to William Irish, the second to Chandler. In reality, each has always relied very heavily on the other.

3. It seems that Ray chooses the more esteemed authors of the genre. *On Dangerous Ground* is adapted from a fine Gerald Butler novel, *Mad with Much Heart*. As for *In a Lonely Place*, it is very freely adapted from an excellent work of the same name by Dorothy B. Hughes (the same writer who inspired *Ride the Pink Horse* [1947]).

4. *Sunlight* is a technical term referring to light reaching a photographed object directly from the sun, whereas *daylight* would include other natural light sources, such as reflected light. By his choice of phrase here, Chabrol seems to intend a reference to the atomic theme of *Kiss Me Deadly* and the blinding light from the box that causes its final explosion. [Note included in this English translation in *"Cahiers du Cinéma," the 1950s: Neo-realism, Hollywood, New Wave*, edited by Jim Hillier (Cambridge, MA: Harvard University Press, 1995), 158–164.]

5. Bezzerides is one of the better current Hollywood scriptwriters. He first came

to the cinema with the adaptation of his own novel *Thieves' Market*, for Jules Dassin (*Thieves' Highway* [1949]), and has since worked as scriptwriter or adapter on *Beneath the 12-Mile Reef* (1953), *On Dangerous Ground*, and other well-crafted films rich in original ideas. The character of Nick in *Kiss Me Deadly* is a typically Bezzeridean creation. To give you some idea of the physical presence of this fascinating personality, he is the one who plays Robert Ryan's second tempter (the one who tries to bribe him) at the beginning of *On Dangerous Ground*.

6. Chabrol's original adjective is *atomique*, to incorporate both the atomic theme of the film and the colloquial meaning given here. [Note included in this English translation in *"Cahiers du Cinéma," the 1950s*, edited by Hillier, 158–164.]

CHAPTER 21

TOWARD A DEFINITION OF FILM NOIR

RAYMOND BORDE AND ETIENNE CHAUMETON
TRANSLATED BY PAUL HAMMOND

The bloody channels through which logic at bay is obliged to pass.
—LAUTRÉAMONT[1]

FILM NOIR IS NOIR *for us*, that's to say, for western and American audiences of the 1950s. It responds to a certain kind of emotional resonance as singular in time as it is in space. It's on the basis of a response to possibly ephemeral reactions that the roots of this "style" must be sought therefore: this is what forges a link between productions as different as *The Shanghai Gesture* (1941) and *The Asphalt Jungle* (1950).

As a result, the method is imposed by and of itself: while remaining on as technical and objective a terrain as possible, it consists in studying the most typical characteristics of films the critics have generally deemed to be noir, and then, by comparing these qualities, in seeking a common denominator and defining the single emotional attitude all the works in the series tend to bring into play.

It's the presence of crime that gives film noir its most distinctive stamp, "the dynamism of violent death," as Nino Frank put it, and the expression is excellent.[2] Blackmail, informing, theft, or drug trafficking weaves the plot of an adventure whose final stake is death. Few series in the history of cinema have, in just seven or eight years, accumulated so many hideous acts of brutality and murder. Sordid or strange, death always emerges at the end of a tortuous journey. Film noir is a film of death, in all senses of the word.

Yet it doesn't have a monopoly here, and an essential distinction is called for. In principle, a film noir is a "police documentary."[3] We know that since 1946 Hollywood has exported a dozen or so movies to France that have the common characteristic of describing a criminal investigation by following the documents in the police file page by page. Furthermore, at the start of the film a title or commentary advises the public that this is a true story occurring at such and such a time, in New York or some other place. And the images on the screen faithfully describe the investigation: a call to headquarters, the discovery of the body, from time to time some seemingly minor incident, a local precinct report that will start the ball rolling. Then the "thankless" task of the police department: detailed and futile inquiries, useless leads, abortive round-ups. At last a glimmer of light, a bit of cross-checking, a testimony, and then the final chase that unmasks a bunch of killers. This series, which has given us some interesting works—Henry Hathaway's *Call Northside 777* (1948) and *The House on 92nd Street* (1945), Elia Kazan's *Boomerang!* (1947) and *Panic in the Streets* (1950), Lázló Benedek's *Port of New York* (1949), Jules Dassin's *The Naked City* (1948), and, on the fringes of the genre, Brentaigne Windust's *The Enforcer* (1951)—has several features in common with film noir: realistic locations, carefully crafted supporting roles, extremely brutal scenes, and bits of bravura in the final chase sequences. On top of that, these police documentaries often have more typically noir features: it will be a long time before we forget the unusual figure of the killers' boss in *The Enforcer* or the impassive gangster in *Panic in the Streets*. It may even be that during his career a director alternates between the two genres. Jules Dassin has put his name to *The Naked City* but also to *Night and the City* (1950). In 1950 Joseph H. Lewis gave us an incontestably noir opus in *Gun Crazy*, yet the year before he'd described the work of some tax officials in *The Undercover Man*.

There are some differences between the two series, for all that—and first and foremost a different angle of vision. The documentary considers the murder from without, from the official police viewpoint, the film noir from within, from the criminals'. In movies of *The Naked City* type, the action begins after the crime, and the murderers, heavies, and their accomplices traverse the screen solely in order to be tailed, spied on, interrogated, hunted down, or killed. If a flashback evokes a scene between gangsters, it's to illustrate a confession or a testimony, the transcript of which figures in the report. The police are omnipresent, so as to intervene or to lend an ear. There's none of this in the film noir, which is set

FIGURE 49. Fact-checking in *The House on 92nd Street* (1945).

in the criminal milieu itself and describes the latter, now through simple touches (*The Big Sleep* [1946] or *Dark Passage* [1947]), now in depth and with obliging subtlety (*The Asphalt Jungle*). In any event, it proposes a psychology of crime that isn't without its echoes, in another domain, of that worldly psychology so appreciated at the end of the nineteenth century: both shed light on forbidden worlds.

The second difference is of a moral, and maybe even more essential, kind. It's part of the tradition of the police documentary to present the investigators as upright, incorruptible, and courageous men. The ship's doctor in *Panic in the Streets* is a hero. A hero, too, albeit more complex, is the short Irish detective of *The Naked City* who believes in God and consecrates his nights to the triumph of justice. An edifying film, the American police documentary is, in fact, a documentary to the glory of the police and belongs in the same bag as such productions, in France, as *Identité judiciaire* (1951) or, in England, *The Blue Lamp* (1950).

None of this exists in the noir series. If there are policemen, they're of dubious character—like the inspector in *The Asphalt Jungle* or that evil-looking, corrupt brute played by Lloyd Nolan in *Lady in the Lake* (1947)—even murderers at times (Otto Preminger's *Fallen Angel* [1945] and *Where the Sidewalk Ends* [1950]). Or at least they allow themselves to get caught up in the machinery of crime, like the attorney in *The File on Thelma Jordan* (1950). It's no accident, then, if scriptwriters have frequently had recourse to the character of the private detective. Casting too many aspersions on the official US police force was a ticklish problem. The private detective, midway between order and crime, running with the hare and hunting with the hounds, not overly scrupulous and responsible for himself alone, satisfied both the exigencies of morality and those of the criminal adventure story. As if by way of compensation, the lawbreakers themselves are rather personable. Of course, the old motto of MGM's prewar short films, "Crime Doesn't Pay," remains the order of the day, and the ending witnesses the chastisement of the guilty. But then the action is so adroitly handled that at certain moments, the public sympathizes and identifies with the gangsters. Think back to that breathtaking scene in *The Asphalt Jungle*, the raid on the jewelers. What spectator isn't instinctively on the side of the crooks? And *Gun Crazy* depicted a couple of killers of an exemplary beauty, if we may say so.

FIGURE 50. John Dall and Peggy Cummins in *Gun Crazy* (1950): killers of "exemplary beauty."

FEW FILMS HAVE SHOWN the instability of the relations between under-world types as well as *The Big Sleep* and, in its noir sequence (Rico's testimony), *The Enforcer*. In this gallery of suspects and criminals, one glimpses the complex and shifting patterns of domination based on money, black-mail, vice, and informing. Who'll do the killing, and who'll get killed? Here is all the ambiguity of a criminal milieu in which the power relationships ceaselessly change.

This equivocation extends to the ambivalence of the characters themselves. The rough-hewn hero, the Scarface-type thug, has disappeared from film noir, making way for a whole host of angelic killers, neurotic gangsters, megalomaniac gang bosses, and disturbing or depraved stooges. Here is the solitary scientific assassin of *He Walked by Night* (1948), here the self-punishing failure of *Night and the City*, here the awesomely mother-fixated fanatic of *White Heat* (1949). Here are the henchmen of *The Enforcer*—vicious, venomous, or spineless.

Ambiguity, too, as to the victims, forever suspect, at least partly. The relationships they maintain with the mob make them first cousins to their torturers. If they're often victims, it's because they haven't managed to be executioners, like the dubious partner in *The Lady from Shanghai* (1947), who meets his death while simulating his own murder and who will long remain the finest example of an equivocal victim. One also thinks of the terrorized heroine of Jacques Tourneur's *Out of the Past* (1947), whom one expects to see done in before the film is over and who sees her executioner off in a carefully prepared trap. A lamb to the slaughter, this heavy secretly marked out for execution.

Contradictions on the hero's side: often he's a man who's already middle-aged, old almost, and not particularly handsome. Humphrey Bogart is the model here. He's also an inglorious victim who undergoes, before the happy end, some appalling beatings. Added to which, he's often the masochistic type, his own executioner, someone hoist by his own petard, someone who gets tangled up in dangerous situations, not so much through a concern for justice or through cupidity as through a sort of morbid curiosity. Sometimes he's a passive hero who is willingly taken to the frontier between lawfulness and crime, like Orson Welles in *The Lady from Shanghai*. We're a long way, then, from the adventure film superman.

Contradictions, finally, on the woman's side: the femme fatale is also fatal unto herself. Frustrated and guilty, half man-eater, half man-eaten, blasé and cornered, she falls victim to her own wiles. While the ambigu-

FIGURE 51. Barbara Stanwyck as the femme fatale in *The File on Thelma Jordan* (1950).

ous behavior of Lauren Bacall in *The Big Sleep* doesn't cost her her life, Barbara Stanwyck will not survive her own murderous schemes in *The File on Thelma Jordan*. This new kind of woman, rubbing shoulders with and masterminding crime, tough as the milieu surrounding her, as expert in blackmail and "vice" as in the use of firearms—and probably frigid—has left her mark on a noir eroticism that is at times merely an eroticization of violence. We're a long way from the chaste heroines of the classic western or the historical film.

IN TERMS OF THE HISTORY of the cinema, film noir has given a new lease of life to the theme of violence. First of all, it has done so by abandoning one of the conventions of the adventure film: the combat with equal weapons. The fair fight gives way to the settling of scores, to the working over, to the cold-blooded execution. Bodyguards bounce a powerless victim between them like a ball, a victim they then leave bleeding on a public square (*Ride the Pink Horse* [1947]), in a blind alley (*The Set-Up* [1949]), or in a yard, among the trash cans (*I Walk Alone* [1948]). Crime itself becomes mechanical, professional, and it's the hired killer who now performs this duty "without anger and without hatred."[4] The first sequence of the Robert Siodmak film *The Killers* (1946), that famous scene in the diner in which two men in search of their victim terrify the clients with contemptible self-confidence, will abide as one of the most striking moments in American cinema, an unforgettable slice of documentary: a hitherto unknown race looms up before us with its tics, its stigmata. This race has its artistes, exceedingly gentle on the whole (Alan Ladd in *This Gun for Hire* [1942]), its unreasoning brutes (William Bendix), and its lucid and fearsome organization men (Everett Sloan in *The Enforcer*). It also has its mental defectives, its overweight killers, oozing cowardice, humiliated by their accomplices, and suddenly let loose (Laird Cregar or Raymond Burr).

As for the ceremony of killing, this remains one of the richest in the entire history of the cinema. Let us cite at random: that unself-conscious gesture of the wealthy publisher who sends a potentially embarrassing witness, busy washing the tiles, hurtling down the lift shaft—all he need do is nudge the man's stepladder with the knob of his cane while shooting the breeze (*High Wall* [1947]); the gruesome razor killing in *The Enforcer*; a tap of the foot given to a hydraulic jack (*Red Light* [1949]). Elsewhere, a paralyzed victim is pushed down a flight of stairs after being tied to her wheelchair (*Kiss of Death* [1947]); a stool pigeon is locked inside a Turkish bath, then the steam turned up (*T-Men* [1947]); a prisoner is gradually driven under a power hammer by threatening him with blazing blow torches (*Brute Force* [1947]); someone is crushed beneath a tractor, while someone else sinks into the quicksand (*Border Incident* [1949]). . . . An unprecedented panoply of cruelties and sufferings unfolds in film noir.

BUT THEN MORE THAN with the violence, the anguish has to do, perhaps, with the strange unfolding of the action. A private detective accepts the vaguest of missions: to find a woman, to halt a blackmail attempt, to deter someone—and straightaway his path is littered with corpses. He's tailed, hit over the head, arrested. Let him ask for information, and he finds himself tied up, bleeding, in some deep cellar. Various men, questioned at night, shoot and then run off. There is, in this incoherent brutality, something dreamlike, yet this is the atmosphere common to most film noirs: *The Big Sleep, Ride the Pink Horse, Lady in the Lake, Chicago Deadline* (1949). On this score, Georges Sadoul suggests that "the story remains opaque, like a nightmare, or the ramblings of a drunk."[5] This is so manifestly true that one of the rare parodies of the genre, Elliott Nugent's *My Favorite Brunette* (1947), begins in just this way. Bob Hope has elected to play at being a detective, and Dorothy Lamour entrusts him with one of those confused investigations the Americans possess the secret of—like, for instance, "Find my brother" or "Find my sister"—by handing him a check. Instantly, the knives are out, corpses bar his way, and the inexorable wheels of fate lead him to the electric chair via a hospital that's a gangster hideout.

At times, the mystery is more convincing: a man who's lost his memory sets off in search of the past, only for crime to rear its ugly head. This theme has been exploited by Robert Florey in *The Crooked Way* (1949) and by Joseph Mankiewicz in *Somewhere in the Night* (1946). But here the stated facts of the problem are such that the public expects a certain amount of confusion in advance. In genuine film noir, strangeness is inseparable from what could be called *the uncertainty of the motives*. What, for instance, are Bannister and his associate seeking through their sinister doings in *The Lady from Shanghai*? The very strangeness of the oeuvre lies in these spineless, mysterious creatures who lay their cards on the table only in death. Elsewhere, will a figure glimpsed in some nondescript nightclub finger an accomplice or an enemy? This enigmatic killer, is he to be executioner or victim? The complexity of criminal relationships, the multifarious intermeshings of blackmail, the mystery as to motives—all this converges in incoherence.

In our opinion, this note of confusion is at the very heart of the oneiric quality specific to the series. A number of titles could readily be found in which the action is deliberately situated at the level of the dream—for example, Fritz Lang's *The Woman in the Window* (1944). There are also works in which the artificial setting relates to symbol and fiction alone; Sternberg's *The Shanghai Gesture* is a case in point. As a general rule, however, the point of departure is realistic, and, taken on its own, each scene could pass for a fragment of documentary. It's the accumulation of these realistic shots on a bizarre theme that creates a nightmarish atmosphere.

One gets the feeling that all the components of noir style lead to the same result: to disorient the spectators, who no longer encounter their customary frames of reference. The cinema public was habituated to certain conventions: a logic to the action, a clear distinction between good and evil, well-defined characters, clear motives, scenes more spectacular than genuinely brutal, an exquisitely feminine heroine, and an upright hero. These at least were the postulates of the American adventure film before the war.

As things stand, though, the public is offered a highly sympathetic image of the criminal milieu, of attractive killers, dubious policemen. Good and evil often rub shoulders to the point of merging into one another. The thieves are average guys; they have kids, love their young wives, and aspire to return to the rural haunts of their childhood (*The Asphalt Jungle*). The victim is as suspect as the executioner, while the latter remains likable. The first of those frames of reference, moral fictions, is blurred.

The heroine is vicious, deadly, venomous, or alcoholic. The hero lets himself be led astray, gets to "take a lot of punishment," as they say in boxing, during ruthless settlings of scores. And the second frame of reference, the myth of superman and his chaste fiancée, goes by the board.

The action is confused, the motives uncertain. This is a far cry from classical drama or the moral tale of the realist era: many of the hoods have murky relationships with each other (*The Big Sleep*); a policeman arrives unexpectedly, proves to be a crook, and his presence only adds to the tension of the viewer (*Lady in the Lake*); proceedings in which a man's life is at stake turn into the craziest of stories (*The Lady from Shanghai*). The film takes on the quality of a dream; the audience searches in vain for the good old logic of yore.

In the end, the violence "oversteps the mark." This gratuitous cruelty and this one-upsmanship in murder add to the strangeness. The sense of dread is dissipated only in the very last images.

It is easy to come to a conclusion: the moral ambivalence, criminal violence, and contradictory complexity of the situations and motives all combine to give the public a shared feeling of anguish or insecurity, which is the identifying sign of film noir at this time. All the works in this series exhibit a consistency of an emotional sort, *namely, the state of tension created in the spectators by the disappearance of their psychological bearings.* The vocation of film noir has been to create *a specific sense of malaise.*

NOTES

1. Since this citation is not, in fact, from Lautréamont's *Les chants de Maldoror* but from *Poésies*, it would be more correct to sign it "Isidore Ducasse." [Trans.]

2. Nino Frank, "Un nouveau genre 'policier': L'aventure criminelle," *L'Ecran Français*, no. 61 (1946): 8.

3. What the authors call a "police documentary" we'd now call a "police procedural." [Trans.]

4. The quotation is from Baudelaire's line "I shall strike you with anger and without hate, like a butcher." The narrator of Georges Franju's infamous documentary about Paris slaughterhouses, *Le sang des bêtes* (1949), quotes the line. [Editors' note.]

5. Georges Sadoul, a review of *The Big Sleep*, in *Les Lettres Françaises*.

CHAPTER 22

PAINT IT BLACK: THE FAMILY TREE
OF THE FILM NOIR

RAYMOND DURGNAT

IN 1946 FRENCH CRITICS, having missed Hollywood films for five years, saw suddenly, sharply, a darkening tone, darkest around the crime film. The English spoke only of the "tough, cynical Hammett–Chandler thriller," although a bleak, cynical tone was invading all genres, from *The Long Voyage Home* (1940) to *Duel in the Sun* (1946).

This tone was often castigated as Hollywood decadence, although black classics are as numerous as rosy (Euripides, Calvin, Ford, Tourneur, Goya, Lautréamont, Dostoyevsky, Grosz, Faulkner, Francis Bacon). Black is as ubiquitous as shadow, and if the term *film noir* has a slightly exotic ring, it's no doubt because it appears as figure against the rosy ground of Anglo-Saxon middle-class, and especially Hollywoodian, optimism and puritanism. If the term is French, it's no doubt because, helped by their more lucid (and/or mellow, or cynical, or decadent) culture, the French first understood the full import of the American development.

Greek tragedy, Jacobean drama, and the romantic agony (to name three black cycles) are earlier responses to epochs of disillusionment and alienation. But the sociocultural parallels can't be made mechanically. Late forties Hollywood is blacker than thirties precisely because its audience, being more secure, no longer needed cheering up. On the other hand, it was arguably insufficiently mature to enjoy the open, realistic discontent of, say, *Hôtel du Nord* (1938), *Look Back in Anger* (1959), or Norman Mailer. The American film noir, in the narrower sense, paraphrases its social undertones by the melodramatics of crime and the underworld: *Scarface* (1932)

Raymond Durgnat, "Paint It Black: The Family Tree of the Film Noir," *Cinema*, nos. 6–7 (1970): 49–56. Copyright © Raymond Durgnat Estate (Kevin Gough-Yates). Reprinted by permission of the estate.

and *On the Waterfront* (1954) mark its limits, both also "realistic" films. It's almost true to say that the French crime thriller evolves out of black realism, whereas American black realism evolves out of the crime thriller.

Evolution apart, the black thriller is a hardy perennial, drawing on the unconscious superego's sense of crime and punishment. The first detective thriller is *Oedipus Rex,* and it has the profoundest twist of all; detective, murderer, and executioner are one man. The Clytemnestra plot underlies innumerable film noirs, from *The Postman Always Rings Twice* (1946) to *Cronaca di un amore* (1950).

The nineteenth century splits the classic tragic spirit into three genres: bourgeois realism (Ibsen), the ghost story, and the detective story. The avenger ceases to be a ghost (representative of a magic order) and becomes a detective, private or public. The butler did it. *Fantômas* (1913), *The Cat and the Canary* (1927), and *Uncle Silas* (1947) illustrate the transitional stage between detective and ghost story. For ghosts the film noir substitutes, if only by implication, a nightmare society, or condition of man. In *Psycho* (1960), Mummy's transvestite mummy is a secular ghost, just as abnormal Norman is, at the end, Lord of the Flies, a Satanic, megalomaniacal hollow in creation. The film noir is as often nihilistic, cynical, or stoic as reformatory; there are fascist and apathetic denunciations of the bourgeois order, as well as Marxist ones.

There is obviously no clear line between the threat in a gray drama, the somber drama, and the film noir, just as it's impossible to say exactly when a crime becomes the focus of a film rather than merely a realistic incident. Some films seem black to cognoscenti, while the public of their time takes the happy end in a complacent sense; this is true of, for example, *The Big Sleep* (1946). *On The Waterfront* is a film noir, given Brando's negativistic and anguished playing, whereas *Edge of the City* (1957) is not, for reasons of tone suggested by the title. *Mourning Becomes Electra* (1947) is too self-consciously classic, although its adaptation into forties Americana with Joan Crawford might not be. *Intruder in the Dust* (1949) is neither Faulkner nor noir, despite the fact that only a boy and an old lady defy the lynch mob; its tone intimates that they tend to suffice. The happy end in a true film noir is that the worst of danger is averted, with little amelioration or congratulation. The film noir is not a genre, as the western or gangster film is, and takes us into the realms of classification by motif and tone. Only some crime films are noir, and film noirs in other genres include *The Blue Angel* (1930), *King Kong* (1933), *High Noon* (1952), *Stalag 17* (1953), *Attack* (1956), *Jeanne Eagels* (1957), *Sweet Smell of Success* (1957), *Lolita* (1962), *Lonely Are the Brave* (1962), *Shadows* (1962), and *2001: A Space Odyssey* (1968).

The French film noir precedes the American genre. French specialists include Feuillade, Duvivier, Carné, Clouzot, Yves Allegret, and even, almost without noticing, Renoir (of *La chienne* [1931], *La nuit du carrefour* [1931], *La bête humaine* [1938], *The Woman on the Beach* [1947]) and Godard. Two major cycles of the thirties and forties are followed by a gangster cycle in the fifties, including Becker's *Touchez pas au grisbi* (1954), Dassin's *Du rififi chez les hommes* (1955), Decoin's *Razzia sur la chnouf* (1955), Allégret's *Méfiez-vous, fillettes!* (1957), and the long Eddie Constantine series to which Godard pays homage in *Alphaville* (1965). *Fantômas* (1913), made for Gaumont, inspired their rival, Pathé, to the Pearl White series, inaugurated by the New York office of this then French firm. *La chienne* becomes *Scarlet Street* (1945), *La bête humaine* becomes *Human Desire* (1954), *Le jour se lève* (1939) becomes *The Long Night* (1947), while *Pépé-le-Moko* (1937) becomes *Algiers* (1938) ("Come with me to the Casbah") and also Pepé Le Pew. The American version of *The Postman Always Rings Twice* is preceded by a French (*Le dernier tournant* [1939]) and an Italian (*Ossessione* [1942]). The fifties gangster series precedes the American revival of interest in gangsters and in group-job themes. Godard was offered *Bonnie and Clyde* (1967) before Penn, presumably on the strength of *Breathless* (1960) rather than *Pierrot le fou* (1965).

The Italian film noir, more closely linked with realism, may be represented by *Ossessione*, *Caccia tragica* (1947), *Senza pietà* (1948), *Bitter Rice* (1949) (neorealist melodramas that pulverize Hollywood action equivalents by Walsh et al.), and *Cronaca di un amore*, Antonioni's mesmerically beautiful first feature. The American black western, which falters in the early sixties, is developed by the Italians. Kracauer's *From Caligari to Hitler*, which details the profusion of film noirs in Germany in the twenties, although the crime theme is sometimes overlaid by the tyrant theme.[1] *Spirits of the Dead*, a compendium of Poe stories, anticipates the Cormans. The Germans also pioneered the horror film. (*Nosferatu* [1922] precedes *Dracula* [1931]; *Homunculus* [1916] precedes *Frankenstein* [1931].) German expressionism heavily influences American film noirs, in which German directors (Stroheim, Leni, Lang, Siodmak, Preminger, Wilder) loom conspicuously (not to mention culturally Germanic Americans like Schoedsack and Sternberg).

The English cinema has its own, far from inconsiderable, line in film noirs, notably the best prewar Hitchcocks (*Rich and Strange* [1931], *Sabotage* [1936]). An effective series of costume bullying dramas (*Gaslight* [1940]), through *The Man in Grey* (1943) and *Fanny by Gaslight* (1944) to *Daybreak* (1947), is followed by man-on-the-run films of which the best

FIGURE 52. John Garfield, Lana Turner, and Cecil Kellaway in *The Postman Always Rings Twice* (1945).

are probably *Odd Man Out* (1947), *They Made Me a Fugitive* (1947), and *Secret People* (1952). The also-rans include many that are arguably more convincing and adventurous than many formula-bound Hollywood cult favorites.

The following subheadings offer inevitably imperfect schematizations for some main lines of force in the American film noir. They describe not genres but dominant cycles or motifs, and many, if not most, films would come under at least two headings, since interbreeding is intrinsic to motif processes. In all these films, crime or criminals provide the real or apparent center of focus, as distinct from films in the first category from noncriminal "populist" films such as *The Crowd* (1928), *Street Scene* (1931), *The Grapes of Wrath* (1940), *The Bachelor Party* (1957), *Too Late Blues* (1961), and *Echoes of Silence* (1967).

1. CRIME AS SOCIAL CRITICISM

A first cycle might be labeled "Pre-Depression: The Spontaneous Witnesses." Examples include *Easy Street* (1917), *Broken Blossoms* (1919), *Greed* (1924), and *The Salvation Hunters* (1925). Two years later the director of

The Salvation Hunters preludes, with *Underworld*, the gangster cycle, which is given its own category below. The financial and industry labor battles of the thirties are poorly represented in Hollywood, for the obvious reason that the heads of studios tend to be Republican and anyway depend on the banks. But as the rearmament restored prosperity, the association of industry and conflict was paraphrased in politically innocent melodrama, giving *They Drive by Night* (1940) and *Manpower* (1941). (Realistic variants like *The Grapes of Wrath* are not noir.) *Wild Harvest* (1947) and *Give Us This Day* (1949) relate to this genre. The former has many lines openly critical of big capitalists, but its standpoint is ruralist-individualist and, probably, Goldwaterian. The second was directed by Dmytryk in English exile, but setting and spirit are entirely American.

Another cycle might be labeled "The Somber Cross-Section." A crime takes us through a variety of settings and types and implies an anguished view of society as a whole. Roughly coincident with the rise of neorealism in Europe, this cycle includes *Phantom Lady* (1944), *The Naked City* (1948), *Nightmare Alley* (1947), *Panic in the Streets* (1950), *Glory Alley* (1952), *Fourteen Hours* (1951), *The Well* (1951), *The Big Night* (1951), *Rear Window* (1954), and *Let No Man Write My Epitaph* (1960). The genre shades into Chayefsky-type populism, and studies of social problems later predominate. European equivalents of the genre include *Hôtel du Nord* (1938), *It Always Rains on Sunday* (1947), *Sapphire* (1959), and even *Bicycle Thieves* (1948), if we include the theft of bicycles as a crime, which of course it is, albeit of a non-melodramatic nature. The American weakness in social realism stems from post-Puritan optimistic individualism and may be summarized in political terms. The Republican line is that social problems arise from widespread wrong attitudes and are really individual moral problems. Remedial action must attack wrong ideas rather than the social setup. The Democratic line is a kind of liberal environmentalism: social action is required to "prime the pump," to even things up sufficiently for the poor or handicapped to have a fairer deal and be given a real, rather than a merely theoretical, equality in which to prove themselves. Either way, the neorealist stress on economic environment as virtual determinant is conspicuous by its absence, although the phrase "wrong side of the tracks" expresses it fatalistically. It's a minor curiosity that English liberal critics invariably pour scorn on the phrases through which Hollywood expresses an English liberal awareness of class and underprivilege.

Two remarkable movies, *He Ran All the Way* (1951) and *The Sound of Fury* (1950), both directed by victims of McCarthy (John Berry, Cy Endfield), illustrate the slick, elliptic terms through which serious social criti-

cisms may be expressed. In the first film, the criminal hero (John Garfield) holds his girl (Shelley Winters) hostage in her father's tenement.
The father asks a mate at work whether a hypothetical man in this position should call the police. His mate replies, "Have you seen firemen go
at a fire? Chop, chop, chop!" A multitude of such details assert a continuity between the hero's paranoid streak ("Nobody loves anybody!") and
society as a paranoid (competitive) network. Similarly, in *The Sound of
Fury*, the psycho killer (Sterling Hayden) incarnates the real energies behind a thousand permitted prejudices: "Beer drinkers are jerks!," "Rich
boy, huh?" His reluctant accomplice is an unemployed man goaded by a
thousand details. His son's greeting is "Hullo, Father. Mother won't give
me ninety cents to go to the movies with the other kids," while the camera notes, in passing, the criminal violence blazoned forth in comic strips.
When sick with remorse, he confesses to a genteel manicurist, who de-
nounces him. An idealistic journalist whips up hate; the two men are torn
to death by an animal mob, who, storming the jail, also batter their own
cops mercilessly.

Socially critical film noirs are mainly Democratic (reformist) or cynical-
nihilistic; Republican moralists tend to avoid the genre, although certain
movies by Wellman, King Vidor, and Hawks appear to be Republican attempts to grasp the nettle and tackle problems of self-help in desperate
circumstances (e.g., *The Public Enemy* [1931], *Duel in the Sun, Only Angels
Have Wings* [1939]).

However, certain conspicuous social malfunctions impose a black social realism. These are mostly connected with crime, precisely because
this topic reintroduces the question of personal responsibility, such that
right-wing spectators can congenially misunderstand hopefully liberal
movies. These malfunctions give rise to various subgenres of the crime
film:

(a) Prohibition-Type Gangsterism. It's worth mentioning here a quiet but
astonishing movie, *Kiss Tomorrow Goodbye* (1950), in which Cagney,
as an old-time gangster making a comeback, corrupts or exploits the
corruption of a whole town, including the chief of police. His plan,
to murder his old friend's hellcat daughter (Barbara Payton) so as to
marry the tycoon's daughter (Helena Carter) and cement the dynasty,
is foiled only by a personal quirk (his mistress's jealousy). The plot
is an exact parallel to *A Place in the Sun* (1951) except that Dreiser's
realistically weak characters are replaced by thrillingly tough ones.
(Its scriptwriter worked on Stevens's film also.) Postwar gangster films

are curiously devoid of all social criticism, except the postwar appeal to conscience, apart from its devious but effective reintroduction in *Bonnie and Clyde*.

(b) A Corrupt Penology (Miscarriages of Justice, Prison Exposés, Lynch Law). Corrupt, or, worse, merely lazy, justice is indicated in *I Want to Live* (1958), *Anatomy of a Murder* (1959), and *In the Heat of the Night* (1967). Prison exposés range from *I Am a Fugitive from a Chain Gang* (1932) to Dassin's brilliant *Brute Force* (1947) and Don Siegel's forceful *Riot in Cell Block 11* (1954). Lynching films range from *Fury* (1936) through *Storm Warning* (1951) to *The Chase* (1966) and, of course, *In the Heat of the Night*.

(c) The fight game is another permitted topic, the late forties springing a sizzling liberal combination (*Body and Soul* [1947], *The Set-Up* [1949], *Champion* [1948], *Night and the City* [1950]).

(d) Juvenile delinquency appears first in a highly personalized family motif concerning the youngster brother or friend whom the gangster is leading astray. The juvenile gang (*Dead End* [1937]) introduces a more "social" motif. *Angels with Dirty Faces* (1938) combines the two themes with sufficient success to prompt a rosy sequel called *Angels Wash Their Faces* (1939), which flopped. The late forties seem awkwardly caught between the obvious inadequacy of the old personal-moral theme and a new sociology-based sophistication that doesn't filter down to the screen until *Rebel without a Cause* (1955) and *The Young Savages* (1961). Meanwhile, there is much to be said for the verve and accuracy of *So Young So Bad* (1950) and *The Wild One* (1953).

Rackets other than Prohibition are the subject of *They Drive by Night* (1940), *Force of Evil* (1947), and *Thieves' Highway* (1949) and drugs in *The Man with the Golden Arm* (1955).

The first conspicuous postwar innovation is the neodocumentary thriller, much praised by critics who thought at that time that a documentary tone and location photography guaranteed neorealism (when, tardily, disillusionment set in it was, of course, with a British variant—*The Blue Lamp* [1950]). In 1945 a spy film (*The House on 92nd Street*) had borrowed the formula from *The March of Time* news series, to give a newspaper-headline impact. The most open-air movies of the series (*The Naked City, Union Station* [1950]) now seem the weakest, whereas a certain thoughtfulness distinguishes *Boomerang!* (1947), *Call Northside 777* (1948), and *Panic in the Streets*. The cycle later transforms itself into the *Dragnet*-style TV thriller. Several of the above films are noir, in that, though the police

FIGURE 53. James Cagney as the old-time gangster with Barbara Payton in *Kiss Tomorrow Goodbye* (1950).

(or their system) constitute an affirmative hero, a realistic despair or cynicism pervades them. A blacker cop cycle is opened by Wyler's *Detective Story* (1951), an important second impetus coming from Lang's *The Big Heat* (1953). The cop hero, or villain, is corrupt, victimized, or berserk in, notably, *The Naked Alibi* (1954), *Rogue Cop* (1954), and *Touch of Evil* (1958). These tensions remain in a fourth cycle, which examines the cop as organization man, grappling with corruption and violence (*In the Heat of the Night*, *The Detective* [1968], *Lady in Cement* [1968], *Bullitt* [1968], *Madigan* [1968], and *Coogan's Bluff* [1968]). Clearly, the theme can be developed with either a right- or a left-wing inflection. Thus, the post-*Big Heat* cycle of the lone-wolf fanatic cop can suggest either "Pay the police more; don't skimp on social services" or "Give cops more power; permit more phone tapping" (as in *Dragnet* and *The Big Combo* [1955]). The theme of a Mr. Big running the city machine may be Democratic (especially if he's an extremely WASP Mr. Big) or Republican ("those corrupt Democratic city machines!"), or anarchist, of the Right or the Left. If a favorite setting for civil rights themes is the southern small town, it's partly because civil rights liberalism is there balanced by the choice of ultraviolent, exotically backward, and Democratic backwoods with which relatively few

American filmgoers will identify. *Coogan's Bluff* depends on the contrast of Republican-fundamentalist–small town with Democratic-corrupt but human–big city. The neodocumentary thrillers created a sense of social networks, that is, of society as organizable. Thus, they helped to pave the way for a more sophisticated tone and social awareness that appears in the late forties.

A cycle of films uses a crime to inculpate not only the underworld, the dead-ends, and the underprivileged, but the respectable, middle-class WASP ethos as well. *Fury* had adumbrated this, melodramatically, in the thirties; the new cycle is more analytical and formidable. The trend has two origins, one in public opinion, the second in Hollywood. An affluent postwar America had more comfort and leisure in which to evolve, and endure, a more sophisticated type of self-criticism.

Challengingly, poverty no longer explained everything. Second, the war helped Hollywood's young Democratic minority to assert itself, which it did in the late forties, until checked by the McCarthyite counterattack (which of course depended for its success on Hollywood Republicans). These films include *The Sound of Fury*, the early Loseys, *Ace in the Hole* (1951), *All My Sons* (1948) (if it isn't too articulate for a film noir), and, once the McCarthyite heat was off, *The Wild One*, *On the Waterfront*, and *The Young Savages*. But McCarthy's impact forced film noir themes to retreat to the western. Such films as *High Noon*, *Run of the Arrow* (1957), and *Ride Lonesome* (1959) make the fifties the western's richest epoch.

Subsequently, Hollywood fear of controversy mutes criticism of the middle class from black to gray (e.g., *The Graduate* [1967]). *The Chase*, *The Detective*, even *Bonnie and Clyde* offer some hope that current tensions may force the relentless social criticism onto the screen.

2. GANGSTERS

Underworld differs from subsequent gangster films in admiring its gangster hero (George Bancroft) as Nietzschean inspiration in a humiliating world. If *Scarface* borrows several of its settings and motifs, it's partly because it's a riposte to it. In fact, public opinion turned against the gangster before Hollywood denounced him with the famous transauteur triptych *Little Caesar* (1931), *Scarface*, and *The Public Enemy*. To Hawks's simpleminded propaganda piece, one may well prefer the daring pro- and contra-alternations of *The Public Enemy*. The mixture of social fact and moralizing myth in prewar gangster movies is intriguing. Bancroft, like Cagney, represents the Irish gangster, Muni and Raft the Italian type, Bogart's dead-

FIGURE 54. Warren Beatty and Faye Dunaway as the eponymous outlaws in *Bonnie and Clyde* (1967) a crime film of social criticism.

pan grotesque is transracial, fitting equally well the strayed WASP (Marlowe) and the East European Jews, who were a forceful gangster element. It's not at all absurd, as National Film Theatre audiences boisterously assume, that Little Caesar and Scarface should love their Italian mommas, nor that in *Angels with Dirty Faces* priest Pat O'Brien and gangster Cagney should be on speaking terms. Gangsters of the 1920s were just as closely linked with race loyalties as today's Black Muslim leaders—the latter have typical gangster childhoods and without the least facetiousness can be said to have shifted gangster energies into civil rights terms. It helps explain the ambivalence of violence and idealism in Black Muslim declarations; dialogues between "priest" (Martin Luther King Jr.) and advocates of violence are by no means ridiculous. Disappointed Prohibitionist moralists found easier prey in Hollywood and the Hays Office and cut off the gangster cycle in its prime. A year or two passes before Hollywood evolves its "antigangster"—the G-man or FBI agent who either infiltrates the gang or in one way or another beats the gangster at his own game. *Angels with Dirty Faces* combines the *Dead End* kids (from Wyler's film of the previous year) with gangster Cagney. When he's cornered, priest Pat

O'Brien persuades him to go to the chair like a coward so that his fans will be disillusioned with him. By so doing, Cagney concedes that crime doesn't pay, but he also debunks movies like *Scarface*. In 1940 *The Roaring Twenties* attempted a naive little thesis about the relationship between gangsterism and unemployment.

Between 1939 and 1953 Nazi and then Russian spies push the gangster into the hero position. A small cycle of seminostalgic gangster movies appear. A unique Hays Code-defying B feature, *Dillinger* (1945), is less typical than *I Walk Alone* (1947). This opposes the old-fashioned Prohibition-era thug (Burt Lancaster) who, returning after a long spell in jail, finds himself outmoded and outwitted by the newer, nastier, richer operators who move in swell society and crudely prefigure the "organization men" who reach their climax in the Marvin-Gulager-Reagan setup of Siegel's *The Killers* (1964). *Murder, Inc.* (1960) is another hinge movie, putting D. A. Bogart against a gang that while actually Neanderthal in its techniques is felt to be a terrifyingly slick and ubiquitous contrapolice network. *Kiss Tomorrow Goodbye* and *White Heat* (1949) are contemporary in setting but have an archaic feel. *The Asphalt Jungle* (1950) is a moralistic variant within this cycle rather than a precursor of *Rififi* and its gang-job imitations (which include *The Killing* [1956] and *Cairo* [1963], a wet transposition of Huston's film).

The next major cycle is keyed by various congressional investigations, which spotlight gangsterism run big-business style. "Brooklyn, I'm very worried about Brooklyn," frowns the gang boss in *New York Confidential* (1955). "It's bringing down our average—collections are down 2 percent." An equally bad sequel, *The Naked Street* (1955), handles a collateral issue, gangster (or ex-gangster?) control of legitimate business (a tardy theme; during the war Western Union was bought by a gangster syndicate to ensure trouble-free transmission of illegal betting results). Executive-style gangsterism has to await *Underworld U.S.A.* (1961) and *The Killers* for interesting treatment. For obvious reasons, the American equivalent of *La mani sulla cittè* (Hands over the city [1963]) has still to be made. *Johnny Cool* (1963) is a feeble "sequel" to *Salvatore Giuliano* (1962).

Instead, the mid-fifties see a new cycle, the urban western, which takes a hint from the success of *The Big Heat*. A clump of movies from 1955 to 1960 includes *The Big Combo*, *The Phenix City Story* (1955), *Baby Face Nelson* (1957), *Al Capone* (1959), *Pay or Die* (1960), and *The Rise and Fall of Legs Diamond* (1960). Something of a lull follows until the latter-day Technicolor series (*The Killers*, *Bonnie and Clyde*, *Point Blank* [1967]). With or without pop nostalgia for the past, these movies exist, like the western, for their action (though their killings relate more to atrocity than heroism). The first phase of the cycle is ultracautious and falters, through sheer repetition of the one or two safe moral clichés, while the second phase renews itself by dropping the old underworld mystique and shading illegal America into virtuous (rural or gray flannel suit) America. The first phase carries on from the blackest period of the western; the second coincides with the Kennedy assassinations and Watts riots.

3. ON THE RUN

Here the criminals, or the framed innocents, are essentially passive and fugitive, and, even if tragically or despicably guilty, sufficiently sympathetic for the audience to be caught between, on the one hand, pity, identification, and regret and, on the other, moral condemnation and conformist fatalism. Notable films include *The Killers*, *The Informer* (1935), *You Only Live Once* (1937), *High Sierra* (1941), *Dark Passage* (1947), *Cry of the City* (1948), *They Live by Night* (1948), *He Ran All the Way*, and a variant, *The Third Man* (1949). *Gun Crazy* (1950), an earlier version of the Bonnie and Clyde story, with Peggy Cummins as Bonnie, fascinatingly compromises between a Langian style and a Penn spirit and, in double harness with the later film, might assert itself as a parallel classic.

4. PRIVATE EYES AND ADVENTURERS

This theme is closely interwoven with three literary figures: Dashiell Hammett, Raymond Chandler, and Ernest Hemingway. It constitutes for some English critics the poetic core of the film noir, endearing itself, no doubt, by the romanticism underlying Chandler's formula: "Down these mean streets must go a man who is not himself mean. . . ."[2] This knight-errant relationship has severe limitations. The insistence on city corruption is countered by the trust in private enterprise, and one may well rate the genre below the complementary approach exemplified by *Double Indemnity* (1944) and *The Postman Always Rings Twice*, in which we identify with the criminals.

The genre originates in a complacent prewar cycle, the *Thin Man* series (after Hammett), with William Powell and Myrna Loy, as well as Asta the dog, being both sophisticated and happily married (then a rarity) as they solve crimes together. The motif is transformed by Bogart's incarnation of Sam Spade in the misogynistic *The Maltese Falcon* (1941) and the bleaker, lonelier, more anxious Hemingway adventurer in *To Have and*

Have Not (1944). In the late forties, Chandler's Marlowe wears five faces: Dick Powell's, Bogart's, Ladd's, Robert Montgomery's, and George Montgomery's, in *Farewell My Lovely* (*Murder, My Sweet* [1944]), *The Big Sleep*, *The Blue Dahlia* (1946), *Lady in the Lake* (1947), and *The High Window* (*The Brasher Doubloon* [1947]). An RKO series with Mitchum (sometimes Mature) as a vague, aimless wanderer, hounded and hounding, begins well with *Out of the Past* (1947) but rapidly degenerates. The series seeks renewal in more exotic settings with *Key Largo* (1948), *Ride the Pink Horse* (1947), *The Breaking Point* (1950), and *Beat the Devil* (1953), but concludes in disillusionment. In *Kiss Me Deadly* (1955), *Confidential Agent* (1945), and a late straggler, *Vertigo* (1958), the private eye solves the mystery but undergoes extensive demoralization. In retrospect, films by well-respected auteurs like Hawks, Ray, Siegel, and Huston seem to me to have worn less well than the most disillusioned of the series—Dmytryk's visionary *Farewell My Lovely* prefiguring the Aldrich-Welles-Hitchcock pessimism. *The Maltese Falcon*, notably, is deep camp—Huston's laughter deflates villainy into the perverted pretension of Greenstreet and Lorre, who are to real villains as Al Jolson is to Carmen Jones. In the scenes between Bogart and Mary Astor (a sad, hard, not-so-young vamp with more middle-class perm than "it"), it reaches an intensity like greatness. Huston's great film noir is a western (*The Treasure of the Sierra Madre* [1948]).

5. MIDDLE-CLASS MURDER

Crime has its harassed amateurs, and the theme of the respectable middle-class figure beguiled into, or secretly plotting, murder facilitates the sensitive study in black. The thirties see a series centering on Edward G. Robinson, who alternates between uncouth underworld leaders (*Little Caesar, Black Tuesday* [1954]) and a guilt-haunted or fear-bourgeoisie (in *The Amazing Dr. Clitterhouse* [1938], *The Woman in the Window* [1944], *Scarlet Street* [1945], *The Red House* [1947], and *All My Sons*). Robinson, like Laughton, Cagney, and Bogart, belongs to that select group of stars who, even in Hollywood's simpler-minded years, could give meanness and cowardice a riveting monstrosity, even force. His role as pitiable scapegoat requires a little excursion into psychoanalytical sociology. Slightly exotic, that is, un-American, he symbolized the loved, but repudiated, father or elder sibling, apparently benevolent, ultimately sinister, never unlovable—either an immigrant father (Little Rico in *Little Caesar*) or that complementary bogey, the ultra-WASP intellectual, whose cold, superior snobbery infiltrates so many late forties movies (Clifton Webb in *Laura*

[1944]). The evolution of these figures belongs to the process of assimilation in America. Robinson's fifties and sixties equivalents include Broderick Crawford, Anthony Quinn, Rod Steiger, and Vincent Price.

The theme of respectable eccentricity taking murder lightly is treated in *Arsenic and Old Lace* (1944), *Monsieur Verdoux* (1948), *Rope* (1948), and *Strangers on a Train* (1951). The theme of the tramp corrupting the not-always-so-innocent bourgeois is artistically fruitful, with *Double Indemnity, The Postman Always Rings Twice, The Woman in the Window, The Woman on the Beach*, and, a straggler, *Pushover* (1954). *The Prowler* (1951) reverses the formula; the lower-class cop victimizes the DJ's lonely wife. The theme can be considered an American adaptation of a prewar European favorite (cf. *Pandora's Box* [1929], *La bête humaine*) and the European versions of *The Postman Always Rings Twice*. The cycle synchronizes with a climax in the perennial theme of Woman: Executioner/Victim, involving such figures as Bette Davis, Barbara Stanwyck, Gene Tierney, Joan Crawford, and Lana Turner. Jacques Siclier dates the misogynistic cycle from Wyler's *Jezebel* (1938),[3] and it can be traced through *Double Indemnity, Leave Her to Heaven* (1945), *Dragonwyck* (1946), *Gilda* (1946), *The Strange Love of Martha Ivers* (1946), *Ivy* (1947), *Beyond the Forest* (1949), *Flamingo Road* (1949), *The File on Thelma Jordan* (1950), *Sunset Boulevard* (1950), *Clash by Night* (1952), *Angel Face* (1952), *Portrait in Black* (1960), and *Whatever Happened to Baby Jane?* (1962). A collateral cycle sees woman as grimly heroic victim, struggling against despair where her man all but succumbs or betrays her (*Rebecca* [1940], *Phantom Lady*). Many films have it both ways, perhaps by contrasting strong feminine figures, the heroine lower class and embittered, the other respectable but callous (like Joan Crawford and her daughter in *Mildred Pierce* [1945]), or by plot twists proving that the apparent vamp was misjudged by an embittered hero (as Rita Hayworth beautifully taunts Glenn Ford in *Gilda*: "Put the blame on Mame, boys . . ."). The whole subgenre can be seen as a development out of the "confession" stories of the Depression years, when Helen Twelvetrees and others became prostitutes and gold diggers and kept women for various tear-jerking reasons. Replace the tears by a glum, baffled deadpan and modulate self-pity into suspicion, and the later cycle appears. Maybe the misogyny is only an aspect of the claustrophobic paranoia so marked in late forties movies.

Double Indemnity is perhaps the central film noir, not only for its atmospheric power, but as a junction of major themes, combining the vamp (Barbara Stanwyck), the morally weak murderer (Fred MacMurray), and the investigator (Edward G. Robinson). The murderer sells insurance; the investigator checks on claims. If the latter is incorruptible, he is unromantically so; only his cruel Calvinist energy distinguishes his "justice" from meanness. The film's stress on money and false friendliness as a means of making it justifies an alternative title: *Death of a Salesman*. This, and Miller's play, all but parallels the relationship between *A Place in the Sun* and *Kiss Tomorrow Goodbye* (realistic weakness becomes wish-fulfillment violence).

6. PORTRAITS AND DOUBLES

The characteristic tone of the forties is somber, claustrophobic, deadpan, and paranoid. In the shaded lights and raining night it is often just a little difficult to tell one character from another. A strange, diffuse play on facial and bodily resemblances reaches a climax in Vidor's *Beyond the Forest*, where sullen Bette Davis is the spitting image, in long shot, of her Indian maid, and, in exile, in Losey's *The Sleeping Tiger* (1954), where dominant Alexis Smith is the spitting image of her frightened maid. A cycle of grim romantic thrillers focused on women who, dominant even in their absence, stare haughty enigmas at us from their portraits over the fireplace. Sometimes the portrait is the mirror of split personality. The series includes *Rebecca*, *Experiment Perilous* (1944), *Laura*, *The Woman in the Window*, *Scarlet Street*, and *The Dark Mirror* (1946). Variants include the all-male, but sexually inverted, *The Picture of Dorian Gray* (1945), *Portrait of Jennie* (1948) (rosy and tardy, but reputedly one of Buñuel's favorite films), *Under Capricorn* (1949) (the shrunken head), and a beautiful straggler, *Vertigo*.

7. SEXUAL PATHOLOGY

In *The Big Sleep* Bogart and Bacall, pretending to discuss horse racing, discuss the tactics of copulation, exemplifying the clandestine cynicism and romanticism that the film noir apposes to the Hays Office. Similarly, "love at first sight" between Ladd and Lake in *The Blue Dahlia* looks suspiciously like a casual, heavy pickup. *In a Lonely Place* (1950) and *The Big Heat* (and, just outside the film noir, *Bus Stop* [1956]) make another basic equation: the hero whose tragic flaw is psychopathic violence meets his match in the loving whore.

The yin and yang of puritanism and cynicism, of egoism and paranoia, of greed and idealism, deeply perturbs sexual relationships, and film noirs abound in love-hate relationships ranging through all degrees of

FIGURE 55. Bruno Antony (Robert Walker, *left*) as the double of Guy Haines (Farley Granger) in *Strangers on a Train* (1951).

intensity. Before untying Bogart, Bacall kisses his bruised lips. Heston rapes Jennifer Jones in *Ruby Gentry* (1952), and next morning she shoots her puritanical brother for shooting him. Lover and beloved exterminate each other in *Double Indemnity* and *Out of the Past*. He has to kill her in *Gun Crazy* and lets her die of a stomach wound in *The Lady from Shanghai* (1947).

Intimations of noneffeminate homosexuality are laid on thick in, notably, *Gilda*, where loyal Glenn Ford gets compared to both his boss's kept woman and a swordstick. A certain flabbiness paraphrases effeminacy in *The Maltese Falcon* (the Lorre-Greenstreet duo repeated in the Morley-Lorre pair in *Beat the Devil*) and in *Rope* and *Strangers on a Train* (where Farley Granger and Robert Walker, respectively, evoke a youthful Vincent Price). Lesbianism rears a sadomasochistic head in *Rebecca* (between Judith Anderson and her dead mistress) and *In a Lonely Place* (between Gloria Grahame and a brawny masseuse who is also perhaps a symbol for a coarse vulgarity she cannot escape). Homosexual and heterosexual sadism are everyday conditions. In *Clash by Night* Robert Ryan wants to stick pins all over Paul Douglas's floozy wife (Barbara Stanwyck) and watch the blood run down; we're not so far from the needle stuck through a goose's head to tenderize its flesh in *The Diary of a Chambermaid* (1946) ("Sounds like they're murdering somebody," says Paulette Goddard).

Slim knives horrify but fascinate the paranoid forties as shotguns delight the cool sixties. Notable sadists include Richard Widmark (chuckling as he pushes the old lady downstairs in her wheelchair in *Kiss of Death* [1947]), Paul Henreid in *Rope of Sand* (1949) (experimenting with a variety of whips on Burt Lancaster's behind), Hume Cronyn in *Brute Force* (truncheoning the intellectual prisoner to the strains of the *Liebestod*), Lee Marvin flinging boiling coffee in his mistress's face in *The Big Heat*, and so on to Clu Gulager's showman-like eccentricities in *The Killers* and, of course, Tony Curtis in *The Boston Strangler* (1968).

8. PSYCHOPATHS

Film noir psychopaths, who are legion, are divisible into three main groups: the heroes with a tragic flaw, the unassuming monsters, and the obvious monsters — in particular, the Prohibition-type gangster. Cagney's *Public Enemy* crisscrosses the boundaries between them, thus providing the moral challenge and suspense that are the film's mainspring. Cagney later contributes a rousing portrait of a gangster with a raging Oedipus complex in *White Heat*, from Hollywood's misogynistic period. Trapped on an oil-storage tank, he cries exultantly, "Made it, Ma. Top of the world!" before joining his dead mother via the auto-destructive orgasm of his own personal mushroom cloud. The unassuming monster may be exemplified by *The Blue Dahlia*, whose paranoid structure is almost as interesting as that of *Phantom Lady*. Returned war hero Alan Ladd nearly puts a bullet in his unfaithful wife. As so often in late forties films, the police believe him guilty of the crime of which he is nearly guilty. The real murderer is not the hero with the motive, not the wartime buddy whom shell shock drives into paroxysms of rage followed by amnesia, not the smooth gangster with whom the trollop was two-timing her husband. It was the friendly hotel house detective.

On our right, we find the simple and satisfying view of the psychopath as a morally responsible mad dog deserving to be put down (thus simple, satisfying films like *Scarface* and *Panic in Year Zero!* [1962]). On the Left, he is an ordinary, or understandably weak, or unusually energetic character whose inner defects are worsened by factors outside his control (*The Public Enemy*, *The Young Savages*). These factors may be summarized as slum environments, psychological traits subtly extrinsic to character (neurosis), and a subtly corrupting social morality. In Depression America, the first explanation seems plausible enough (*The Public Enemy*, with exceptional thoughtfulness, goes for all three explanations while insisting that he's become a mad dog who must die). In 1939 *Of Mice and Men* prefigures a change of emphasis, and in postwar America, with its supposedly universal affluence, other terms seem necessary to account for the still festering propensity to violence. Given the individualism even of Democratic thought, recourse is had to trauma, either wartime (*The Blue Dahlia, Act of Violence* [1948]) or Freudian (*The Dark Corner* [1946], *The Dark Past* [1948]). A second group of films, without exonerating society, key psychopathy to a tone of tragic confusion (*Of Mice and Men, Kiss the Blood Off My Hands* [1948]). A third group relates violence to the spirit of society (*Force of Evil* [1948], *The Sound of Fury*). A cooler, more domestic tone prevails with *Don't Bother to Knock* (1952), with its switch-casting (ex-psychopath Richard Widmark becomes the embittered, kindly hero, against Marilyn Monroe as a homicidal babysitter). This last shift might be described as antiexpressionism, or coolism, with psychopathy accepted as a normal condition of life.

Critics of the period scoff at the psychopathic theme, although in retrospect Hollywood seems to have shown more awareness of American undertones than its supercilious critics. *The Killers, Point Blank*, and *Bonnie and Clyde* resume the "Democratic" social criticism of *Force of Evil* and *The Sound of Fury*. A highly plausible interpretation of *Point Blank* sees its hero as a ghost; the victims of his revenge quest destroy one another, or themselves. The psychopathy theme is anticipated in prewar French movies (e.g., *Le jour se lève*) with a social crisis of confidence, a generalized, hot, violent mode of alienation (as distinct from the glacial variety, à la Antonioni). With a few extralucid exceptions, neither the French nor the American films seem to realize the breakdown of confidence as a social matter.

9. HOSTAGES TO FORTUNE

The imprisonment of a family, an individual, or a group of citizens by desperate or callous criminals is a hardy perennial. But a cycle climaxes soon after the Korean War, with the shock, to Americans, of peacetime conscripts in action. A parallel inspiration in domestic violence is indicated by *The Petrified Forest* (1938), *He Ran All the Way*, and *The Dark Past*. But the early fifties see a sudden cluster, including *Suddenly* (1954), *The*

Desperate Hours (1955), *Violent Saturday* (1955), and *Cry Terror!* (1958). The confrontation between middle-class father and family, and killer, acts out, in fuller social metaphor, although, often, with a more facile Manichaean-ism, the normal and abnormal sides of the psychopathic hero.

10. BLACKS AND REDS

A cycle substituting Nazi agents and the Gestapo for gangsters gets under way with *Confessions of a Nazi Spy* (1939). The Cold War anticommunist cycle begins with *The Iron Curtain* (1948), and most of its products were box-office as well as artistic flops, probably because the Communists and fellow travelers were so evil as to be dramatically boring. The principal exceptions are by Samuel Fuller (*Pickup on South Street* [1953]) and Aldrich (*Kiss Me Deadly*). Some films contrast the good American gangster with the nasty foreign agents (*Pickup on South Street*); *The Woman on Pier 13* (1949) links Russian agents with culture-loving waterfront union leaders and can be regarded as ultra-Right, like *One Minute to Zero* (1952) and *Suddenly*, whose timid liberal modification (rather than reply) is *The Manchurian Candidate* (1962). *Advise and Consent* (1962) is closely related to the political film noir.

11. GUIGNOL, HORROR, FANTASY

The three genres are clearly first cousins to the film noir. Hardy perennials, they seem to have enjoyed periods of special popularity. Siegfried Kracauer has sufficiently related German expressionist movies with the angst of pre-Nazi Germany. Collaterally, a diluted expressionism was a minor American genre, indeterminate as between film noir and horror fantasy. Lon Chaney's Gothic grotesques (*The Phantom of the Opera* [1925], *The Unknown* [1927]) parallel stories of haunted houses (*The Cat and the Canary*) that conclude with rational explanations. Sternberg's *The Last Command* (1928) can be considered a variant of the Chaney genre, with Jannings as Chaney, and neorealistic in that its hero's plight symbolizes the agonies of the uprooted immigrants who adapted with difficulty to the tenement jungles.

The Depression sparked off the full-blown, visionary Guignol of *Dracula*, *Frankenstein* (with Karloff as Chaney), *King Kong* (1933) (with Kong as Chaney!), *The Most Dangerous Game* (1932), *Island of Lost Souls* (1932), and so on (the Kracauer-type tyrant looms, but is defeated, often with pathos). Together with gangster and sex films, the genre suffers from the Hays Office. After the shock of the Great Crash, the demoralizing stagnation of the depressed thirties leads to a minor cycle of black, brooding fantasies of death and time (*Peter Ibbetson* [1932], *Death Takes a Holiday* [1934]). The war continues the social unsettledness that films balance by cozy, enclosed, claustrophobic settings (*Dr. Jekyll and Mr. Hyde* [1941], *Flesh and Fantasy* [1943], *Cat People* [1942]). A postwar subgenre is the thriller, developed into plainclothes Gothic (*The Spiral Staircase* [1945], *The Red House, Sorry, Wrong Number* [1948]). *Phantom Lady* (in its very title) indicates their interechoing.

A second monster cycle coincides with the Korean War. A connection with scientists, radioactivity, and outer space suggests fear of atomic apocalypse (overt in *It Came from Outer Space* [1953], *Them!* [1954], and *This Island Earth* [1955]; covert in *Tarantula* [1955] and *The Thing from Another World* [1951]). *Red Planet Mars* (1952) speaks for the hawks, *The Day the Earth Stood Still* (1951) for the doves. *Invasion of the Body Snatchers* (1956) is a classic paranoid fantasy (arguably justified). As the glaciers of callous alienation advance, the Corman Poes create their nightmare compensation: the aesthetic hothouse of Victorian incest. *Psycho* (1960) crossbreeds the genre with a collateral revival of plainclothes Guignol, often revolving around a feminine, rather than a masculine, figure (Joan Crawford and Bette Davis substitute for Chaney in *Whatever Happened to Baby Jane?*). The English anticipations of the Corman Poes are the Fisher Frankenstein (*The Revenge of Frankenstein* [1958]) and *Dracula* (1958). With *Dutchman* (1967), the genre matures into an expressionistic social realism.

The sixties obsession with violent death in all forms and genres may be seen as marking the admission of the film noir into the mainstream of Western pop art, encouraged by (a) the comforts of relative affluence; (b) moral disillusionment, in outcome variously radical, liberal, reactionary, or nihilist; (c) a post-Hiroshima sense of man as his own executioner, rather than nature, God, or fate; and (d) an enhanced awareness of social conflict. The cinema is in its Jacobean period, and the stress on gratuitous tormenting, evilly jocular in *The Good, the Bad and the Ugly* (1966), less jocular in *Laughter in the Dark* (1969), parallels that in Webster's plays. Such films as *Paths of Glory* (1957), *Eva* (1962), and *The Loved One* (1965) emphasize their crimes less than the rottenness of a society, or, perhaps, man himself.

NOTES

1. Siegfried Kracauer, *From Caligari to Hitler: A Psychological Study of the German Film* (Princeton, NJ: Princeton University Press, 1947). The most recent edition was revised and expanded by Leonardo Quaresima in 2004. [Editors' note.]

2. Raymond Chandler, "The Simple Art of Murder" (1944), in *Later Novels and Other Writings*, edited by Frank McShane (New York: Library of America, 1995), 991–992. [Editors' note.]

3. Jacques Siclier, "Misogyny in Film Noir" (1956), reprinted in *Perspectives on Film Noir*, edited by R. Barton Palmer (New York: G. K. Hall, 1996), 66–75. [Editors' note.]

CHAPTER 23

INTRODUCTION TO *THE GANGSTER FILM*

JOHN BAXTER

"ORDINARY PEOPLE OF YOUR CLASS," says a character contemptuously in Don Siegel's *The Lineup* (1958), "you don't understand the criminal's need for violence." The remark is typical of the modern gangster film. Like them, it implies that the rules of crime are different from those of ordinary society and force on those who live by them a unique and rigorous ethic. "Crime is only a left-handed form of human endeavor," Louis Calhern says in *The Asphalt Jungle* (1950), conveying in one sentence the code of these haunted people.

Characteristic too is the way in which *The Lineup*'s comment hints at social generalization. It is not only the criminal commenting on other criminals; it is the criminal commenting on society and the forces that encouraged him to enter the half-world of crime. Few gangster films are free of the imputation that criminals are the creation of society rather than rebels against it. It is because this was often in the past true, and may still be, that the gangster film has become the province of men whose political and social views are unconventional.

Our ambiguous attitude to criminals, figures of both menace and glamour, has formed the basic gangster film character, the urban wolf. He is the product of his harsh environment, violent, laconic, and tough, but his involvement in crime seems a matter of chance rather than choice. An urban wolf can equally well be killer or detective, warden or prisoner. The ethics are similar, and all speak the same discursive language. When early gangster films took as their theme the conflict between boyhood friends

John Baxter, introduction to *The Gangster Film* (New York: Zwemmer/ London: A. S. Barnes, 1970), 9–14. Copyright © 1970 by John Baxter. Reprinted with permission of I. B. Taurus and the author.

FIGURE 56. Planning the heist in *The Asphalt Jungle* (1950).

who end up on opposite sides of the law, the writers, although always giving equal time to statement from both sides on the desirability of the alternatives, were usually forced by the subtlety of the distinction to settle the matter by violence.

True to the traditions of the entertainment film, the urban wolves, like western heroes and the characters of science fiction and fantasy films, have strict and limited dimensions. They are almost always men in early middle age, only they have had the chance to live and to cultivate the strict moral code that justifies their existence. (The real gangsters were usually young—Al Capone's golden period ended in 1929, when he was thirty-four—but the cinema has never been sensitive to the truth in recording reality, as the sections in this book on real criminals and their screen incarnations show.)

A certain ironic humor and mordant philosophy are also common to both gangster and cop, each seeming able to express himself with wit and perception about his relative role in a way real men would find ludicrous. And they are united in their contempt for the amateur, the unprofessional, the "punks" interested only in profit, the "freaks" who kill for fun or terrorize without point. In *The Asphalt Jungle* this coincidence of attitude is intelligently underlined. Cop John McIntire early in the film orders his men to squeeze a witness of information by locking him up, frightening him some more. "Don't you know your job?" he snaps. And later, in an identical mood, gunman Sterling Hayden beats up a man who has tried to double-cross him and snarls, "What kind of guy are you anyhow? Try to shake us down and don't have the guts to go through with it." For both, the rituals of professionalism seem more important than the formal necessities of crime and detection.

It is idle to generalize too much about gangster films, or any other field of cinema, so immense are the variations, particularly in Hollywood, where most genres have been crossed successfully. Gangsters have appeared in comedies, musicals, horror, and science fiction films; Shakespeare has been done as a gangster film; and there have been films about dogs reincarnated as private eyes and hardened killers moved to repent after hearing Billy Graham. But in general, the best have been tied closely to the reality of crime, reflecting public interest in a particular criminal, robbery, or illegal activity. The history of the gangster film is in a sense the history of crime in the United States, and few of the best films have not taken some of their material from the reality of organized crime that is a part of modern urban life.

CRIME IN AMERICA IS AN imported vice. No doubt it would have existed had the first waves of migration in the late nineteenth century not brought to the United States many of the underworld elements of European cities, but it would have been a lesser kind of crime, neither so ferocious nor so well organized as it was to become. With the migrants came representatives of the tightly organized street gangs of French and Italian cities, the violent political activists of Ireland and the Balkans, the blood-loyal mafiosi of Sicily. The influx laid the foundations of the fanatical and brutal criminal society of the twenties. As Kenneth Allsop points out, "The gangster of the Prohibition era was almost invariably second-generation American; he was almost invariably a Sicilian, an Irishman or a Jew."[1] It was mainly from the sons of the 1880s' immigrants that the underworld drew its most apt recruits.

Although the Mafia was in New York in the 1890s, its activities were limited by the meager sources of revenue. D. W. Griffith in *The Musketeers of Pig Alley* (1912) showed how the street gangs of the time existed, ruling a few blocks, getting along on the proceeds of extortion and petty theft, a far cry from the profitable and well-organized activity of Italy, where in many communities the Mafia and local government were often indistinguishable. But the tempo of criminal life quickened in the period following the First World War, when soldiers, demobbed to unemployment, social unrest, and injustice, turned to civil disobedience, union agitation, and sometimes crime as a means of satisfying their taste for violence and their need for the necessities of life.

Into this potentially explosive situation the US government in 1920 introduced prohibition of liquor, the nation's most disastrous social experiment. The European gangs found themselves with the ingredients of an illegal industry, bootlegging. Fattened by a rising market, already dissatisfied with a lax and cynical government, the public was not inclined to obey a puritan injunction to abstain and welcomed as social institutions the illegal liquor merchant and secret bar. From among the unemployed ex-soldiers, the gangs drew men who had little respect for a government that denied them social justice, a workforce at once eager to advance and careless of whom they hurt in doing so. All over the United States, but particularly in Chicago where geographical and social conditions favored the illegal liquor industry, the gangs fastened onto this new source of revenue and used it greedily to establish themselves.

WITH PROHIBITION, THE LEGENDS of crime began. By the middle twenties, the public was becoming aware of certain individuals in the underworld who carried off their careers with flair, arrogance, and a style unusual in the characteristically anonymous world of crime. One was Arnold Rothstein, New York bootlegger, gambler, and racketeer, the original Meyer Wolfsheim in F. Scott Fitzgerald's *The Great Gatsby*, Nathan Detroit in Damon Runyon's *Guys and Dolls* sketches, as well as of films like *Street of Chance* (1930), *King of the Roaring 20's: The Arnold Rothstein Story* (1959), and a score of others. The stereotype of the brightly dressed, clever, and arrogant gang boss is derived directly from him.

The second figure who emerged as big news was Al Capone, the boy from Castel Amaro who, before he was thirty, had taken over Chicago and the national bootlegging industry. Public interest in Capone, Rothstein, and people like them led to a string of biographical films, many based on actual figures. Most sought only to tell the story of a gangster's rise and fall and were usually riotously amoral and violent until the last reel, when, as a sop to the pious, he was shown shot down by the law. Ben Hecht's observation that "the forces of law and order did not advance on the villains with drawn guns but with their palms out like bellboys" was seldom observed in these phony fantasies of violence and sadoeroticism.

Rothstein was killed in 1928 and Capone jailed in 1931, but they left

FIGURE 57. David Janssen (*left*) as the flashy Arnold Rothstein in *King of the Roaring 20's* (1959).

behind a legacy that would rack America for decades, and also provide Hollywood with the basis for its next cycle of crime films. Both men had realized that profit depended on organization and cooperation between gangs. Rothstein in New York and Capone in Chicago had put order above all, welding the dissident gangs into efficient mobs even if mass extermination was the only means whereby this could be achieved. After Rothstein's death, Capone called a meeting in New York of the major criminal powers and suggested the logical extension of this policy, a national syndicate to coordinate criminal activity. Although the plan was rejected by the mutually suspicious gangs, the meeting did lead to cooperative projects like the execution service later known as "Murder Incorporated" and the national illegal betting service that was to provide the gang's main income after the repeal of Prohibition.

The gangs' new standing in national society was reflected in films that showed crime as a highly organized industry. Warner Brothers, experts in entertaining the masses, had produced many of the biographical gangster films: *Little Caesar* (1931), based on Capone; *The Public Enemy* (1931), based on Hymie Weiss; as well as many others. The first all-sound film, *The Lights of New York* (1928), was also drawn from the genre that Warner recognized as a potential gold mine. A glance at the newspapers gave their writers dozens of plots, particularly when, after repeal, the gangs moved in on prostitution (*Marked Woman* [1937]), the cab business (*Taxi!* [1932]), trucking, banking, and politics. Often imitated by other studios but seldom anticipated, Warner pioneered the private detective film, the prison drama, and most of the subsections that make up the modern crime film.

WHILE HOLLYWOOD EXPLORED the possibilities of organized crime, another phenomenon was catching public interest. This was the rise of the rural bandits, independent bank robbers, kidnappers, and petty thieves thrown up by the Depression who briefly ravaged the Midwest and South in 1933 and 1934. Racing across Oklahoma, Ohio, Kansas, Missouri, and Arkansas, they struck at isolated banks and filling stations in daring daylight raids, often shooting up buildings and people with submachine guns before roaring off in their stolen cars. Mostly small-town sports and embittered petty criminals, they traded on a corrupt and inefficient state police force to satisfy their simple needs, money, excitement, and fame.

With the possible exception of John Dillinger, these bandits—"Ma" Barker and her sons, Charles "Pretty Boy" Floyd, Bonnie Parker and Clyde Barrow, George "Machine Gun" Kelly, Lester "Baby Face Nelson" Gillis, and the rest—stole only a tiny percentage of the money that Capone and his associates looted from the country. The gangs looked on them contemptuously as small-time thieves, thrill seekers, and freaks. Their notoriety stemmed solely from their value as news subjects and the bloody childlike violence of their lives. The Depression society, weary of corruption in government and apathy in business, welcomed the stories of banks held up and policemen baffled. It was not, after all, their money in the banks, and few public servants had proved themselves as corrupt and useless as the state police. Flattered by newspaper attention and their legendary status, the bandits responded, writing to the papers and the officers who hunted them, appearing casually in town to buy food, and returning home to visit friends and family, gestures of their contempt for the impotent police force.

This arrogance was their downfall. Left to compete solely with the state police, most of them would have lived for years, but their growing popularity encouraged the federal authorities to intervene. Given sweeping power by Congress after the Lindbergh kidnapping, the Federal Bureau of Investigation (FBI), with its biblically righteous leader, J. Edgar Hoover, swept down on the bandits, and within a few months in 1934 most were dead, pursued with icy determination across America by the

G-men and shot down with dubious legality by men who knew they had nothing to lose. In 1933, at the height of the hunt, the Production Code authority issued an order that no film on Dillinger, or by implication any of the other bandits, should be made. No longer nourished by publicity, the legends died, not to be revived for another thirty years.

With the big crime rings, Hoover kept an uneasy truce. Even his power was unequal to that of the gangs, and to attack them would be to invite a costly battle that might eventually lead the FBI into the same disrepute as the state police. His neutralization of Capone in 1931 had merely been the end of a process begun by the gangs, who found Capone's rule galling. Beyond that, Hoover dared not go. Crime films, reflecting this agreement, became panegyrics to the fearless G-men, stories of prison, of racketeering on the city level with civic groups or alert police smashing the small gangs, or individual stories of crime and retribution peopled by private eyes and gentlemen gangsters who were already becoming figures of heroic mythopoetry, conveniently distant from the real facts of national graft and corruption.

THE REALITY OF WAR and of organized crime burst on the United States at roughly the same time. In the thirties, special investigator Thomas A. Dewey set about cleaning up New York, convicting Mafia leaders and deporting criminal heads. Continuing this work in 1939, other investigators found during a probe into crime in Brooklyn that "the big fix" extended far deeper than anybody had realized. A small-time killer named Abe Reles admitted that for years he had been a paid assassin for a criminal group that carried out executions for the nation's gangs, the group that became known as "Murder Incorporated." His testimony uncovered evidence of gambling, prostitution, and union rackets covering the whole country, of corruption extending into government on all levels, into the state and federal police, into industry.

War and America's growing involvement in it blunted the effect of these revelations and diverted Hollywood from making films based on them. It was not until 1946 that the first films on criminal corruption emerged, and when they did it was with a precision and power that nobody had expected. Many of them reflected the socialist/humanist views of men who had been attracted to communism during the periods of Soviet reconstruction in the thirties and the wartime entente. Few of the productions were more fiery than the political parables of Warner Brothers in the early thirties (e.g., *Wild Boys of the Road* [1933]), but the Depression was gone and with it the memory of injustice and graft. In the postwar mood of relaxation, optimism, and nostalgia, the realism of *Body and Soul* (1947), *Brute Force* (1947), *Crossfire* (1947), *Force of Evil* (1948), and *The Naked City* (1948) forced social awareness and civic indignation once again on a careless public, and the world's filmgoers turned with new interest to Hollywood.

Regretfully, the liberal spirit of the time was ephemeral, giving way abruptly to a more typical isolationism and xenophobia. The men whose talents had made these films great—Dassin, Dmytryk, Polonsky, Rossen, Trumbo, Garfield, Hayden—were first to suffer in the McCarthy witch hunts of the early fifties, and the spring of social comment that had welled briefly to the surface sank below once more, not to return for many years.

DESPITE THE FRANKNESS of these socialist-oriented films, they had little effect on public opinion toward organized crime, now an invisible industry of immense influence and wealth. Since the forties, the small mobs had been quietly consolidating themselves into a loose confederation of independent area groups with the Italian/Jewish Mafia as an informal link. In New York, a committee of Joe Adonis, Willy and Solly Moretti, Albert Anastasia, and Anthony "Tony Bender" Strollo met at Duke's Restaurant near Palisades Park through the war, planning strategy and maintaining the "Murder Incorporated" and Continental Press Service gambling machinery. The press ignored crime, but it was widely understood that a "Combination" of top gangsters ran the rackets in America. Gordon Wiles's *The Gangster* (1947) was one of the first films to call it "the Syndicate."

The word became the accepted one for organized crime in 1952, when Senator Estes Kefauver published the findings of the Senate Special Committee to Investigate Crime in Interstate Commerce, of which he was chairman from May 1950 to May 1951. "A nationwide crime syndicate does exist in the United States of America," he announced in a widely quoted report, and went on, "This nationwide syndicate is a loosely organized but cohesive coalition of autonomous crime 'locals' which work together for mutual profit. Behind the local mobs which make up the national crime syndicate is a shadowy criminal organization known as the Mafia." Once again, as in 1939, the public was made aware that crime had become far more than a matter of simple theft but now penetrated into the highest levels of business and politics, even as far as the White House itself.

The fifties spawned a rash of exposés that purported to tell the truth about graft in a number of cities. Some, like *The Phenix City Story* (1955), were honest attempts to show how apathy led to corruption. Others—

Kansas City Confidential (1952), *Hoodlum Empire* (1952), *Crime Wave* (1954), *Chicago Syndicate* (1955), *New Orleans Uncensored* (1955), *The Case against Brooklyn* (1958)—settled for a trite formula in which a crusading cop or private citizen shows that behind the well-cut suit of some local dignitary is a gang boss with contacts in the Mafia or the mobs. Respecting the FBI's truce with big-time crime, these films confined themselves to corruption on a city level, limiting any reference to national organization to a veiled comment that the Syndicate or "the Big Boy" was worried. Lacking film-makers of social consciousness, the crime film degenerated into another aspect of the Hollywood experience, distinguishable from the cowboy and horror film only in the variety of its attitudes and realism of its settings.

GENRES RISE AND FALL, fertilizing the ground for new growth, and the gangster film today has been plowed back to nourish the James Bond cycle, with its suave supercrooks and elaborate gadgetry, or the smooth professionalism of "big caper" films like *Robbery* (1967) or *The Split* (1968). Films about fantastic robberies, most of them inspired by real-life crimes like the Brinks armored car robbery or the Great Train Robbery in England, have become so common that the best of them—*Rififi* (1955), *The Asphalt Jungle*, *The Big Caper* (1957)—are a subgenre of their own, with special rules deriving more from the imagination of their writers than the realism of the news. As scenarist vies with scenarist to work out more elaborate plots, the underworld looks on, notebook ready, in case one comes up with a new wrinkle.

That the cinema should have become the criminal's university is par-ticularly appropriate. For decades crime and film have had a close and mutually responsible relationship. Not only has the cinema played to crime by recording and glorifying its activities, but criminals have re-sponded with interest to the pictures painted of them. Capone demanded that he be consulted over the script of *Scarface* (1932), and actors from George Raft to Alain Delon have been unwilling to draw a line between their screen personae and real life. Films like *Yokel Boy* (1942), with Albert Dekker as a gangster invited to star in a film of his own life, and *The Hollywood Story* (1950), where Richard Conte solves a twenties murder while directing a film about it, are no more odd than *Broadway* (1942), starring George Raft as himself in a film that often looks and sounds like a thirties gangster romance. Both in the public eye, both dependent on the protection of their charisma to survive in an uncertain world, both doomed to short-lived careers, gangsters and actors seem too close for true separation.

Tied to the period that creates it, the gangster film has no more durability than the year from which it springs. For this reason today's crime
films are thin. The poorest are rooted in nostalgia, pastel memoirs of forties detective dramas or thin parodies of a genre that in its time was brisk
and relevant. Others, like *Madigan* (1968), record without comment the
commonplace brutality of the city streets and hope for some truth about
our time to emerge from the grim catalog. But in truth the gangster film
seems gone for good, as the gangster is gone. With the trench coat replaced by the well-cut suit, the prison pallor by a Palm Springs tan, and
guns by more subtle means of persuasion, he has passed beyond the area
where cinema could say anything about him except that he once existed
and gave rise to some of American cinema's most powerful dramas.

NOTE

1. Kenneth Allsop, *The Bootleggers: The Story of Prohibition* (New Rochelle, NY:
Arlington House, 1968), 210.

Page numbers in *italics* indicate photographs.